Fields
of
Glory

Fields *of* Glory

A History and Tour Guide of the
Atlanta Campaign

JIM MILES

RUTLEDGE HILL PRESS
Nashville, Tennessee

To my wife, Earline,
       my driver and research assistant,
and our children,
       Paul and Melanie

Published in Nashville, Tennessee, by Rutledge Hill Press, Inc., 211 Seventh Avenue North, Nashville, Tennessee 37219.

Typography by Bailey Typography, Inc.
Design by Harriette Bateman. Studio Six.
Drawings by Tonya Pitkin, Studio III Productions.

Unless noted differently, photographs are by the author. Pictures credited to *Mountain Campaigns in Georgia* courtesy of the Atlanta Historical Society.

Library of Congress Cataloging-in-Publication Data

Miles, Jim.
   Fields of glory : a history and tour guide of the Atlanta campaign
Jim Miles.
      p.   cm.
   Bibliography: p.
   Includes index.
   ISBN 1-55853-023-1
   1. Atlanta Campaign, 1864. 2. Georgia—History—Civil War,
1861-1865—Battlefields—Guide-books. 3. United States—History—
Civil War, 1861-1865—Battlefields—Guide-books. 4. Historic
sites—Georgia—Guide-books. 5. Georgia—Description and
travel—1981-   —Guide-books. 6. Automobiles—Road guides—Georgia.
I. Title.
E476.7.M636   1989
973.7′36—dc20   89-6389
                                                                          CIP

Printed in the United States of America
3 4 5 6 7 8—99 98 97 96 95

Introduction

MADE IN ATLANTA.

General William T. Sherman kicked at the shell casing in disgust. All around him lay the debris of war—cannon abandoned in haste by their gunners, wagons with broken axles, rifles dropped by panicked or wounded men, canteens, and dead Rebels who lay scattered across the ground. Stamped or stenciled on virtually every last item, even the buttons on uniforms of the casualties, was that hated slogan, *Made in Atlanta.*

Sherman had seen that script on a dozen battlefields extending from Mississippi to Tennessee. Gazing south from Lookout Mountain, he imagined he could see the young, bustling city that had become the manufacturing center of the Confederacy. New factories turned out enormous quantities of cannon, rifles, pistols, shells and cartridges, wagons, uniforms, spurs, shoes, and swords. An Atlanta rolling mill even produced steel plate for the dangerous Rebel ironclad warships.

Across the heartland of the Confederacy—Mississippi, Alabama, and Georgia—farmers had abandoned their traditional cotton crops to raise vegetables, grains, and fruits of every kind; and herds and flocks grew fat. This food was funneled into Atlanta where, along with the war materiel, it was shipped on a nearly continuous stream of trains to supply not only his adversary, the Army of Tennessee, but allowed the resilient Army of Northern Virginia to keep fighting in the east. The four railroads that met in Atlanta were also the key to transportation in the Confederacy.

Within a few months Sherman took charge of all armies in the west. U. S. Grant, appointed commander in chief of the Federal Army, gave Sherman this order: "You I propose to move against Johnston's army, to break it up, and to get into the interior of the enemy's country as far as you can, inflicting all the damage you can against their war resources."

In Sherman's mind, before the war could be brought to a victorious conclusion, this meant that Atlanta had to be destroyed and the Confederacy denied her precious products. From that day, Atlanta was a doomed city.

Tips for Enjoying the Tour Guide

The driving tour to historic sites has been exhaustively researched. However, readers need to bear in mind that highways and streets occasionally are altered, and the names and designated numbers of roads are often changed. That is why we have included written directions, mileage, and maps. These should enable you to circumvent any changes that might be made to the tour route in coming years. *(We will update with each new printing.)* Also, remember that odometers can vary considerably. Our .8 might be your .9, so please take this into account. When in doubt about your location, don't hesitate to ask local residents for directions. While preparing this guide, we were frequently "misplaced."

For safety's sake, it is obviously best to tour the Atlanta campaign with a companion. While one drives, the other can read and direct. It is also advisable to read the touring information before hitting the road. Familiarizing yourself with the tour will enable you to choose the sites you would like to visit beforehand.

Traffic in parts of metropolitan Atlanta can be fast and hazardous, so please exercise caution in stopping to view historic sites and in reentering the traffic flow.

By all means, be respectful of private property. Do not trespass on land or call on the residents of a private historic home. It is extremely difficult to live in or on a part of history, and there are too many vandals and arsonists around to expect owners to be tolerant toward uninvited visitors. Fortunately, many historic homes are open as part of community tours around Christmas and during the spring. Check calendars of events for specific dates.

The tour route is designed to follow historic events of the Atlanta campaign. In doing so, it traverses some neighborhoods where crime is common. Exercise caution in determining when and under what circumstances you should visit sites in these areas.

The route is seldom far from Interstate-75, a very busy north–south artery. Food of every variety, hotels, campgrounds, and service stations abound for the weary and hungry explorer.

Contents

Fields of Glory

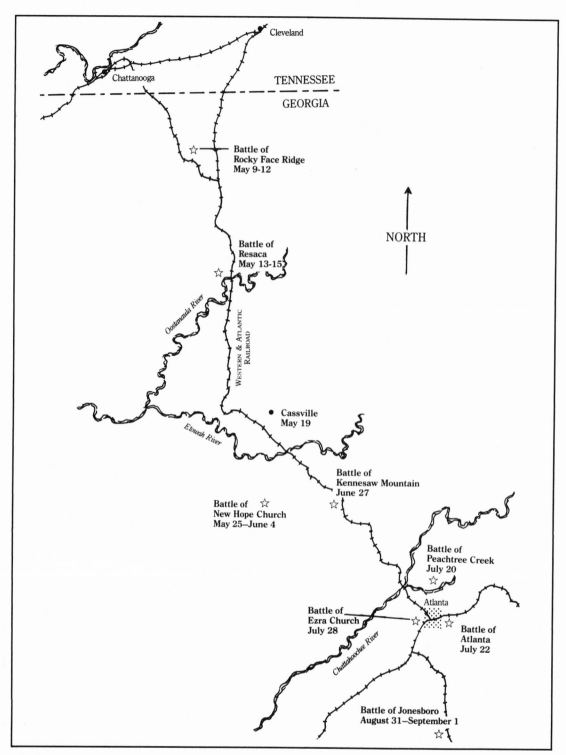

Map 1: Major battles of the Atlanta campaign.

CHAPTER 1

The Path of War Leads to Georgia

During the first days of May 1864, the roads leading south from Tennessee into Georgia were choked by the traffic of 100,000 marching soldiers. An incredibly destructive force was advancing on Atlanta.

The fighting in the Civil War was entering its fourth catastrophic year. Four years of the most intense and deadly warfare experienced by any nation had brought the full fury of war to Georgia. Numerous bloody battles had been fought, and many more remained to be waged before the war would draw to a close in another year. What happened in Georgia during the next three months would contribute heavily to that final outcome.

The Civil War was fought on two fronts. According to traditional thought, the major theatre was in the east, where enormous Federal armies under a succession of inept commanders attempted to destroy the Army of Northern Virginia and capture the capital of the Confederacy, Richmond. Every attempt to attain these goals was thwarted by the brilliant strategist Robert E. Lee, the Confederacy's beloved Gray Fox, whose tattered soldiers consistently delivered devastating defeats to far superior forces. However, Lee's two efforts to invade the North and end the war victoriously for the South had also failed. In the spring of 1864, the situation in the east was at stalemate.

Only in the western theatre had Union forces prevailed. Early in the war, President Abraham Lincoln directed that the South be divided in half by the Federal seizure of the Mississippi River. A long and costly effort, it ultimately was successful.

In 1862 Ulysses Grant skillfully combined infantry and a fleet of armed river boats to subdue the Confederate fortresses of Henry and Donelson, thereby securing Federal control of the Tennessee and Cumberland rivers and establishing a stout reputation for himself. In April Grant beat back a furious Confederate assault at Shiloh to win the first great battle in the west.

Union control of Missouri and Arkansas was assured after a Federal victory at Pea Ridge, Arkansas. Following successful battles for New Madrid and Island Number Ten, Federal forces had cleared the upper Mississippi River of Confederates; the southern end of the river was closed when Admiral David Farragut's fleet courageously captured New Orleans.

A Controversial Plan

Patrick R. Cleburne was one of the Confederacy's best generals. He had been born in Ireland and served in the British army before joining his family in immigrating to America, where they settled in Arkansas. His Confederate service had been exemplary, and for his valor at Ringgold Gap, Cleburne had been nicknamed "Stonewall of the West."

Joseph Johnston had been commander of the Army of Tennessee less than a week when Cleburne approached him with a stunning proposal. After three years of costly war, the Irishman announced, the South needed additional soldiers. Therefore, slaves should be allowed to fight for the Confederacy; their reward would be emancipation for all slaves. This would solve the South's manpower shortage, encourage European recognition of the Confederacy, and remedy a terrible social problem.

Johnston found himself mediator between generals who maintained an open mind on the issue and generals like William T. Walker who called the proposal "treason." Cleburne's idea was quickly silenced in Richmond, and the general's outstanding career came to a sudden standstill.

Cleburne was killed a year later leading his men at Franklin, and his visionary plan did not come to light until 25 years after the war ended. ■

An attempt by Confederate Braxton Bragg, commander of the Army of Tennessee, the South's second great army, to wrest control of Kentucky from the Federals failed when he was repulsed at Perryville by Don Carlos Buell. Bragg retreated to central Tennessee, where William Rosecrans, Buell's replacement, won a narrow, but costly, victory at Stones River.

Grant and William Tecumseh Sherman, Grant's chief lieutenant, had initiated operations against Vicksburg, the last remaining obstacle to Union control of the entire Mississippi River, late in 1862; but their first advances ended in dismal failure. Throughout 1863, Grant moved against Vicksburg, overcoming many obstacles and eventually surrounding the city. On July 4, 1863, Vicksburg was starved into submission, resulting in the closure of the Mississippi River to the Confederacy. The fledgling nation was split into two halves.

Rosecrans spent six months rebuilding his army, and in September 1863, he finally moved against Chattanooga. Bragg, outmaneuvered, abandoned the city; but at Chickamauga Creek, just across the Georgia border, he turned and assaulted Rosecrans with great ferocity. On the second day of battle, Confederate James Longstreet pierced the Federal line; and Rosecrans, with most of his army, literally ran for the safety of Chattanooga. At Chickamauga, one of the bloodiest battles in American history, 36,000 men fell in two days of bitter fighting.

Bragg's victory had cost his own army so dearly that he was unable to follow it up vigorously, and he had to be content with besieging Chattanooga, surrounding the city in hopes of forcing its surrender. Unfortunately for this strategy, Grant, after his magnificent victory at Vicksburg, was promoted to lead all western armies and arrived outside Chattanooga with 60,000 additional troops from Mississippi.

After opening a supply line into Chattanooga in November, Grant launched several attacks against the Confederates entrenched atop Lookout Mountain and Missionary Ridge. The Southern defenders were routed, and the Army of Tennessee reeled into Georgia.

Grant was soon recalled to Washington and made lieutenant general, the first since George Washington. As supreme commander of all Union armies, Grant assumed personal control of the eastern troops in Virginia and immediately promoted Sherman to command the western forces. Grant then formulated a plan to bring about a Federal victory in the war. For the first time there would be coordinated offensives in the east and west. When spring arrived, he would launch an attack against Lee and shatter the Army of Northern Virginia with his legions, while Sherman would advance south from Chattanooga, destroy the Army of Tennessee, and divide the Confederacy once again by capturing Atlanta and driving to either the Atlantic Ocean or the Gulf of Mexico.

Grant instructed George Meade, commander of the Army of the Potomac, "Lee's Army will be your objective point. Wherever Lee goes, there you will go also." For Sherman: "Joe Johnston's Army being the objective point and the heart of Georgia his ultimate aim."

After realizing that Atlanta provided food, clothing, munitions, and equip-

Evidence of a revival in the Army of Tennessee's spirits—a famous snowball battle fought in March 1864. [ALFRED WAUD]

ment of all kinds to the Confederate armies in the field, Grant was determined that the city must fall. If Lee were denied the enormous natural resources of Georgia, Grant was convinced he could not continue the fight.

Another factor that made Atlanta's destruction imperative was its railroads. Atlanta was one of the Confederacy's last remaining transportation centers. Four major railroads converged there from throughout the South. The Western & Atlantic extended north to Chattanooga and into Tennessee; the Georgia Railroad line to Augusta, Charleston, Wilmington, and Richmond was a direct funnel to Lee in Virginia; the Macon & Western served Macon and Savannah; and the Atlantic & West Point extended to one of the South's last major ports, Mobile. Atlanta was the economic, manufacturing, political, and transportation center of the remaining southernmost states in the Confederacy, and it had to be destroyed to bring the war to a successful conclusion.

A triumph in Georgia was also a political necessity. The capture of Atlanta was needed to guarantee the reelection of Lincoln, which seemed in doubt during much of 1864. The Republic needed some decisive military victories to convince the northern people to persevere and bring the war to a victorious military conclusion. Without the capture of Atlanta, an antiwar candidate could conceivably win the presidency and make a settlement with the South that would permanently split the United States. That must not be allowed to happen.

The conduct of the Atlanta campaign was determined by two factors: the disparity in numbers between the contending armies and the personalities of the commanders. Sherman had 110,000 troops at his disposal, while his adversary, Joseph Eggleston Johnston, started the campaign with only 40,000 men.

Sherman had been a dissatisfied peacetime soldier, but he proved himself an effective fighter during war. After graduating sixth in his West Point class, he left the military after seventeen years, later writing, "I was not considered a good soldier." In civilian life he was a failure in law and banking, then became superintendent of Louisiana State Seminary, which later became Louisiana State University. He reentered military service at the start of the war, and at Bull Run his brigade was one of those that panicked and ran from the field. Transferred west, his antics convinced northern newsmen that he was dangerously insane; and he was nearly driven from the army. While commander of the Army of the Tennessee, Sherman won fame while helping Grant capture Vicksburg.

Sherman was held in high esteem by his men. They called him "Uncle Billy" and preferred his rumpled appearance and grumpy demeanor to the more stiff formality of other officers.

Sherman's forces were divided into three armies. Commanding the enormous 60,000-man Army of the Cumberland was George "Pap" Thomas, one of the few Virginians who had remained with the Union. Thomas gained fame at Chickamauga when the rest of the army, including Rosecrans, fled the field in panic. Thomas organized his men into a defensive position and repulsed numerous Confederate assaults, saving the army from destruction by buying time for its escape to Chattanooga. When Grant arrived, he relieved Rosecrans and placed Thomas in command. Sherman's only complaint with the "Rock of Chickamauga" was his tendency to caution when Sherman expected immediate and vigorous action, prompting Sherman's personal nickname, "Old Slow Trot."

The Army of the Tennessee, 23,000 strong, formerly commanded by Grant and Sherman, was transferred to James Birdseye McPherson, a young favorite of his superiors who had risen from captain to major general in one year. Before the campaign began, he had asked Sherman for leave so he could marry his fiancee in Baltimore; but Sherman had refused, explaining that marriage would have to wait until the war was over.

Sherman's smallest corps, the 17,000-man Army of the Ohio, was led by John McAllister Schofield, an intellectual who would become Secretary of War and Commander-in-Chief of the U.S. Army after the Civil War.

The Union cavalry was led by Hugh Judson Kilpatrick, a youngster who started the war with the famous New York Zouaves and rose to command George Meade's cavalry at Gettysburg.

Grant had great confidence in Sherman, as his orders indicated. Sherman was instructed to destroy the Army of Tennessee, capture Atlanta and render it useless to the prosecution of the war, and inflict as much damage on Georgia's productive breadbasket region as possible. How Sherman accomplished these broad goals was left to his discretion. From Atlanta, Sherman would be free to advance on Andersonville, Columbus, Mobile, Macon, Savannah, or wherever he thought he would have the greatest effect.

When he marched south from Chattanooga, Sherman had a rough plan for the campaign. Thomas would attack Johnston's front to keep the Confederates pinned down, while McPherson would flank Johnston to the west and Schofield, usually accompanied by Joseph Hooker's corps, circled to the east. These maneuvers would force Johnston to continuously retreat closer to the first objective: Atlanta. It also raised the possibility of Sherman cutting off the Confederate supply line and severing their line of retreat, which would force Johnston to fight on Sherman's terms.

At some point Johnston would have to attack in an effort to stop the offensive, and Sherman's huge army of seasoned veterans would be ready to stop the assault. They would then counterattack and destroy the inferior Confederate command.

Johnston was born in Virginia fifteen days after Robert E. Lee and graduated with him from West Point in 1829. During his military career, Johnston was wounded ten times, leading Lee to remark that he seemed to attract lead. When Virginia seceded, Johnston resigned from the United States Army and offered his services to the Confederacy. He was soon embroiled in controversy with President Jefferson Davis, who ranked him fourth among Confederate generals. Johnston felt that his service and seniority earned him first ranking. This reignited a long-running feud that began at West Point when Johnston allegedly bested Davis in fisticuffs over the affections of a young lady. Johnston originally commanded the Confederate armies in Virginia, but he was wounded at Fair Oaks in 1862 and was replaced

A Commanding General First and Last ■ Joseph E. Johnston

[LIBRARY OF CONGRESS]

Johnston, who had been wounded in combat with Indians and the Mexicans, was a senior officer in the U.S. Army when he chose to fight for his home state, Virginia. Now he would face his own countrymen in battle.

When the first major conflict of the Civil War was fought, Johnston commanded the Rebel forces, rushing his men by rail to Manassas, where they turned the tide for the South. A year later, in 1862, Johnston demonstrated his skill in executing deft withdrawals (a cursed habit, his critics believed), down the Yorktown Peninsula before George McClellan's massive force. With the Union army within sight of Richmond, Johnston launched

a furious counterattack at Fair Oaks to blunt the Federal advance; but while reconnoitering in the early twilight, Johnston (exercising his propensity for attracting lead), was seriously wounded. Although initially few expected his replacement to work out, Robert E. Lee did just fine.

Transferred to recuperate and take nominal command of the Confederate west, Johnston was ineffective in stemming the Union tide that flowed through Tennessee and down the Mississippi River. After Braxton Bragg's retreat from Chattanooga, Jefferson Davis grudgingly appointed Johnston, an old and bitter enemy, to command the Army of Tennessee.

Johnston kept the army intact, but he retreated to Atlanta's outskirts without initiating a major battle to stop Sherman's remorseless advance. Distressed by Johnston's reticence to communicate his plans, Davis dismissed Johnston at Atlanta's gates.

Eight months later—with the Army of Tennessee reduced to tatters—Johnston was returned to command. He rushed his men to North Carolina and threw his lean ranks against Sherman at Bentonville. Caught unaware, Sherman fought hard to regain his advantage. Two weeks after Lee surrendered to Grant, Johnston capitulated to Sherman. ■

by Lee. After convalescing, he directed the Department of Mississippi during the Vicksburg campaign in 1863.

Following the Army of Tennessee's rout from Missionary Ridge in November 1863, Bragg asked Davis to relieve him. William Joseph Hardee, a corps commander, was given the position; but he gallantly refused to keep it, insisting that Johnston deserved the command. On December 27, 1863, Johnston arrived at the railroad depot in Dalton to lead one of the Confederacy's most distinguished armies. Unfortunately, Davis recalled the disgraced Bragg to act as his principal military adviser. This dreadful mistake allowed the embittered Bragg to reinforce Davis's distrust of Johnston by continually criticizing his strategy.

Johnston inherited a ruined army. In the rout from Chattanooga, the once proud Army of Tennessee had abandoned thousands of rifles, a number of cannon, and supplies of every sort. At Dalton, Georgia, Johnston found a pitiful force of tattered, hungry men. They were 6,000 rifles short; and "the number of bare feet was painful to see," the general wrote.

Johnston immediately ordered an amnesty, influencing thousands of men who had deserted since Chattanooga to rejoin the army and redeem themselves by fighting selflessly for their new leader. He furloughed the entire army in shifts, allowing his men, some of whom had not seen home in two years, to visit their families. Johnston requisitioned better food and new uniforms and found boots for the soldiers. A program of intense drilling and training instilled a sense of pride, confidence, and discipline in the army. Morale was bolstered by battles fought throughout the winter with snowballs; and when Johnston judged their progress as satisfactory, a formal review of the troops was held. Forty thousand men paraded past his reviewing stand with bands playing and regimental banners flying. The army even experienced a religious revival. By spring, Johnston believed the Army of Tennessee was ready once more to defend the Confederacy's heartland.

But defense of the fledgling republic was not what Davis expected. During the winter he plagued Johnston with telegraphed orders to take the offensive, to recapture Chattanooga and invade Tennessee to claim it for the Confederacy. Sherman had massed 110,000 troops in Chattanooga; Johnston had 40,000. Sherman had 254 cannon; Johnston had 124. The odds prohibited offensive action; so Johnston informed Davis that when Sherman advanced, he planned to defeat the enemy, then drive north. A trifle impertinent, Johnston added that if Davis would send him all the idle soldiers in the deep South who were on useless garrison duty, he could recapture Tennessee. Davis did order the 15,000-man Army of the Mississippi, under Leonidas Polk, to join Johnston in early May.

Johnston's army was divided into two corps. Hardee, a Savannah native and author of West Point's standard strategy textbook, led one corps. The second was commanded by John Bell Hood. Hood, from Kentucky, had been one of Lee's best divisional commanders in Virginia. A wound suffered at Gettysburg cost Hood the use of an arm, and he lost a leg at Chickamauga. The courageous general had to be helped into the saddle where straps held him in place, and he could walk only with the aid of crutches. Although there is evidence that Hood took pain medicine for his wounds that impaired his judgment, he was made a corps commander. Hood considered Johnston cowardly for assuming a defensive posture and was highly critical of how he handled the army, attitudes he expressed in letters to Davis and Bragg.

Johnston, an intelligent, formal man, kept his own counsel, sharing his thoughts and strategy with no one. This trait made Davis, Bragg, and Hood suspect that he had no master plan. Davis's distrust of Johnston increased as the campaign progressed, a feeling partially fueled by false reports from Hood.

Polk, who had resisted Bragg's attempts to take the offensive at Chickamauga, continued to be obstinate; so Johnston could not trust two of his three corps commanders to conscientiously carry out his orders. "If I were President," Johnston stated, "I would disperse the generals of the army over the Confederacy." Of his corps commanders, Johnston trusted only the loyal and reliable Hardee.

Johnston's cavalry was led by the impetuous Joseph Wheeler, who had gained a reputation in the Tennessee campaign as being Jeb Stuart's equal. The colorful soldier announced his raids on Union lines by crying, "The war child rides tonight!"

Like Sherman, the uncommunicative Johnston won the admiration of the soldiers who fought for him. He was concerned for the common infantrymen and took care not to waste lives in foolhardy actions. His men loved, trusted, and admired Johnston, who wrote that the army "was my true friend"—he had few enough in Richmond.

Johnston had formed his own counterstrategy while awaiting Sherman's offensive. He would establish strong defensive positions and entice Sherman to attack in hopes of whittling down the enemy. Johnston planned to

The Man Who Made War Hell: ■ William T. Sherman

[LIBRARY OF CONGRESS]

Sherman, considered to be one of the greatest generals in American history, was definitely one of the country's most unusual military minds. Named Tecumseh at birth for the famous Indian warrior, William was added by his adoptive parents, whose daughter Ellen he later married.

Weary of trying to earn a living in the military, Sherman entered civilian life in 1853 and failed miserably in business. He seemed to have found his niche as commandant of a military school, which would later become Louisiana State University, when the Civil War began. Sherman rejected a Confederate commission, one of the few offered a native Northerner, and rejoined the U.S. Army.

Sherman's volatile temper and absolute contempt for a free press embroiled him in conflicts that almost led to his dismissal; the general even considered suicide. Fortunately, his star began to rise when he assisted Grant in the capture of Vicksburg; and after the pair relieved the Confederate siege of Chattanooga, Grant left his trusted friend in charge of the western armies.

Sherman's brilliant maneuvering won him Atlanta, and his virtually unopposed March to Savannah and through the Carolinas was a stroke of genius that pierced the hollow shell of an exhausted Confederacy. Paradoxically, when that devastating campaign was over, Sherman was harshly censured by Congress for granting generous terms to surrendering Confederates.

After the War, Sherman refused to challenge Grant for the Presidency and served in the army until 1883. To the North, Sherman was a conquering hero; to the South, evil incarnate. To all, he was a tempermental, unpredictable military phenomenon. ■

withdraw deeper into Georgia, stretching Sherman's supply lines while constricting his own. Sherman would be forced to leave troops behind to guard each depot, railroad bridge, and town he occupied. While Sherman would have to cope with the ever present danger of Confederate cavalry raids cutting the vital railroad, Johnston would gather strength as his garrisons joined the main army. After attrition had taken a toll on Sherman's forces, Johnston planned to attack him at a time and position favorable to the Confederates.

This grand chess game would be played for two months in the beautiful countryside of northern Georgia. Sherman attacked and flanked; Johnston established successive defensive positions. Compared to the awful carnage taking place between Grant and Lee at Virginia's Wilderness, Spotsylvania, and Cold Harbor, losses were light. Several times Sherman would become impatient with his own strategy and play Johnston's hand, with bloody results. When Sherman relied on his own strategy, he steadily gained ground. Johnston, busy much of the time executing deft retreats, attempted on several occasions to take the offensive to isolate and shatter parts of Sherman's giant army, but his efforts always failed.

Sherman had tremendous respect for his opponent, stating that Johnston was "in all the elements of generalship equal to Lee." Sherman praised Johnston's "lynx-eyed watchfulness" and his habit of remaining in an exposed position until the last second to inflict all possible casualties on an enemy, then slipping away unscathed. His "model of defensive warfare," Sherman declared, neutralized his own numerical superiority.

In turn, Johnston had a healthy respect for Sherman, for he had been ineffective in stopping Grant and Sherman from seizing Vicksburg while he was in charge of the Department of Mississippi. Johnston was well aware of Sherman's consummate military skill and of the large number of men and enormous amount of supplies that the Union commander would have available. He fully realized that the impending campaign would determine the fate of the Confederacy.

On the first of May 1864, Grant telegraphed Sherman that he was moving against Lee. The struggle for Atlanta was about to begin.

CHAPTER 2

Feints, Fights, and Flanks

T he quiet valleys of northern Georgia came alive with activity as an irresistible wave of Federal skirmishers swept Confederate cavalry pickets from Ringgold and other outposts north of Tunnel Hill. Behind this screen advanced miles-long columns of blue-clad soldiers—110,000 of them—accompanied by hundreds of artillery pieces, brass bands, and a seemingly endless wagon train carrying supplies to sustain an enormous army on an extended campaign.

The soldiers marched slowly south from their winter quarters in Chattanooga and Cleveland, Tennessee. The ponderous force could not move quickly over the few country lanes leading south; so the armies spread out on a wide front, taking advantage of the narrow roads and natural gaps through the rugged ridges that dominate this part of Georgia. Johnston's army was waiting at Dalton behind a strong natural barrier: Rocky Face Ridge. Sherman intended to assault it frontally while sending a force around the ridge to outflank the Confederate position.

Thomas's massive Army of the Cumberland occupied Ringgold on May 4 and advanced along the western slope of Taylor's Ridge in the Chickamauga Creek Valley. On the morning of May 5, he crossed Taylor's Ridge at Nickajack Gap, emerging into the Dogwood Valley near Mill Creek Gap. Kilpatrick's cavalry led the advance and screened the troop movements through this gap and others to the south so the Confederates could not determine the strength of the offensive or the primary direction of the thrust.

Schofield's Army of the Ohio marched to the east of Ringgold from Cleveland and Red Clay. Federal units that had camped at the antebellum watering hole of Catoosa Springs on May 6 advanced on Tunnel Hill and the Crow Creek Valley past Lee's Chapel on the following day. Sherman, Thomas, and Schofield watched the troops advance from a ridge near the church, which is considered the spot where the Atlanta campaign began.

The route of the Federal armies was lightly contested by Wheeler's cavalry. Confederate skirmishers established temporary firing positions in the woods and felled trees across the roads to delay the march, but they were forced to fall back under heavy pressure.

Schofield occupied Varnell after a sharp skirmish with Wheeler, then

Horse Soldiers ■ The Cavalry

Both sides in the Civil War produced a number of dashing cavalry leaders like J.E.B. Stuart, Philip Sheridan, Joseph Wheeler, and James Wilson; but their roles were changed drastically by this war.

In earlier conflicts, cavalry was expected to crash into the enemy, riding down infantry and slashing away with sabers from their mounts. The new rifles made the cavaliers, and particularly their huge horses, easy prey. After several thousand years of war, the infantry had finally triumphed over the horsemen.

Cavalry in the Civil War used their mobility to strike deep behind the enemy in lightning raids to destroy supplies and lines of communications, but these raids were frequently more flashy than constructive. Cavalry also served as the eyes of the army, engaging in vital reconnaissance. The best horse soldiers, as typified by Nathan Bedford Forrest, were the equal of any infantry when fighting dismounted. ■

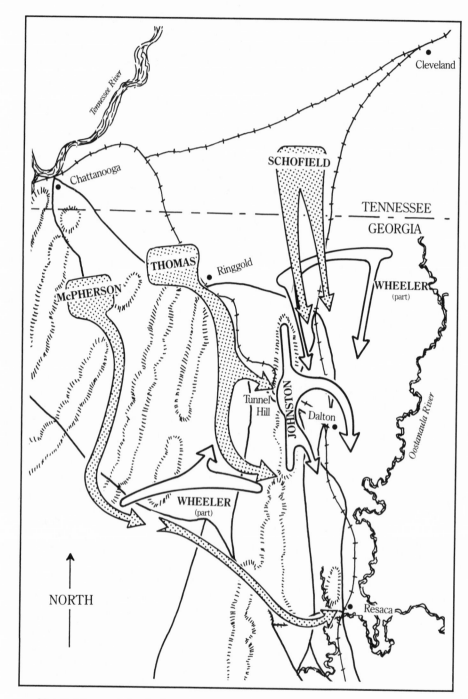

Map 2: The campaign begins.

marched through Harris Gap, where Rocky Face Ridge breaks up into a series of small hills. He then approached Tunnel Hill, his first major objective. When the Federals arrived at 9:00 A.M. on May 7, they forced the Confederate cavalry out of town but found Chetoogeta Ridge over the railroad tunnel bristling with a slight line of cavalry and a few small guns. The Federal skirmishers charged, and the Confederate cavalry fired a volley, then mounted up and galloped off for scouting duties west of Dug Gap. Federal General O. O. Howard remarked simply, "The ball is opened."

The Confederates had neglected to close the railroad tunnel with explosives, an oversight that presented Sherman with an unexpected, but greatly appreciated, gift. His supply trains would be able to keep pace with the offensive. Sherman would maintain his headquarters in Tunnel Hill during the Dalton operations.

From the top of Chetoogeta Ridge, Sherman and Howard had their first view of Rocky Face Ridge, a high, formidable wall of stone. Through his glasses, Sherman studied the impressive Rebel defenses. The first barrier on the road to Atlanta lay before him.

To the west, the third Federal force, McPherson's Army of the Tennessee, was quietly sneaking around Rocky Face Ridge through Snake Creek Gap to attack Johnston's weak flank by surprise. The gap, which skirts the southern edge of Rocky Face fourteen miles south of Dalton,

Ringgold depot, damaged by artillery fire in November 1863, was repaired with lighter colored stones.

Catoosa Springs was an antebellum resort and camp for Federal troops advancing into Georgia in May 1864.

opens into Sugar Valley and leads to the small town of Resaca, ten miles south of Dalton along the railroad. If the rails could be severed, Johnston would be trapped in Dalton between two Federal armies.

On May 7, McPherson marched through the old Chickamauga battlefield and turned southeast. He camped for the night at Chestnut Flat, dispatching a brigade to seize Ship's Gap (Maddox Gap on modern maps) over Taylor's Ridge. The next morning McPherson marched over winding Ship's Gap into the beautiful West Armuchee Valley and seized Villanow, a small crossroads settlement, then continued east to seize Snake Creek Gap with no opposition.

North of Villanow was Gordon Springs Gap, where two corps of the Army of the Cumberland crossed into Dogwood Valley opposite Rocky Face Ridge to participate in the assault against Dug Gap and Mill Creek Gap. Kilpatrick's cavalry, having screened Federal infantry movements from Ringgold to Mill Creek, crossed Gordon Springs Gap in the opposite direction and led McPherson's advance out of Snake Creek Gap. The Federal armies were in position.

Dalton was a strategic city, located 30 miles southeast of Chattanooga and 80 miles north of Atlanta on the Western & Atlantic Railroad. It was protected by the strongest natural obstacle in north Georgia: Rocky Face Ridge, a long, 1,500-foot-high ridge with a razor-sharp summit that extends north to south three miles west of the city.

After the Confederate army was routed from Missionary Ridge in November 1863, Bragg halted his troops at Dalton and fortified the ridge, expecting immediate pursuit by the Federals. When the Yankee advance was blunted by Patrick Cleburne's heroic rearguard stand at Ringgold, the Army of Tennessee camped in Dalton during the winter of 1863.

When Johnston replaced Bragg, he strengthened the works along the ridge, particularly at three accessible routes over and around the mountain barrier. The first was Mill Creek Gap, a natural passage just northwest of Dalton that was carved out of the mountain by Mill Creek. The railroad and main wagon road to Chattanooga passed through this bottleneck. Two miles to the south is narrow Dug Gap, an 800-foot-high passage over the mountain. A third point of concern was the Crow Creek Valley, which lies several miles north of Dalton and east of the protection afforded by Rocky Face. To repulse an expected attack from that direction, Johnston established a defensive line along a string of high hills that ring the exposed valley.

This was Sherman's second attempt to capture Dalton. In February 1864, Sherman learned that Johnston had weakened his army by sending Hardee to reinforce Polk in Mississippi, and he responded to this opportunity by sending the Army of the Cumberland to test Dalton's strength. Thomas occupied Ringgold and Tunnel Hill, then assailed the fortifications at Mill

The now abandoned railroad tunnel through Chetoogeta Ridge was Sherman's first objective.

Union soldiers struggle up Rocky Face Ridge to attack Confederate defenders at Dug Gap. [ALFRED WAUD]

Creek Gap, Dug Gap, and Crow Creek Valley simultaneously. When every attack was repulsed by the defenders, Sherman withdrew to Chattanooga to wait for the arrival of spring, when he planned to launch a general offensive with additional troops promised by Grant.

Confederate cavalry scouts immediately alerted Johnston to Sherman's initial movements south from Ringgold. On the morning of May 8, he ordered his men to take up their stations in works along the ridge and in the passes.

Later in the day, the powerful Federal armies appeared north and west of Rocky Face, which Sherman called the "terrible door of death." Even without McPherson, his forces dwarfed Johnston's. The warriors in blue marched up to the killing grounds in parade ground formations, proudly flying Old Glory and the flags of their individual units. Bands played "The Star-Spangled Banner," "America," "Hail, Columbia," and other martial airs with passion. The music wafted upon the breeze to the Confederate troops, moving patriotic feelings for the United States in the most staunch of Rebel hearts.

From their vantage points on the heights, the Confederates had a grand view of Sherman's approach. The ragged, but proud, Rebel troops were impressed by the spectacle, but not awed. Legend states that a Federal soldier stepped forward at Mill Creek Gap and boldly read Lincoln's Emancipation Proclamation. The Southerners listened politely; then, when the Yankee had finished, the Confederates punctured the document with a hail of musket fire.

The defenders hoped the Federals would launch direct assaults on their lines. The common thought was that all the Union soldiers would be killed in short order, and they could go home. Cleburne said he could hold this line indefinitely and destroy all attackers. But Sherman knew, and Johnston surely suspected, that this was a grand charade. Sherman would not cripple his army by dashing it against what was called Georgia's Rock of Gibraltar. The purpose of this demonstration was to distract Johnston's attention from his rear, so McPherson could push around the Rebel flank undetected.

Mill Creek Gap, known then as Buzzard Roost Gap, is a bold opening in Rocky Face Ridge. The heaviest fortifications around Dalton were erected here, giving the Confederates a great defensive advantage. Batteries of concealed artillery, which had been laboriously hauled up the vertical slope by hand, fired punishing salvos that the Federals could not return. Thousands of infantrymen crouched along the slopes, hidden from the enemy by thick foliage; but their view of the troops below was unimpaired. Confederate marksmanship devastated the Union ranks as they advanced in smartly dressed lines to meet death.

When the major Federal attack began, Hood's men lurked behind heavy entrenchments in the gap and virtually impregnable stone breastworks on the slopes to either side. Combat engineers had dammed Mill Creek to create an artificial lake that barred entrance to the gap. On May 8 Thomas's troops made three valiant, but futile, efforts to destroy the dam so Federal troops could storm through the gap; then they attempted to bridge the lake to no avail. A concerted attack up the southern slope of the ridge was bloodily repulsed by a hail of fire from all along the heights.

Sherman watched this grim, but expected, slaughter of his men from the

A Bright Star Lost: ■ James B. McPherson

[LIBRARY OF CONGRESS]

"If he lives, he'll outdistance Grant and myself."

That was William Sherman's assessment of his protegé, the 35-year-old McPherson; and his opinion was shared by all who knew the Ohioan. McPherson had graduated from West Point first in his class and was a fine engineer before returning to the Military Academy to teach.

McPherson had fought valiantly in all the Army of the Tennessee's encounters, and Grant and Sherman groomed him for further advancement. Their perception of his potential was shared by soldiers of all ranks who revered his intelligent, energetic leadership.

The handsome six-footer attracted many female admirers, but he had made his decision concerning matrimony. When the war allowed, he would marry Emily Hoffman, the proud exception to a Baltimore Secessionist family.

The Atlanta campaign did not embellish McPherson's sterling reputation. His timidity at Resaca wasted a golden opportunity to destroy Johnston, and his assault at Kennesaw Mountain had been easily repulsed. At the moment when his career should have crested, when Hood launched a crushing attack against his army, McPherson was slain.

"You have killed the best man in our army," his orderly told the Confederates who had just shot McPherson. Thousands of soldiers, including Sherman, echoed that sentiment in their hearts. ■

peak of Blue Mountain. He could only hope that McPherson was having greater success at Resaca.

Dug Gap is a narrow pass in Rocky Face Ridge. Early pioneers cut a road to it from the sheer cliff to connect Dalton and LaFayette, and just east of the gap lay Johnston's vital railroad supply line. A Confederate officer said the terrain surrounding the gap was such a strong natural defense that a handful of resolute men could hold it without adding fortifications.

Keeping the Confederates at Dug Gap from scouting to the west was important to Sherman's plans. Across the Dogwood Valley to the west were two passes leading over Taylor's Ridge; and beyond it was McPherson, stealthily marching toward Snake Creek Gap, only twelve miles southeast of Dug Gap.

To screen McPherson's movements, Joseph Hooker's XX Corps had crossed Taylor's Ridge via Nickajack Gap on the afternoon of May 7 and had camped in the Dogwood Valley near Liberty Church, midway between Dug Gap and Mill Creek Gap. On the morning of May 8, John Geary's division marched over Taylor's Ridge via Gordon Springs Gap to attack Dug Gap.

At the foot of western Rocky Face was a small community centered around Joel Babb's plantation. Confederate cavalry commanded by Colonel W. C. P. Breckinridge had withdrawn from Tunnel Hill and Mill Creek to camp here below Dug Gap and patrol the valley. At 1:30 P.M. on May 8, they discovered Federal troops swarming through Dogwood Valley. Two hours

Confederate infantrymen crouched behind this stone wall and repulsed a Federal assault at Dug Gap.

later Geary arrived at Babb's, deployed a brigade to either side of the gap, and began his assault. A battery of guns was unlimbered to cover the attacking men, and shells began falling among Confederate positions on the mountain.

Southern boys were thickly sown across the lower slopes, crouching behind logs, trees, and rocks to snipe at the approaching enemy. Geary called their fire "galling and destructive." They took a toll on the attackers, then scrambled to defensive positions farther up the ridge.

Geary's men fought well, springing between the cover of rocks and trees. The Confederates—Arkansas troops and Breckinridge's dismounted Kentucky cavalry—took up their main works: a stout stone wall erected along the summit of the knife-edged ridge. To keep the advancing enemy off balance, the defenders rolled huge stones down the slope onto them. In postwar accounts, outraged Federals expressed the belief that this was a breach of fair play.

A Northern newspaper correspondent wrote that there was a "fierce fire behind every cliff or rock. Huge rocks were even rolled from the top of the ridge, which came plunging down from crag to crag, crushing and tearing among the trees and sweeping through the advancing line."

The following Southern account of that famous episode was written by Breckinridge.

> At first, in a mere spirit of exuberant fun, some of the men rolled stones down the mountain-side; but when the effect was noticed they were directed to use these means as part of our defense; great stones were rolled down on the supporting lines on the mountain-sides or at its foot; and as these boulders would go leaping, crashing, breaking off limbs, crashing down saplings, we fancied we could see the effect of the unexpected missiles. It also proved a valuable resource for us, for without them our ammunition would have given out, indeed it was about exhausted when the attacks ceased.

A second assault was also parried successfully, and the thin line of defenders held the Federals at bay until two Confederate brigades arrived to reinforce Dug Gap; but they were not needed. A few Union soldiers had gallantly struggled to the summit of Dug Gap, but the pass was so narrow that only five men could enter at one time. The Confederates, crouched behind the stone wall to either side of the gap, quickly cut them down and cleared the crest of Yankee troops. The fighting subsided as a smoky dusk fell over the battlefield.

Geary lost 49 men killed, 257 wounded, and 51 missing, to 50 Confederate casualties. Concluding that he had accomplished his objective of diverting Confederate attention away from Snake Creek Gap, Geary wisely elected not to renew the uneven contest on the following morning. He camped at the foot of the mountain and threw an occasional and ineffective shell up at the defiant Rebels.

The cries of Federal wounded scattered across the slope haunted the mountain that night. At dawn Confederate soldiers rescued the enemy casualties and carried them down into Dalton for care. Cleburne said the assaults

A Rifleman's War

The Civil War was the first conflict that was dominated by firearms. Muskets employed in earlier wars were one-shot smoothbores, which were inaccurate and extremely limited in range. Reloading was a difficult, time-consuming job; and the primitive flintlocks would not work when wet, and only 80 percent of the time under ideal conditions.

Percussion caps for ignition soon replaced the unreliable flintlocks, and experiments with rifled muskets were initiated. A revolution in infantry warfare was sparked by a Frenchman, Claude E. Minié, who in 1849 designed a bullet (not a "ball," as most Civil War participants referred to it) that was smaller than the diameter of the gun barrel and could easily be inserted. When fired, the base of the projectile expanded to fit the rifling, giving the bullet a stabilizing spin for greater accuracy and range.

Napoleon's muskets could be used at 200 yards against a column of men, and only 100 yards against an individual. The rifled minié slug was effective against targets 600 yards distant. Its high velocity impact inflicted terrible damage to chests and skulls, and was responsible for the awful piles of amputated limbs that resulted from every Civil War battle.

Riflemen on the defensive ruled the Civil War. Few assaults could survive the hail of fire that started at long range and increased in horrible intensity as the troops advanced. Civil War battles started as stand-up fights between infantry, in the old European style; but rifled muskets soon drove Civil War soldiers into earthworks that presaged World War I trench warfare. ■

The statue of a Confederate soldier guards the graves of Southern warriors in Dalton.

were "repulsed with great slaughter" and contended that the Union fallen equaled the number of defenders present at Dug Gap when the fight began.

A third battle took place in Crow Valley, where the Confederate defenses began atop Rocky Face just north of Mill Creek Gap. It extended across several wooded ridges to Potato Hill, where artillery was emplaced to anchor the line.

On May 9 two of Schofield's divisions deployed in battle lines before Crow Creek. Rebel skirmishers delayed the Federal drive, then fell back until the enemy was deep in the valley. Shells from masked Confederate batteries on Potato Hill and volleys of musketry from invisible infantry on top of eastern Rocky Face stopped the charge cold.

Federal forces remained in front of the Confederate positions at Dalton for several days, maintaining a constant pressure to keep the Confederates occupied. Sherman did not order them to renew the suicidal assaults. He was waiting for McPherson's bold strike on Resaca.

A DRIVING TOUR
■ Ringgold to Dalton ■

Our tour of the Atlanta campaign begins in Ringgold, twenty miles south of Chattanooga and ten miles north of Dalton in Catoosa County. Rugged Taylor's Ridge, which runs north to south immediately south of the town, is visible for miles. Piercing the mountain is narrow, steep-sided Ringgold Gap. The old wagon road and railroad hugged the southern slope of the gap, and U.S. 41–GA 3 and the railroad still follow the same path; Interstate 75 was laid out below the western slope. When passing through on I–75, notice the stone terraces carved out to prevent rock slides.

Turn off Interstate 75 at Ringgold (exit 140 onto GA 151) and proceed east to U.S. 41–GA 3 (Nashville Street). Turn right. At the southern end of U.S. 41–GA 3, just before the railroad underpass, is the old stone depot on the left. Turn in.

The depot is now listed on the National Register of Historic Places. Both slopes of Ringgold Gap are visible beyond the railroad underpass from the parking area in front of the depot. Erected in 1849 with locally quarried sandstone blocks, the walls of the depot are fourteen inches thick. It was in continuous use on the Western and Atlantic Railroad until recent decades, and although badly damaged by artillery fire during the battle of Ringgold Gap in November 1863 (see Appendix A), it was later repaired with lighter colored blocks. The extensive damage suffered at the southern end and along the roof line is easy to distinguish. By comparing its large size and strong, skillful construction to other depots found along the Western and Atlantic in northern Georgia, you will understand the importance that Ringgold once enjoyed in the region's economic life.

By the spring of 1864, Ringgold had seen more Civil War activity than any other community in Georgia and had been largely destroyed. Only a few homes and churches survived the war. In April 1862, the famous Great Locomotive Chase ended just north of town when Federal saboteur James Andrews, who had stolen the engine *General* in Big Shanty, eighty miles south of Ringgold, abandoned his daring mission because of William Fuller's heroic pursuit on the *Texas*. In September 1863 William Rosecrans's Union army and the Confederate Army of Tennessee under Braxton

Bragg collided just a few miles to the west in the second bloodiest battle of the Civil War: Chickamauga. Touring the battlefield, museum, and monuments of the Chickamauga and Chattanooga National Battlefield Park would be a day well spent. Following the battle of Ringgold Gap, Ringgold became a no-man's land between Federals in Chattanooga and Confederates in Dalton.

At 309 Tennessee Street is the Whitman-Anderson House (1850), listed on the National Register, which was used by U. S. Grant as headquarters after Ringgold Gap. Legend states that Grant offered the woman of the house fifty U.S. dollars for her trouble, but she refused, asking for Confederate currency instead. "She certainly is not whipped yet," Grant commented, and Federal soldiers cheered her spirit. The family had watched the fighting in Ringgold from their second floor. At Nashville and Guyler streets is the Evans home, where Confederate nurses boarded. The Catoosa County Chamber of Commerce has a full color brochure, called "Catoosa County, Georgia, Battlefields and Backroads," pointing out fourteen sites,

Map 3: Ringgold area.

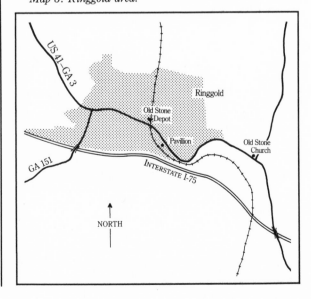

seven of them related to the Civil War and the others springs, stores, etc.

In 1862–63 Ringgold was host to many military hospitals. More than twenty thousand Confederate soldiers convalesced in churches, homes, the court-house, hotels, and warehouses, cared for by many gracious Southern ladies. The hospitals evacuated south in September 1863 to avoid capture by advancing Federal forces in the Chickamauga campaign.

Turn left from the depot onto U.S. 41–GA 3 and pass beneath the railroad. Note the twin stone pillars that welcome visitors to Ringgold; immediately on the right at .5 is the first of five unique interpretive pavilions.

Each of the pavilions about the Atlanta campaign was erected by the Works Progress Administration during the 1930s and has enhanced historical interest along U.S. 41, which was the main traffic artery for the region at that time. These enchanting fieldstone constructions are equipped with picnic tables, a metal plaque describing the actions that occurred nearby, and a large stone table in the center containing a giant relief map of the area that accurately depicts the battles and movements of both armies in the campaign. The markers were designed by John Steinichen and cast at the Georgia Tech Foundry. Construction was delayed by World War II and completed in 1946. The total budget was $27,500. There are occasional efforts to clean and restore the pavilions and replace missing markers and maps. At the rear of this one is a short path to a large granite monument with a bronze plaque near the railroad that marks the spot of furious fighting at Ringgold Gap. It honors Col. John Ireland's New York Brigade. The pavilions provide ideal places to orient yourself to the details of the campaign, allow the children to romp a bit, eat lunch, or lounge on the stone benches within the enclosures while enjoying the shade on a hot day.

The Atlanta campaign is considered to have begun on a ridge several miles east of here near Lee's Chapel on GA 2, where Sherman, Thomas, and Schofield watched their armies advance on Dalton. Thomas marched west of this spot along the route of GA 151, on the opposite side of Taylor's Ridge, to approach Mill Creek Gap. He camped for the night of May 6 at Pleasant Grove Church, Peavine Church, and Leet's Tanyard, where Bragg maintained his headquarters during the battle of Chickamauga. Schofield advanced to the east to seize Tunnel Hill and enter the Crow Valley.

With good maps, travelers can explore rugged Peavine Ridge around Beaumont and cross Taylor's Ridge over narrow, beautiful Nickajack Gap on SR 192–326 off GA 151 at Wood's Station, and approach Dalton through Trickum on Thomas's route. Gordon Springs Gap to the south, through which Geary moved to attack Dug Gap, is in southwest Whitfield County off GA 201 (Lookout Mountain Scenic Highway), but the road no longer crosses the ridge. West of GA 201 on Dunnagan Road near Liberty Church in the Dogwood Valley is the Anderson House, which was Hooker's headquarters during the Dalton operations. Catoosa Station was not far from here. Braxton Bragg maintained his headquarters in the station's freight room during the battle of Chickamauga, and Longstreet's Corps was forced to disembark at the station to join the battle because the bridges farther north had been burned.

Continue south on US 41–GA 3 through Ringgold Gap.

This portion of north Georgia is particularly beautiful as the highway hugs the sheer stone face of White Oak Mountain and twists beside Chickamauga Creek to the right. As the narrow gap broadens into a valley, beautiful farm country is framed against towering Taylor's Ridge in the background.

After 1.8 miles, at the intersection of U.S. 41–GA 3 with GA 2 at Tiger Creek, turn immediately left into the Old Stone Church.

Organized in 1837 by Scotch-Irish Presbyterians, this church was constructed in 1850 with sandstone quarried from White Oak Mountain, which stands to the north. After the battle of Ringgold, the church was used as a hospital, as evidenced by blood stains that are still visible on the floor. The sanctuary, which retains the original altar and pews and bullets in the stone walls, has since been used by many different denominations and remains in use today.

Catoosa County was famous in antebellum days for its hundreds of mineral springs. Believed to be healthful, they were spas where the wealthy traveled each summer to vacation and "take the cure," drinking and bathing in mineral-enriched water. On 388 to the east, in beautiful Cherokee Valley, was Cherokee Springs, used as a Confederate hospital from 1862 to 1863. Thousands of soldiers were treated for battle wounds or disease there, including General Bragg and his wife.

East on GA 2 and northeast on a county road is

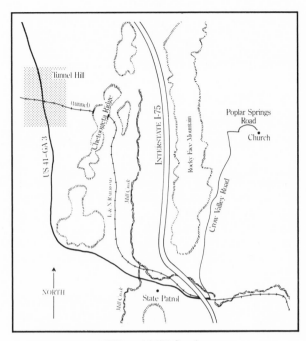

Map 4: Tunnel Hill and Mill Creek areas.

Catoosa Springs, perhaps the finest spa in pre–Civil War Georgia; it also was used as a Confederate hospital. Skirmishes were fought between Confederate and Federal cavalry on the grounds, and the Federals later used the facilities for campsites while awaiting the push on Atlanta. The hospitals at Cherokee Springs and Catoosa Springs both accommodated five hundred beds. The fine homes, hotels, and other facilities have vanished, but a businessman recently bought the land and maintains the grounds and ponds created by the springs. Although several bathhouses remain, Catoosa Springs is not open to the public.

Also in the area was a saltpeter cave, an important Confederate facility that produced material for the manufacture of gunpowder.

Rejoin U.S. 41–GA 3 as it turns south opposite Old Stone Church to Tunnel Hill. At 5 miles cross the railroad bridge on 41–3 and immediately turn left onto Oak Street. Round the curve; up the railroad tracks at .2 to your right are the tunnels through Chetoogeta Ridge.

The larger modern tunnel is to the left, the original to the right. The town of Tunnel Hill sprang up after the railroad was completed in 1850. The tunnel, the first in the deep South, was hewn through the ridge by two

separate parties that started from opposite ends and met in the center of the mountain. The Confederates maintained a camp there throughout the winter and spring of 1864; when the Federals arrived, the Confederates made a brief stand on the ridge over the tunnel, then retreated.

Turn right on the road alongside the railroad tracks (Clisby Austin Road).

As you approach a small, modern covered bridge spanning a trickling stream, look across the tracks to your left for the Tunnel Hill depot, now part of a fertilizer company. It was constructed of stone dug from the tunnel. To your right is the Clisby Austin House, also known as Meadowland, which was built as a resort hotel to take advantage of the scenery and springs. After John B. Hood's leg was amputated in the Armuchee Valley following Chickamauga, he recuperated here. On a grim note, because he was expected to die from infection, as large numbers of amputees did during the war, the leg was brought with him so his entire body could be buried together. Hood of course survived, and his leg was interred in the family cemetery. Austin, a unionist who welcomed Sherman and encouraged him to use Meadowland as headquarters during the fighting around Dalton, wisely slipped away under cover of night when the Federals withdrew. While being renovated in the 1980s, a horror movie was filmed here. The story line of the *Offspring* was that Southern war orphans who occupied a ruined mansion watched as Yankees captured and executed a

A relief map explains Union and Confederate moves at Mill Creek Gap.

squad of Confederates. The orphans kidnapped the Union leader and burned him at the stake.

Just before the road starts to climb Chetoogeta Ridge at .3, turn around in the road to your left.

The fourteen-hundred-foot-long tunnel is nearby, but it is on private property and large chunks of masonry fall from the roof and sides, making it dangerous to enter.

The tunnel remained in use until 1920, when the larger tunnel was constructed adjacent to it. Older area residents remember when railcars became larger and occasionally got stuck in the old, narrow tunnel.

This quiet village was a busy railroad town 130 years ago when James Andrews and his raiders emerged from the tunnel and raced through Tunnel Hill, closely followed by the *Texas,* which must have presented a curious sight rushing up the tracks backward.

Return to U.S. 41–GA 3, and turn left toward Dalton.

East on GA 201 is the Varnell House, which was used as a Confederate and Federal hospital and served as headquarters for several Federal generals. A number of skirmishes were fought around the house, including one on May 12, 1864, when Wheeler swung around the Federal left flank and drove them briefly from the town, inflicting 150 casualties and capturing 100 prisoners, including nine officers.

Rugged Rocky Face Ridge blocked Sherman's advance to Dalton.

US 41 through Dalton and Calhoun was once known as the capital of the hand-tufted and chenille bedspread industry. Numerous billboards attest to their continued leadership in carpet manufacturing.

On the outskirts of Dalton, at 4 miles, turn right into the State Patrol Post.

The patrol post is perched on the southern slope of Rocky Face Ridge. In front of a parking area below the station and overlooking the highway is the well-maintained second Atlanta Campaign National Park Service pavilion. The relief map describes Sherman's unsuccessful attacks on Mill Creek Gap, the Crow Valley, and Dug Gap, McPherson's successful flanking movement to the southwest, and Johnston's evacuation of Dalton (events of May 7–13, 1864).

You are in Mill Creek Gap, and the ridge rises abruptly in front and behind you. Here Thomas's troops fruitlessly assaulted the Confederate works in the gap and on the ridge. The northern slope, directly across the highway, was also held by the Confederates. Blue Mountain is north of Mill Creek Gap. Sherman observed Union operations from its summit.

Continue south on U.S. 41–GA 3 toward Dalton, but turn sharply left at .3 and cross the bridge that spans Mill Creek on Willowdale Road. Cross the railroad, pass under I–75, and turn left onto Crow Valley Road at .2.

Traveling north on Crow Valley Road, the eastern slope of Rocky Face rises abruptly to your left. Note the beautiful bands of exposed stone.

At 2 miles, a historical marker indicates the point where the Confederate defensive line in Crow Valley began.

The line began high on top of the mountain, where a signal station was maintained, extended to the valley floor, and continued several miles to the hills on the east. Schofield's forces were stopped cold before this stalwart line.

Continue .8 to the stop sign, turn right onto Poplar Springs Road, and drive around the sharp curve to turn right at .4 into a church parking lot.

The large hill to the northeast is Potato Top, the Confederate artillery position instrumental in turning back the Federal attack. Dalton's eastern defenses began there and extended south along the ridge tops of Hamilton Mountain. As part of Johnston's efforts to improve discipline in the ranks when he first assumed command of the army, a number of deserters were shot in the valley. As you drive back down Poplar Springs Road to Crow Creek Valley Road, one of the finest views available of dramatic Rocky Face will appear before you. At the intersection of GA 2 and GA 201 in Varnell is the Varnell House, still bearing bullet scars from nearby skirmishing.

Return to U.S. 41–GA 3.

With very good maps, the adventuresome visitor can trace Schofield's scenic path from Red Clay to Cohutta and Varnell, through Harris Gap just north of here, to the Crow Valley. Red Clay, only yards across the Tennessee line, was an important Cherokee council site

Map 5: Mill Creek and Dalton areas.

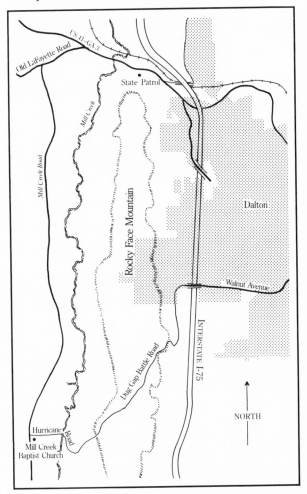

(their last eastern capital) and a vital Federal supply depot. It has been preserved as a Tennessee state park and features a visitors center-museum, a reconstructed Cherokee farm and cabins, a sacred council spring called "The Blue Hole," and other interesting attractions.

The three-story Prater's Mill, on the National Register, is two miles east of GA 71 on GA 2. Built in 1859, the mill has three underwater turbines that turn huge milling stones, sifters, and grinders. On February 23, 1864, when Thomas probed Dalton's defenses, six hundred Union soldiers camped on the grounds. On April 13, as the Atlanta campaign began, twenty-five hundred Confederates spent the night. Twice a year—on Mother's Day weekend and the second weekend in October—one of Georgia's finest fairs is held here, offering Civil War encampments, great country food, entertainment, arts and crafts, and even canoeing. The setting is idyllic. For information, call (706) 275-6455.

Before turning right onto 41–3, examine the rugged ridge facing you. Up there is the grave of English-born George Disney, a member of the Orphan Brigade who was killed while on picket duty during the Federal probe of Dalton's defenses in February 1864 and buried on the spot. Boy Scouts who discovered the grave on a hike in 1912 had it properly marked with a marble headstone.

Turn right (returning the way you came past the State Patrol Post). At .9 is Mill Creek.

To your left a trail leads beside the creek to a point where a strong Federal attack up the southern slope was repulsed. In this area was the large artificial lake created for defense when the Confederates dammed the stream.

At .4 turn left from U.S. 41–GA 3 onto the Old LaFayette Road.

To your right before you turn is Blue Mountain, where Sherman observed the assaults on Mill Creek Gap.

At .6 turn left onto Mill Creek Road.

Here you enter beautiful Mill Creek Valley. Rocky Face Ridge rises boldly to your left beyond forests, homes, and farms. Other ridges appear equally grand to the right.

At 5 miles, turn left beside Mill Creek Baptist Church onto Hurricane Road at what was Babb's Settlement.

Here Geary deployed his men and set up his artillery to fire on Confederate defenders on the ridge.

Take the next left at .8 onto Dug Gap Battle Road and wind to the razor-sharp summit of Rocky Face Ridge. Dug Gap Battlefield Park is at 1.4 on your left.

The scenery on both sides of the ridge is spectacular; the best views are available at the park. A small parking area affords a wonderful view of Dalton and ridges to the east, and a path leads to a 1,237-foot-long segment of the defensive stone wall from which a few brave Confederate soldiers repulsed Geary's men. It is easy to imagine how they could stop the Federals laboring up the sheer sides. Enormous boulders like the ones Confederates levered down on their approaching enemy are near the parking area on the west side of the ridge. The two-and-a-half-acre park was established by the Dalton Civil War Roundtable. To arrange tours, call the Murray-Whitfield County Historical Society at Crown Gardens and Archives, (706) 278-0217.

Continue east down the mountain on Dug Gap Road toward Dalton. At 1.3 turn right into the Northwest Georgia Trade and Convention Center.

Joseph E. Johnston, commander of the Army of Tennessee, is honored with this statue in Dalton.

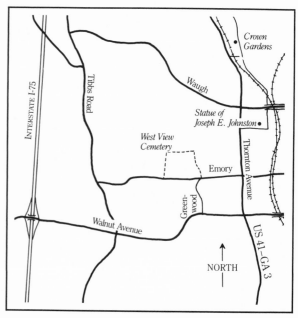

Map 6: Dalton.

A wide selection of information about Dalton is available here, as well as information about many attractions in northwest Georgia.

Continue east as Dug Gap Road becomes GA 52–Walnut Avenue, then turn left at 2 miles onto Greenwood to the stop sign at Emory at .3. The rolling, terraced hills of Westhill Cemetery will be in front. Take the entrance nearly straight ahead of you and the second right within the cemetery to the Confederate Cemetery, which is to the left in front of the maintenance buildings.

The enclosure, shaded by several large oak trees, contains the graves of 421 unknown and four known Confederate soldiers, and four unknown Federal soldiers. These soldiers died of wounds suffered at Stones River, Perryville, Chickamauga, Lookout Mountain, Missionary Ridge, raids on Dalton, and of disease in camp. Four hospitals in town nursed thousands of men to health, but they were evacuated south in May 1864. A small granite monument to the unknown soldiers who died in local hospitals was dedicated on May 10, 1892. At the opposite end of the fence is a monument topped by a simple statue of a Confederate soldier, dedicated April 26, 1884, to honor the men who died at Chickamauga, Rocky Face, Dug Gap, and Resaca.

The Western & Atlantic railroad depot in Dalton was used by Confederate and Union troops during the Civil War.

Return to Emory, turn left, and travel east .3 to U.S. 41–GA 3 (Thornton Avenue), and turn left.

The fourth house on your left at 506 Thornton is the Blunt House (1848). The Blunt family fled to Illinois during the Civil War, and occupying Federals used the house and grounds for a hospital, covering the yard with temporary shelters called brush arbors. Following the Civil War the U.S. government paid the family $1,815. The Murray-Whitfield Historical Society acquired and restored the house, which is on the National Register. Tours can be arranged through Crown Gardens and Archives, (706) 278-0217.

Turn right at .4 onto Crawford and drive through the next two intersections (Sedvidge and Pentz); at .2 to your left is a statue of Joseph E. Johnston.

The bronze statue, the work of Belle Kinney of Nashville, was raised in 1912 by the Bryan M. Thomas Chapter of the United Daughters of the Confederacy. Johnston, a controversial Confederate leader, led the Southern armies in Virginia before Lee and was twice commander of the Army of Tennessee. Hated by Confederate politicians, he was loved by his men and respected by Federal opponents. While Virginia has erected numerous statues of Lee, Jack-

son, Davis, and lesser Confederate notables, it has snubbed this son. Only Dalton has honored the service of Joseph Johnston.

Turn left onto Hamilton.

To your right down the next street is the Dalton Western and Atlantic railroad depot. Constructed in 1852 and in service until 1978, it is one of only two surviving original Western and Atlantic depots and saw a great deal of Civil War activity. James Andrews sped the *General* through Dalton, pursued closely by the *Texas,* which dropped a young man here who telegraphed Chattanooga for assistance. In 1863 cheering citizens showered food on Longstreet's corps, en route to Chickamauga. Days later the railroad cars returned, loaded with thousands of wounded, and the women of Dalton stripped their beds of sheets to make bandages. After a million-dollar renovation in 1992, the depot now serves as a restaurant.

Several streets east is Fort Hill, a prominence where Sherman established a blockhouse to protect the railroad during the Atlanta campaign. When Hood drove into Tennessee in the fall of 1864, Wheeler's cavalry captured the isolated Federal garrison there. The Huff House (1850s) on Sedvidge was Johnston's headquarters, and Walnut Grove, on Five Springs Road, saw service as a Union headquarters. The family believed the house was saved from destruction because they painted a large U.S. flag on the roof. Much of Dalton was ruined during the long Federal occupation.

At .2 turn left onto Hawthorne for 20 feet, and immediately right onto Chattanooga. At .3 proceed straight through the intersection with Tyler.

On your left is the beautiful Hamilton House (1840) and a stone spring house. During the winter of 1863–64, the commander of the Orphan Brigade, Joseph M. Lewis, maintained his headquarters in a tent near the spring. Both armies used the residence for a hospital from 1863 until the end of the war.

At .2 turn left into Crown Gardens and Archives.

This is the headquarters of the Dalton-Whitfield Historical Society. There are exhibits of Civil War artifacts, some excavated on the grounds from the Orphan Brigade camp by the Dalton Civil War Roundtable. The Society has a collection of Civil War books, local Confederate records, and historical, genealogical, cemetery, and Daughters of the American

Revolution files. There is also a picnic area and large scenic spring.

In 1864, residents of Murray County just to the east found a sixteen-year-old Federal soldier dead in a barn, apparently lost or deserted from his company. He was buried in an unmarked grave at the Spring Place Cemetery, and in 1976 the local American Legion Post gave him a headstone that read, "Little Unknown Soldier." Also interred there is a Confederate officer killed during a Federal expedition to clear the mountains of guerrillas in April 1865.

Return to Tyler and turn right for .1, then left onto U.S. 41–GA 3 (Thornton). If you are continuing on with the next section of the tour, at 9.1 you may turn left onto Tilton Road. If you forego the Tilton side trip, continue south. At 2.8 the Tilton loop emerges on East Nance Springs Road.

CHAPTER 3

A Clash of Armies

McPherson's troops threaded through the narrow, five-mile-long passage between Mill Creek Mountain and Horn Mountain, emerging unopposed into Sugar Valley on May 9. McPherson's message announcing his arrival at the strategic position prompted Sherman to shout triumphantly, "I've got Joe Johnston dead!" His optimism was premature.

McPherson immediately deployed his troops to advance across Sugar Valley and occupy Resaca, certain that he would trap Johnston between his army and the bulk of Sherman's forces. The enemy would be destroyed before the campaign was fairly begun.

If Johnston had bothered to fortify the narrow gap with a few guns and men, he could have bottled up McPherson indefinitely; but for some unknown reason he failed to do so. The situation was made more critical by the failure of his cavalry to discover McPherson's maneuver until the Federal army was pouring out of the pass and into Sugar Valley. One of Johnston's subordinates blamed this serious oversight on disobeyed orders. That was a common infantryman's complaint, that the horse soldiers preferred exotic, flashy deeds of derring-do over routine, but vital, reconnaissance. Regardless of whose fault it was, McPherson was able to slip into the Confederate rear unopposed, where his orders from Sherman were to break the railroad at Resaca, then return to Snake Creek Gap to dig in and await reinforcements. He would hit the Confederate flank when Johnston hurriedly withdrew from Dalton.

As McPherson advanced, dismounted Confederate cavalry bravely threw themselves at the advancing Federals. The skirmishers, including boys from the Georgia Military Institute in Marietta, drove back the first line of advancing Yankees. They fought desperately among abandoned cotton fields and farm buildings, then fell back to prepared works erected on a ring of hills west of Resaca, stubbornly resisting all the way. They had accomplished their purpose—to give the surprised Rebel defenders precious hours to ready their positions.

When the Union troops marched within range, Resaca's garrison met them with a withering fire. McPherson, stunned by the fierce resistance,

Federal troops launch a spirited attack against Confederate defenders at Resaca in May 1864. [CURRIER & IVES]

was further confounded to find the eastern ridges of Camp Creek honeycombed with freshly dug earthworks and bristling with Confederate cannon and muskets.

The ever crafty Johnston had sent a small force of infantry and cavalry to Resaca to guard the railroad bridge over the Oostanaula River at his rear. These men had prepared the extensive works that caused McPherson's consternation, and providence had provided soldiers to man the line. The first 5,000-man division of Polk's Army of the Mississippi conveniently arrived from Rome to put up the skillful resistance; but their commander, James Cantey, had considerable cause to worry. He had 5,000 men to counter McPherson's 23,000.

When word of McPherson's threat reached Johnston, he dispatched Hood and Hardee to inspect Resaca's defenses. The corps commanders arrived as Cantey calmly awaited the seemingly inevitable and doubtless disastrous Federal strike. "We must hold until dark," Hood said simply; but the expected attack never materialized.

McPherson had been surprised to find the town, so far behind Johnston's main line, defended. In reaction, he supposed there were more Confederates than there actually were. The young general, noting his supplies were running low and fearing Johnston would isolate him from the main Federal army and destroy his force, moved cautiously. The Yankees slowly inched forward, pushing in the Rebel skirmishers and sharpshooters. Late in the day, McPherson decided he could not capture Resaca and ruin the railroad before nightfall; so he fell back to the gap and entrenched. McPherson penned a second message to Sherman, informing him that Resaca was too strongly fortified to be captured by assault.

Sherman, directing feints at Dalton's tough defenses from his Tunnel Hill headquarters, was exasperated. He grudgingly admitted that McPherson's actions were justified by his orders which, Sherman grimaced, he had worded poorly. Later the Union commander would write that McPherson's fumbled opportunity to destroy an entire enemy army "does not occur twice in a single life."

McPherson had advanced to within a mile of the strategic railroad. With his overwhelming numerical advantage, he could easily have broken through the thin gray line; but he lacked boldness to accomplish the mission. McPherson would sit idly in his works at the mouth of Snake Creek Gap for

Map 7: The Battle of Resaca.

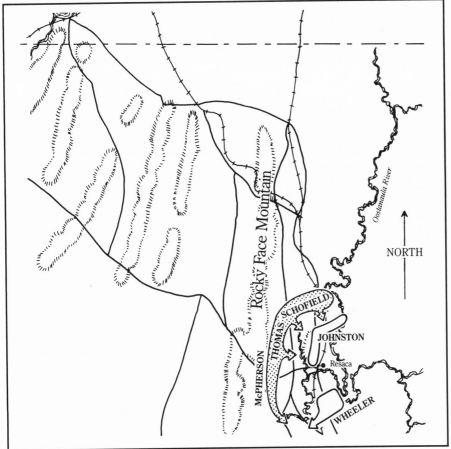

three days waiting for the rest of Sherman's army to join him. The first opportunity to win a quick victory had been lost.

Sherman had never intended to waste his men by dashing them against Dalton's deadly ridges. He left a small force under General O. O. Howard to hold the Confederates in place and to occupy Dalton when Johnston withdrew. Then he sent Thomas on the 11th, and Schofield on the 12th, south over Taylor's Ridge at Gordon Springs Gap to follow McPherson through Snake Creek Gap and around Rocky Face Ridge. He would unite his entire force in Sugar Valley for a full assault on Resaca and destroy whatever Confederate force held it.

The bulky Federal army moved slowly over the primitive mountain roads, choking the narrow passages with masses of men, horses, wagons, and cannon. Rain turned the dirt tracks into quagmires that forced soldiers to wrestle their heavy equipment through knee-deep mud.

Johnston was in no hurry to leave his comfortable Dalton camp, refusing to evacuate the army until the night of May 12. With his usual foresight, Johnston had previously sent his wagons and draft animals south of Resaca so his withdrawal would not be hindered. He had improved the country roads leading to Resaca and knew that his troops using these roads and rail trans-

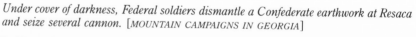

Under cover of darkness, Federal soldiers dismantle a Confederate earthwork at Resaca and seize several cannon. [MOUNTAIN CAMPAIGNS IN GEORGIA]

portation could easily beat Sherman to Resaca. Besides, he had a much shorter distance to travel and had faith that his men could hold off McPherson, if he attacked, until relief arrived.

Johnston's cavalry reported as each Federal unit was withdrawn, but he continued to rest his men in Dalton. He knew where the Yankees were going and how long it would take them to get there. His own officers were terrified that the army would be trapped, and General Howard feared the unpredictable Rebel leader would assail and eliminate him before the Confederates withdrew.

At midnight on the 12th, the remaining Federals reported fierce fighting still occuring with the Confederates. Four hours later, there was silence. Johnston's army had vanished as cleanly as if it had never existed. One of Sherman's officers reported that he was "profoundly impressed by the skill of the withdrawal." Johnston had decamped south with 40,000 soldiers in a matter of hours without leaving a single biscuit behind. At 10:00 A.M. Johnston slipped into the works before Resaca as easily as he had left Dalton, dumbfounding the enemy and originating a legend about his mysterious ability to anticipate an opponent.

Howard occupied Dalton and marched directly to Resaca from the north. He drove against a stubborn Confederate rearguard and was temporarily checked by a sharp skirmish at Tilton. He termed the pursuit "slow and spasmotic."

The Confederates had just settled into their prepared works when McPherson's troops deployed opposite them on the ridge west of Camp Creek. On the march McPherson had fought a fierce action with Confederate cavalry that left Kilpatrick, the Union cavalry commander, wounded. The Confederates, dressed in butternut, watched quietly as the rest of Sherman's blue-clad army emerged over the hills and took up positions alongside McPherson.

At Resaca, Johnston was delighted to find Leonidas Polk, who had fortuitously arrived from Mississippi with 10,000 more infantrymen. Polk, the famous Bishop-General of the Confederacy, had attended West Point but had left the military in 1827 for the ministry. He had been the Episcopal Bishop of Louisiana for several decades, but in 1861 he offered his services to the Confederacy.

The Confederates occupied a double row of trenches that extended for three miles along the low, wooded hills west and north of Resaca, forming a rough semicircle overlooking Camp Creek Valley. Their left lay south on the Oostanaula River and continued north parallel to Camp Creek, protecting Resaca and the railroad, which were several hundred yards east of the line, then turned sharply east and ended at the railroad and Conasauga River. The Federal position paralleled the Confederates. Hood held the right opposite Thomas; Hardee, the center opposite Schofield; and Polk, the left against McPherson. A Federal officer stated that this horseshoe-shaped defensive alignment was similar in strength to the Confederate position at Fredericksburg, Virginia, site of a bloody Union defeat in 1862.

The two armies spent the remainder of the first day skirmishing to obtain

Attack and Die ■ Civil War Tactics

America's Civil War generals were schooled principally in the tactics developed by Napoleon, who had fought his final battle in 1815. Napoleon advocated assaults on a narrow front by massed columns of infantry. His human battering rams smashed into the opposing ranks; then French soldiers dispatched the enemy with bayonets.

Such tactics worked at the turn of the nineteenth century only because muskets were notoriously inaccurate, difficult to reload, and had a limited range. Attackers were subjected to only one or two volleys before they overran the defenders.

By the time of the Civil War, musket range and reloading time had increased up to 300 percent. Confederate General William J. Hardee had modified American military thinking to adjust for this development in his textbook, *Tactics*. Civil War troops advanced in an extended line shoulder-to-shoulder and two ranks deep. A company of 100 men covered 25 yards; a regiment 3,000 yards; a brigade 9,500 yards. In addition, skirmishers who preceded the main attack skillfully scrambled from one point of concealment to another, firing sporadically to force defenders to keep their heads down.

Unfortunately for the infantry in both armies, generals still expected soldiers to march across hundreds of yards of open land in the face of devastating rifle and cannon fire, then dispatch the opposition with the "cold steel" of bayonets. Few Civil War assaults reached the enemy's works; they were usually shattered far from their objective. ■

The Resaca battlefield: trenches in the foreground, town and bridges over the Oostanaula River in the background. [GEORGE N. BARNARD, LIBRARY OF CONGRESS]

better positions. When the action started, Polk occupied a bald hill west of Camp Creek; but McPherson's batteries commenced a furious shelling that inflicted heavy Confederate casualties and weakened Polk's works. McPherson's men charged forward, initiating a furious three-hour battle that forced Polk to the east side of Camp Creek. Polk dug in along the ridge overlooking Resaca, which was occupied by the rest of the Confederate army; but on the afternoon of May 14, the Federals stormed across Camp Creek and drove the Rebels from this second line. Polk's vigorous attempts to retake it proved fruitless; so he withdrew to establish a new position in front of the railroad on the outskirts of Resaca. Discovering that his captured ridge overlooked the Resaca river crossings, McPherson brought up his guns and began to shell Johnston's only line of retreat.

This was the only advantage the Federals would gain at Resaca, because the valley of Camp Creek was not favorable to offensive action. Attackers were forced to leave the security of their works on a heavily wooded ridge, march down a steep slope to the floor of a broad valley, crawl through thickets of brush and trees, flounder through pools of deep water, struggle through bogs, cross ravines, and charge up a steep ridge in the teeth of massed infantry and artillery fire.

On May 14 Schofield's troops surged across the valley to strike the center of the Confederate line. They climbed halfway up the opposite slope before being hurled back with heavy losses. The survivors took shelter below the creek bank until dark, then crept back to their own lines. One of them termed the Confederate fire "terribly deadly."

Sherman launched a second assault that day on the angle of the Confederate line where it turned east toward the railroad. The men charged forward in a line five deep, bands playing stirring airs and regimental banners snapping in the breeze. The Confederate gunners were so eager to cut down this parade ground spectacle that their officers could hardly restrain them until the Federals were within effective range, about 200 yards. They opened up a murderous fire that cost the Yankees 600 soldiers; the rest took refuge in Camp Creek bed. Three successive waves of attackers were handily repulsed by the spirited Confederates, who enjoyed the gunnery practice. The approaching enemy made such an inviting target that artillery crews were "double shotting," firing two deadly charges at once. A few Federal soldiers reached the Rebel reentrant line but were rapidly driven out. The Union general responsible for these poorly coordinated attacks was subsequently relieved for incompetence.

A northern newsman recorded one of the mad charges. "Over the hill they swept, down the valley in double quick time, across it, raked by withering fire from the Rebel artillery; up the opposite hill toward the crest, where they met a regular shower of shell and bullets. Yet on they swept, plunged through the woods, striving desperately to gain its ascent." Few did, and those were cut down.

The Confederates did not escape unscathed. Volleys of well-aimed Federal artillery fire, faithfully signaled by a bugle call, had nearly leveled the Confederate earthworks at the angle by day's end.

Acting on intelligence from Wheeler's scouts that the northeastern flank of the Union line was lightly held, Johnston ordered Hood to lash out with an attack at 3:30 P.M. Hood's men rushed over the Yankee parapets, carried the enemy entrenchments, and surged around the left end of the Federal position. Regiments started to break for the rear, but Sherman thrust in reinforcements at this critical moment and restored the line. The Confederate advance stalled; and Hood was forced back to his original line, denied a

The War Child: ■ Joseph Wheeler

[LIBRARY OF CONGRESS]

The short history of the Confederacy produced many able, flamboyant cavalry leaders, and Wheeler deserves to be ranked with J.E.B. Stuart and Nathan Bedford Forrest. Wheeler, a self-professed "War Child," fought in an incredible 127 battles and skirmishes. He suffered three wounds; and sixteen horses bearing him in combat were killed. The attrition rate among his staff officers was legendary.

The diminutive warrior—he was only five feet, five inches in height and weighed 120 pounds—commanded the Army of Tennessee's cavalry in all its major campaigns, which made him the country's acknowledged expert in covering retreats. His most important role was harrassing the Federal March to the Sea, which he accomplished with such vigor that Jefferson Davis praised him for constricting Sherman's area of destruction.

After the Civil War, Wheeler served in Congress and entered private business. When the Spanish–American War broke out, he reenlisted in the United States Army and led a division of cavalry against the Spanish in Cuba. Rumor persists that Wheeler, flushed once again with the heat of battle as he led his men into combat, yelled, "Come on boys, let's whip those damn Yankees!" He later averred that he did not curse during the occasion in question.

Wheeler retired as a Brigadier General in the U.S. Army and was buried with full military honors in Arlington Cemetery. ■

Confederate troops vainly try to recapture Lay's Ferry and save Johnston's position at Resaca. [MOUNTAIN CAMPAIGNS IN GEORGIA]

critical victory. Sherman, the master flanker, had come perilously close to seeing his own flank turned and rolled up.

Throughout the day Johnston, who had been wounded in the Mexican War and earlier in the Civil War, rode his horse to the scenes of conflict. Bullets from Union snipers whipped past him, but he disdainfully refused to take cover. The ground trembled from the cheers of his men as he rode among them with encouraging words. They were outnumbered and outgunned, but their spirits were excellent.

When darkness fell, artillery batteries shelled the opposing ridges as both armies extended their lines in efforts to outflank each other. The Federals made one attempt to surprise the Southern defenders in the dark; but their advance was detected by Confederate pickets, and the alarm was sounded. The Confederates fired a large barn to illuminate the field, then twelve cannon opened a punishing fire against the attackers in blue. One participant, torn from sleep, wrote, "Volcanic fire leaps forth from the cannon's mouth . . . the air trembles violently with the din of battle." The Union foray was quickly repulsed, and the soldiers went back to sleep.

A far different activity was taking place just behind the Confederates' lines that night. After Hood and Polk were reunited at Resaca, the two generals were inspecting their lines when Hood remarked to the bishop that he had never received the communion of his church and asked that Polk perform the rite. Polk immediately agreed, and Hood soon stood before him on crutches (Hood's numerous wounds prevented his kneeling) in a candlelit field tent. Polk, resplendent in his robes which were worn over the full uniform of a Confederate general, baptized Hood from a tin basin with Hood's staff present as witnesses. A participant later wrote that Hood's face was "like that of an old crusader" as Polk administered the religious act.

Several days later Joseph Johnston approached Polk with the same request. In a similar ceremony in a tent at Cassville, Polk baptized this old campaigner.

The first day of battle had ended inconclusively. Sherman's test of the Confederate defenses had proved them impregnable to frontal assault, but the Confederates had come close to winning a significant victory. Sherman noted that the exchanges "rose all day to the dignity of a battle" that turned the area into a forest of shattered stumps. Resaca was shaping up as the first major conflict between Federal and Confederate forces in the Atlanta campaign.

At noon on the 15th, Schofield and Thomas concentrated for a strike against Hood's sector, but the Rebel works could not be pierced. The attack was marked by general confusion—Federal brigades fired volleys at each other, then the units milled together, making an organized assault impossible. The Yankees did manage to overrun an exposed four-gun battery, unwisely placed 80 yards in front of the gray infantry line; but other Confederate positions opened a withering fire on the attackers, forcing a hasty retreat. The Federals crept back after dark, quietly dismantled the

After several days of hard fighting, Federal forces occupy Resaca. [HARPER'S WEEKLY]

front of the log and earth lunette, and dragged the four guns back to their own lines by hand as trophies of war.

When Sherman deployed along Camp Creek two days earlier, he had dispatched his cavalry to search the north bank of the Oostanaula River for an undefended crossing. If one were found, he could threaten Johnston's flank as he had at Snake Creek Gap by driving troops into the Confederate rear, exposing their railroad supply line to attack, and possibly trap them between two Federal forces.

On May 14 the cavalry crossed the river at Lay's Ferry, near the mouth of Snake Creek, on two pontoon boat bridges. They drove off a fierce attack by Confederate cavalry guarding the opposite bank of the river, but the game of lost advantage continued. The Union horsemen withdrew because of a rumor that the Confederate army was crossing the river above them. Fearing they would be cut off, the Federal cavalry retreated to the northern shore and dug in for the night.

Johnston responded to the threat at Lay's Ferry by sending a division to throw the Federals back across the river. Finding the crossing deserted, the men marched back to Calhoun to await developments. On May 15 the Federals recrossed the river and were reinforced by McPherson's troops, who were shifted south from Resaca. This development, coupled with the Union shelling of his bridges, presented a serious danger to Johnston.

Hood had prepared a second attack against the Federal left flank late in the afternoon, but his troops were recalled when Johnston learned that Federal troops were crossing in force at Lay's Ferry. It was time for another strategic withdrawal.

Once more Joe Johnston's army disappeared like the night mist at dawn. When the sun rose on May 15, Sherman found the field deserted of Confederate defenders who left nothing behind except hundreds of bodies that littered the battlefield. The dead lay scattered across no-man's-land, cut down by bullets and shells long before they reached the enemy. A few attackers who breached the opposing trenches lay dead in the works, skulls crushed by rifle butts or bellies laid open by bayonets.

The corpses of Rebel and Yankee soldiers were intermingled in death. There are no accurate casualty figures for this small battle, but the best estimates are that Sherman lost 3,500 men killed and wounded at Resaca, Johnston 2,600.

Veteran officers on both sides of the field must have wondered about a curious coincidence. Many had fought in the Mexican War at the battle of Resaca de la Palma, and here they fought each other at a small Georgia village named for that American victory.

Resaca set the tone for the remainder of the campaign. It was immediately obvious that determined defenders positioned behind stout works could confidently hold off a much larger attacking force. Direct assaults would always fail, with great loss of life to the attackers. Sherman would react to this discovery by using his numerical advantage to outflank his adversary, while Johnston would try to maneuver Sherman into positions where either he would be goaded into attacking the Confederate defenses or Johnston would have an opportunity to successfully strike Sherman.

A DRIVING TOUR

■ Tilton and Resaca ■

This portion of the driving tour begins between Dalton and Resaca at the intersection of US 41–GA 3 and Tilton Road. To get there, turn off Interstate 75 on exit 134 (Carbondale Road). Turn right (east) and proceed .2 to the intersection. Turn right onto US 41–GA 3.

An optional tour route is to drive straight ahead across 41–3 on Tilton Road, which loops to Tilton near the pretty Conasauga River. The road intercepts 41–3 farther south. The countryside is beautiful, the town attractively sleepy. Sherman's advance was sharply checked at Tilton by a Confederate rear-guard action, and after the fighting moved south, the Federals built a wooden blockhouse on the northern edge of the town and garrisoned it with three hundred soldiers. When Hood's army attacked on October 13, 1864 (after the Atlanta campaign), the Federals retreated into the blockhouse, but Hood brought up his artillery, and after several hours the fort was battered into submission. Two years earlier, Andrews's Raiders had stopped here for wood and water.

After the Confederate evacuation of Resaca, some of Schofield's troops crossed the Conasauga near here at Hogan's Ford and several ferry points to advance on Adairsville from the east, camping at Old Holly Post Office in Murray County.

At 2.8 on US 41–GA 3, East Nance Springs Road is to the left, where the optional Tilton Loop ends. If you took the Loop, turn left to regain 41–3.

Before you turn left, there is a small monument designating Nance's Spring, where an old church cemetery still exists. At the railroad near Nance's Spring was John H. Green's wood station, a fueling stop on the Western and Atlantic in the 1860s. On May 9, 1864, at the start of Sherman's offensive, Federal raiders burned the station and cut the telegraph wires between Dalton and Atlanta. Two local women—Miss Carrie Sims and her sister, a Mrs. Bachman—became heroines after that attack by splicing the telegraph wires together to maintain Confederate communications.

Just before the Gordon County line at .4, a historical marker draws attention to a ridge which the highway cuts through.

The Federal line at Resaca occupied the crest of this ridge. Union troops advancing to attack Hood's position marched in formation along this route.

At .4 to your left is a small country road that leads to a hilly area where much of the Resaca fighting occurred.

Each year during the third weekend in May, an important reenactment of the battle is staged here, where the hills form a natural amphitheater for the simulated fighting. The reenactment includes infantry combat, cavalry clashes, and artillery duels. The event is sponsored by the city of Resaca, the Gordon County Chamber of Commerce, and the Gordon County Historical Society. Check locally for specific information.

Just across the Gordon County line to your left at .5 is the third Atlanta campaign pavilion.

Here a marker and relief map describe the battle of Resaca and the Federal flanking movement at Lay's Ferry, which forced Johnston to evacuate Resaca and retire farther south. This station is well-maintained, and on the corner is a small monument that commemorates the establishment of the Resaca Confederate Cemetery.

Take County Road 297 (Confederate Cemetery Road) beside the pavilion .4 to the Confederate Cemetery. Memorial services are held during the reenactment and on Confederate Memorial Day.

In this area the Confederate line ran west to east from the Camp Creek Valley to the railroad and Conasauga River just north of this road. Here Hood almost broke Sherman's left flank with a determined assault, and Hood's four-gun battery was captured nearby. The earthworks still exist in woods not far from U.S. 41.

When the armies had continued south, a local resident—Miss Mary J. Green—organized the women of Resaca to give the dead decent burials. They gathered more than four hundred bodies of Confederate soldiers and buried them here, where many had fallen on Hood's battlefield. A sturdy stone wall with a high entrance arch now surrounds the cemetery; on it is a bronze marker erected by the Atlanta Chapter of the United Daughters of the Confederacy. This marker

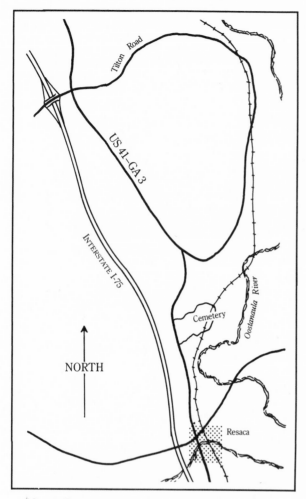

Map 8: Resaca area.

Also buried here is Mrs. E. J. Simmons, who helped establish and maintain the cemetery.

Return to U.S. 41–GA 3 and turn left to pass through the village of Resaca.

No longer a stop on the Western and Atlantic, it consists of a post office, one gas station, an arts and crafts exchange, and several stores. It was recently incorporated with a population of 350.

At 1.8 turn right onto GA 136 toward LaFayette. Cross I–75 and at .6 park on the right side of the road by Camp Creek. Walk to the bridge.

Sherman's armies marched to Resaca along this route over the gap on the western horizon to establish a position on the western ridge. Northwest of here is McPherson's route through Snake Creek Gap (see Appendix C). The Confederate line was to the east, considerably altered by the construction of 41–3 and I–75. The line extended nearly three miles parallel to Camp Creek from the Oostanaula River to the south, then turned sharply east to Hood's position near the cemetery and to the Conasauga River. The ridges were heavily wooded, and the meandering brook was choked with trees, underbrush, and quicksand. At no other site of the Atlanta campaign is it possible to view so much of the battlefield. Near this spot McPherson swept Polk back, brought up artillery, and started shelling the river bridges.

The women of Resaca gathered the Confederate dead after a battle and buried them in a special cemetery.

honors Miss Green's service in establishing the first Confederate Cemetery in Georgia.

The graves of 421 unidentified Confederate soldiers killed at Resaca are laid out in circles around a central stone monument topped by a granite cross that honors the "Unknown Dead." Some of the graves were later marked by family members who traveled from across the South to locate the resting places of sons, brothers, fathers, and husbands. Carefully cultivated flowers surround the monument, and a stand of giant oak trees shades the cemetery and imbues it with a serenity that stands in marked contrast to the manner in which these men died. On Confederate Memorial Day, small Confederate flags are placed on each grave.

A Works Project Administration monument was erected in memory of Cassville, a community destroyed by Federal troops after the Atlanta Campaign concluded.

Federal troops deployed their battle lines, worked their way down the western ridge under deadly accurate cannon fire from the Confederate defenders, plunged through the creek, charged up the eastern slope in the face of a galling fire from screaming Rebel infantry, then retired in disarray to lie in the creek until darkness hid the field. It is easy to visualize the carnage left in the valley by the clear fields of fire enjoyed by the Confederates, and it seems incongruous to watch cattle grazing on the western slopes of the peaceful farms and the traffic and intrusive signs along the Interstate.

Return to 41–3 and turn right toward Calhoun if you are continuing the tour.

To the southeast is Lay's Ferry, where McPherson flanked Johnston out of Resaca. The site is no longer accessible, but by proceeding north off Grogan and Leg roads from GA 156 west of Calhoun, you can approach the site, which occupies a scenic setting.

You will soon cross the Oostanaula River. The railroad bridge to the left was constructed on the original foundations of the bridge that Confederates torched as they retreated. On a ridge east of the railroad bridge are the ruins of a Union fort constructed to protect Sherman's supply route.

CHAPTER 4

Race to the Etowah

J ohnston's men evacuated their lines soon after dark on May 15 and withdrew from Resaca across two pontoon bridges and the railroad trestle that spanned the Oostanaula River. The Confederates destroyed the railroad bridge at 3:30 A.M. on the 16th and removed the pontoon boats to delay pursuit, then retreated toward Calhoun in search of a new defensive position. Hardee remained behind to slow the Federal advance and to prevent an attack on the cumbersome Southern wagon train.

To facilitate rapid movement on a broad front over the rough country roads, Sherman split his massive force into three groups, hoping to trap Johnston's army while it was scattered in withdrawal. McPherson crossed the river over two pontoon bridges six miles south of Resaca at Lay's Ferry and moved to the west toward Rome, sending J. C. Davis's division to capture that important industrial center. Thomas quickly built two bridges over the Oostanaula at Resaca and followed Johnston directly to Calhoun, while Schofield, accompanied by Hooker's corps, spanned the Coosawattee River at Field's Ferry and marched east of Calhoun through Cash and Sonoraville in an attempt to slip around the Confederate right at Adairsville.

Johnston found the terrain south of Resaca lacking in strong defensive features. Below Dalton there were no rugged mountains, only low, gently rolling hills that were easy to flank and valleys too wide for his limited number of troops to hold. In this terrain Johnston would find himself constantly frustrated in his attempts to hold a defensive position, always outflanked by Sherman's superior numbers. The open country placed Johnston at a disadvantage, but it was perfect territory for Sherman to maneuver his large armies.

Johnston had hoped to fight at Calhoun, but the open plain before the town was split by the swollen Oothkalooga Creek. Johnston could not risk separating his army to defend both banks, but he did stop to allow his exhausted men a few hours of precious sleep.

When the Confederates withdrew south of Calhoun, Hardee still commanded the rear guard, with orders to fight a delaying action. On May 16 at the Battle of Rome Crossroads, he engaged two divisions of McPherson's army and stopped them for 24 hours, ensuring the escape of the long wagon train below Adairsville. When McPherson exerted strong pressure against the Rebel position, Hardee withdrew to Adairsville and rejoined the main Confederate column.

Johnston had reason to be optimistic as he approached Adairsville on May 17. Maps showed a narrow, defensible gap between two ridges north of the town, but a personal survey of the area shattered his plans. The valley was wider than indicated, and Johnston worried that he lacked the men to hold it. The Confederate commander warily ordered his soldiers to establish a line and seriously considered bringing Sherman to battle here, but intelligence gathered by cavalry scouts indicated that Federal troops were flanking his position to the east and west of town. As Thomas deployed on the valley below, Johnston decided to abandon Adairsville.

Johnston disliked surrendering more territory, but according to his military philosophy this was preferable to wasting men in an unwise battle. Furthermore, during the days of retreat he had developed an offensive strategy. Feeling that the situation south of Adairsville was perfect for its execution, Johnston ordered the plan put into effect. Sherman would be lured into a trap.

When Johnston began his withdrawal south, Cheatham's division of Hardee's corps was left to fight another delaying action in the trenches be-

Map 9: Confrontation at Cassville.

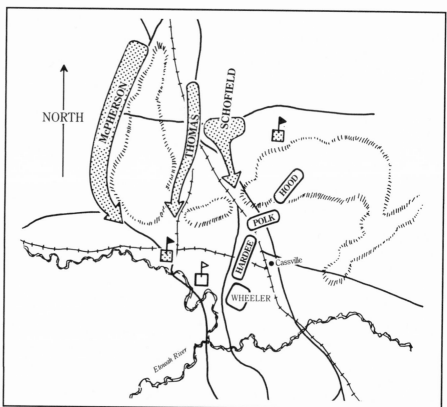

fore Adairsville to buy time for the wagons to safely reach Kingston. The skirmish raged for several hours with heavy exchanges of artillery and musket fire, but Cheatham held the Federals until several divisions deployed in line of battle for a full attack on his works. Then he skillfully withdrew during the night and marched to Kingston on the morning of May 18.

When Sherman arrived at Adairsville, he took his staff forward to reconnoiter the enemy position. There an alert Confederate battery opened fire on them, killing several horses. Sherman wryly remarked that it was probably a mistake to expose the army's general staff to such danger and they retired to a safer observation post.

Sherman noted that the Confederate action at Adairsville approached the intensity of a full battle. During the afternoon of the 17th, 200 Union soldiers were killed; but the dawn of the 18th revealed that Johnston had pulled his vanishing act once again. Except for the stout fieldworks, there was no evidence that an army had ever occupied the ground. After the Confederate evacuation, Sherman briefly rested his armies at Adairsville while preparing to march on Kingston, where he assumed the Confederates would finally make a stand. Before following Johnston south, Sherman cared for his wounded, replenished his supplies, and destroyed a Confederate arsenal at Adairsville and nearby factories.

Behind Sherman's advance, Union engineers performed a miraculous job of repairing the railroad. While men fought at Resaca, Federal supply trains entered Dalton; when Union troops seized Calhoun, the rails reached Resaca; and engines chugged into Adairsville while Sherman briefly tarried there. The repair of telegraph lines kept pace with the railroad, keeping Sherman in constant communication with his supply bases in Tennessee.

Sherman split his forces for the pursuit from Adairsville, intending to outflank Johnston and cause the Confederates to retreat closer to the ultimate objective: Atlanta. Thomas followed directly to Kingston; McPherson passed to the west; and Schofield and Hooker pursued to the east, in a repetition of their earlier pattern. Johnston was counting on that.

As the Confederates continued to retreat, refugees became a growing problem. Some people chose to remain in federally controlled territory to care for their farms and businesses, but thousands flocked before the Southern army, clogging the roads, straining local resources, and often panicking other citizens with frightening stories of destruction. As each mile of territory was relinquished, there were more civilians urging Johnston to turn and destroy the hated Yankee invaders. He intended to do just that.

Johnston had retreated 30 miles from Dalton; but he was determined to stop Sherman before the Union general forced him across the Etowah, the last river barrier remaining before the Chattahoochee. Johnston had studied his adversary's accomplished flanking maneuvers at Snake Creek Gap, Resaca, Calhoun, and Adairsville. Now he planned to turn Sherman's tactics against him.

Johnston anticipated that Sherman would send the bulk of his army to Kingston, following the railroad and major wagon roads. Johnston believed Sherman would split his forces as he had done before, sending the smallest

Drill, Drill, Drill ■ The Soldier's Guide to Battlefield Survival

Successfully loading a Civil War musket was an exercise in exasperation. It was an involved process, and performing it amid the din and slaughter of battle—with an enemy shooting back—required iron discipline and constant training in camp.

In order to teach the proper procedure to green troops, Confederate General William J. Hardee broke the reloading process down into nine steps in his *Tactics*:

1. Hold the rifle barrel up, stock firmly on the ground;
2. Take a cartridge from belt and tear it open with teeth;
3. Pour the gunpowder down the barrel, followed by the paper cartridge as wadding and place bullet in barrel, pointed end up;
4. Take rammer from beneath barrel;
5. Ram bullet down the barrel;
6. Cock hammer halfway back and extract old percussion cap;
7. Take new cap from pouch and place on nipple under hammer;
8. Cock hammer back fully, bring rifle to shoulder, and sight;
9. Fire.

It seems amazing that a well-trained soldier could actually get off three shots a minute.

Curious things happened in combat. Often a gun would fail to fire, but with the sounds of battle surrounding him, the rifleman might not notice. He would reload, and the gun might fire the two loads; or it might explode. A number of men were impaled by rammers that excited soldiers had neglected to extract from the barrel before they fired. ■

command—Schofield's Army of the Ohio, accompanied by Hooker's corps—
to the west toward Cassville, the next stop after Kingston on the railroad, to
flank Johnston out of Kingston. Johnston decided he would mass his army at
Cassville to destroy Schofield and Hooker before the other armies could
arrive to assist their beleaguered colleagues.

Johnston sent Hardee and Wheeler's cavalry, with all the wagons, to
Kingston, ten miles south of Adairsville. That would make the road look
obviously well traveled to Sherman's scouts. The bulk of the Confederate
army, the corps of Hood and Polk, marched to Cassville, five miles south of
Adairsville and east of Kingston, on a minor road that led directly from
Adairsville. The wagon train continued immediately from Kingston to Cassville; but Hardee was to execute a fighting withdrawal, tearing up the railroad tracks and obstructing the roads behind him in order to delay
McPherson and Thomas from coming to relieve Schofield and Hooker.

Johnston was delighted by the terrain he found at Cassville. North of the
town was a ridge where he would entrench Polk's army. In front of Polk was
a wide, open plain over which Schofield would advance: a perfect killing
field. Behind the town was another ridge where the Confederates emplaced
their artillery, and a rear guard stationed there could protect their flank.

Hood was positioned northeast of Polk. His assignment was to assault
Schofield's left flank, then Polk would pour out of his works to hit the badly
outnumbered and thoroughly surprised Federals from the front. Hardee,
advancing from Kingston, would strike the Federals from the west and roll
up their right flank. Schofield and Hooker would be destroyed before reinforcements could intervene, and Sherman might be forced to retreat to
Chattanooga to regroup.

Johnston began to evacuate the women and children of Cassville, a thriving commercial and cultural center of northern Georgia. He hurriedly converted a women's college into a hospital to receive the inevitable flood of
casualties. The attack was scheduled for dawn on May 15.

Johnston announced the impending combat in an order which was read to
all his troops. The Confederate commander congratulated the men for having "repulsed every assault." He praised their courage and skill in facing the
enemy. Then he delivered the message for which they had long waited: "You
will now turn and march to meet his advancing columns. I lead you in battle!"

A Confederate officer later noted, "The men were burning to fight," particularly those Southerners whose homes had been occupied in Kentucky,
Tennessee, and northern Georgia, and those whose families lay in the path
of hostilities to Atlanta. Great cheers echoed among the hills as each regiment heard the order, but the ragged Rebels were due another disappointment.

As Schofield marched unwittingly into the trap, Johnston waited anxiously
for the sounds of battle. They never came. The plan failed when Hood
claimed he had been outflanked by powerful Federal forces, which turned
out to be a small contingent of lost Yankee cavalry. Hood promptly fell back
to establish a defensive position on the ridge beside Polk. Johnston, bitterly
disappointed by the loss of a perfect opportunity to turn the tide of this

New Echota, near Calhoun, was the capital of the Cherokee nation. Here they published a Cherokee language newspaper, the Phoenix.

campaign, was outraged that Hood had not bothered to ask for instructions. Instead, the crippled general had withdrawn, then informed Johnston of his action hours later. Johnston called Hood's conduct "extraordinary disobedience."

The bulk of Sherman's armies followed Hardee to Kingston, camping at Conesena Creek on the 18th and arriving in Kingston at 8:00 A.M. on May 19. Sherman was extremely puzzled, and more than a little troubled, when he reached the town. His troops met only light resistance on the march, and Kingston had been relinquished without a fight. Since Johnston had not defended Calhoun, Adairsville, or Kingston, Sherman believed the wily Confederate had retreated across the numerous bridges and shallow fords along the serpentine Etowah River just south of Kingston. A hasty cavalry reconnaissance reported no Rebels across the river and no evidence that an army had recently used the roads.

At midday on the 19th, Schofield, not realizing his narrow escape from disaster, stumbled upon Johnston's army entrenched at Cassville. Riders quickly informed Sherman, who saw Schofield's danger and immediately shifted Thomas and McPherson from Kingston as rapidly as he could push through Hardee's interference. Sherman's hard ride over primitive roads brought him to Cassville an hour before dark. Thomas's huge corps and the bulky wagon train advanced over the main roads and deployed in front of Cassville, then waited for McPherson, who marched cross country and over poor back lanes to arrive several hours later.

For the assault against Schofield, Johnston's position on the ridge north of Cassville was perfect; but it was not a good line of defense. Johnston was unable to attack the entire Federal army advantageously, which was once again united in front of him, from his position. At 4:00 P.M. Johnston ordered his forces to establish a new line on the ridge south of town. He and Polk reconnoitered the terrain and marked positions they wanted occupied.

As the withdrawal progressed in the late afternoon, an aggressive Federal strike drove the Confederates back from the women's college in Cassville. The Southern trenches were rapidly seized by an Ohio artillery battery that opened a deadly fire on the retreating Confederates. Under a heavy bombardment in the oppressive evening heat, the Rebels tumbled into their new line. A Confederate officer made this note in his diary, "Late in afternoon, considerable skirmishing and artillery (fire), enemy's skirmishers occupy town."

Amid much noise, dust, and confusion, the Confederate wagon train, artillery, cavalry, and infantry fell back to the southern ridge under constant fire from Federal batteries. Experienced officers coolly waded into the melee and restored order, directing the wagons to wait while the fighting men and cannon took up positions from which they returned the galling Union fire.

The terrified people of Cassville suddenly found themselves dangerously exposed in a free-fire zone. The Confederate diarist recorded, "Many flee, leaving all, some take away few effects, some remain between hostile fire."

The new Confederate position extended four miles, from a point east of Cassville to west of the railroad at Cass Station. Arriving from Kingston, Hardee anchored the western end of the line, Polk occupied the center, and Hood was to the east. Ironically, the line skirted the home of General W. T. Wofford, who at that moment was fighting desperately in Virginia's Wilderness with Robert E. Lee, unaware that war was ravaging his home.

When Sherman arrived at Cassville, Howard informed him that the Confederates had withdrawn in perfect order to the opposite ridge. Surveying the heights through his glass, Sherman found it covered with freshly dug works. *At last,* he must have thought, *Johnston has found a favorable place to fight.*

Federal troops occupied the evacuated Confederate works, and throughout the night of May 19th a furious artillery duel took place between Rebel and Yankee batteries. Shells shrieked across the beautiful valley as skirmishers fiercely fought in the streets of Cassville. Fine homes and buildings were riddled with shot and shell, and some structures were fired by troops for illumination. Civilian casualties among those who remained are unknown.

The Confederate rear guard barely escaped capture in the town by swarming Union soldiers. One of the last Confederates who fell in Cassville was Legare Hill, son of Joshua Hill, a Congressman from Madison who knew

Sherman's brother John, a U.S. Senator from Ohio. Federal troops watching from nearby hills held their fire as two friends carried Hill's body into a house, pinned his name to his clothes, and left. The Federals who occupied the town buried the young man and marked the grave by carving his name on a piece of wood, thus sparing him the ignominy that many soldiers on both sides of the Civil War feared and faced—an unknown grave.

After surveying his new lines, Johnston believed he had a good defensive position. The ridge towered 140 feet above the valley floor, commanding the ground over which Sherman would have to advance. The eager Confederates had an unobstructed field of fire. Johnston called the position "the best that I saw occupied during the war." Having been denied victory here once, Johnston decided it would still be the site of the first decisive battle in the Atlanta campaign.

After riding along the line to encourage his men, Johnston entered his tent to rest. There he found an invitation to supper with Hood and Polk. When he arrived at Polk's headquarters, Hood immediately argued that his position was vulnerable to artillery fire from the side as well as from the front, a dangerous situation known as being enfiladed. He claimed the Union guns were in a position to slaughter his troops. Johnston responded that the problem had been noted, and engineers were digging traverses to protect Hood's works; but Hood insisted that his line could not be held. Polk concurred, leading historians to believe they had conspired to induce Johnston to change his plans. Hood and Polk advised their commanding general to withdraw behind the Etowah and fight on a better field.

Johnston was dumbfounded. These two officers, particularly Hood, had frequently criticized him for not meeting Sherman in aggressive battle. Hood grossly violated the proper chain of command by writing letters to President Davis in which he condemned Johnston's strategy. And Hood was

The Unsung Rock: ■ George H. Thomas

[LIBRARY OF CONGRESS]

During the Civil War, a number of notably incompetent generals rose to command Union armies, but one of the Union's greatest leaders has long remained unheralded. Thomas was born in Virginia in 1816, but he lost his family in 1861 when he chose to fight for the North. His sisters turned his picture to the wall and never spoke his name again.

Thomas assumed an early role in the Army of the Cumberland, fighting at Shiloh, Perryville, and Stones River. At Chickamauga he very probably saved the Union. The Federal army was put to flight, but Thomas and his men established a precarious hilltop position and repulsed furious Confederate attacks until nightfall, preventing the Rebels from completely destroying William Rosecrans's army. For this heroic action, Thomas was nicknamed "The Rock of Chickamauga."

After steady service in the Atlanta campaign, Sherman dispatched Thomas to contain Hood in Tennessee. Hood laid a pathetic siege to Nashville while Grant harried Thomas to attack. When "Old Slow Trot" was ready and Grant was boarding a train to relieve him, Thomas launched a shattering assault that inflicted the worst defeat suffered by a Confederate army in the entire war.

Thomas was one of the Union's best tacticians; but when many of his plans were successfully implemented, more colorful generals reaped the rewards. Thomas refused to seek the presidency in 1868 and died two years later, at his post. As a public demonstration of Thomas's contributions to the outcome of the Civil War and of the regard in which he was held, over 10,000 people attended his funeral. ■

the man who just that day had thrown away a golden opportunity to destroy Schofield's entire army. Johnston surely remembered that Polk had given Braxton Bragg grief in 1863 when he had wanted to take the offensive. Bragg had relieved Polk of command for failing to attack at Chickamauga, but his decision was countermanded by Jefferson Davis. Now these two wanted to withdraw when Johnston had decided to confront the enemy.

Johnston's reflections were interrupted by the arrival of Hardee at the conference. The respected tactician was outraged that Hood and Polk had confronted Johnston with such a suggestion. His own position was the least desirable, but Hardee foresaw a great Confederate victory on this ground.

The final decision was Johnston's. Considering the possibility of victory in a battle where two of three corps commanders questioned his judgment and felt that defeat was probable, he angrily determined to retreat.

During the night the bewildered Confederate soldiers received orders to withdraw. By dawn not a trace of the Army of Tennessee remained at Cassville. After the sun rose to reveal that the enemy had disappeared, Sherman wandered among the empty Confederate trenches. His astonishment was matched by that of the Confederate soldiers who were tramping across the Etowah River and burning the bridges behind them.

Johnston was severely criticized by Southern newspapers from Atlanta to Richmond for retreating behind the Etowah without bringing Sherman to battle, but they did not realize that the decision had been forced on him by two sullen subordinates. The "Cassville Controversy," Hood's failure to attack followed by his confrontation with Polk against Johnston, would be fought on paper for decades after the Civil War ended.

A DRIVING TOUR
■ Adairsville to Cassville ■

This portion of the driving tour begins at the intersection of Interstate 75 and U.S. 41–GA 3. Those coming from Atlanta, should turn left and under the interstate on 41–3; those coming from Chattanooga should turn right. The tour continues south on 41–3 toward Calhoun.

This is the route followed by Johnston and Thomas, while Schofield crossed the Conasauga River to the east, and McPherson advanced to the west. The covered railroad bridge here was James Andrews's primary target during the Great Locomotive Chase, but close pursuit by Fuller forced him to abandon the attempt. Andrews backed up to "throw" a boxcar at the *Texas,* but Fuller coupled it and continued the chase. The foundation of the railroad bridge to your left stood during the war.

At the intersection of 41–3 and GA 225 at 1.8, pull over to inspect the two interesting monuments in the traffic island.

At the entrance to the little park is an arch with a figure of a Confederate soldier on the left and a World War I doughboy on the right. One suspects that when this monument was erected no one could imagine America involved in a larger or more destructive war than those represented here. Through the arch is a bronze statue of Sequoya, the Indian who developed an alphabet for his language and established a Cherokee newspaper at New Echota, a fascinating state historical development to the east on GA 225. New Echota was capital of the Cherokee Nation before the forced removal of the Cherokee Indians on the Trail of Tears. Historical buildings have been moved there and restored, or recreated. There are houses, a tavern, a supreme court building, a print shop, and an interesting museum.

Continue South on 41–3 through downtown Calhoun.

During the Great Locomotive Chase, Andrews nearly collided with a southbound passenger train here. Hardee delayed McPherson here for twenty-four hours in an action along the banks of Othcalogo Creek just west on GA 53.

On the right in Calhoun at 2.4 is Oakleigh.

Sherman is said to have established temporary headquarters here. It is now home to the Gordon County Historical Society and houses a doll collection.

Map 10: From Adairsville to Kingston.

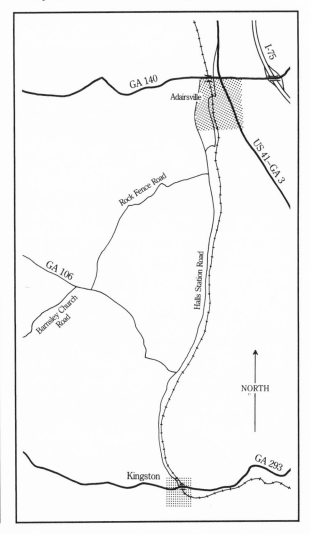

If you are in no hurry, there is an unusual attraction along I–75 two miles south of GA 53: the World Aircraft Museum, which consists of thirteen aircraft, including five jet fighters, two DC-3s, two helicopters, and a transport.

The highway between Calhoun and Adairsville passes through beautiful, pastoral country situated in a broad valley. It is easy to see why Johnston had to retreat through Calhoun and south to Adairsville; the ridges east and west—actually low, rolling hills—were too widely separated to establish a defensive line across the valley. Johnston and Thomas traveled this route; Schofield passed east through Cash and Sonoraville, and McPherson west, sending a detail to occupy Rome and destroy its industrial facilities.

If you have plenty of time, county maps, patience, and a sense of humor, you may want to explore the river crossings east of here and the lovely countryside that Schofield traversed on his route to Adairsville and Cassville. Bridges span the Coosawattee River just before it joins the Conasauga to form the Oostanaula at the sites of Field's Ferry, McClure's Ferry, and Harlan's Crossroads. County roads run from Redbud, which sports a red double-decker bus along the road, to Cash, where Schofield camped beside Dew's Pond, which has a beautiful mill and falls, and to Sonoraville, with a roadside wooden Indian. Schofield advanced into Bartow County via Mosteller's Mills, a plantation-manufacturing center of the 1860s where little remains today, and crossed Cedar Creek to proceed through Pleasant Valley toward Cassville. Drive back to Calhoun to avoid long periods of being lost while exploring this route.

You can trace the route of Federal cavalry and infantry to Rome east of here. On May 15 Garrard's cavalry left Villanow and camped at Floyd Springs on GA 156. The next day he continued four miles to Farmers Bridge (Armuchee), skirmished briefly with Confederate cavalry, crossed the creek at the U.S. 27 bridge, and rode eight miles to DeSoto Hill on the east bank of the Oostanaula River near the railroad underpass on U.S. 27. That day, Confederate General French arrived to prepare a defense, but he soon received orders to withdraw and assist in the planned Confederate attack at Cassville.

Garrard was scouting for Federal Gen. Jefferson Davis's infantry, which reached DeSoto Hill on May 17; on the following day, Davis forced a crossing under fire to capture the city. He remained until May 24, then followed McPherson to Dallas through Aragon on GA 101. The city was garrisoned until November and

was reinforced during Hood's erratic campaign into Alabama. Sherman rested in Rome on October 17 and returned on October 28. When the March to the Sea began, all military equipment and factories were destroyed. The city was abandoned on November 10.

When Garrard left the Rome area, he protected McPherson's right flank on the move to Kingston via Barnsley's Gardens, breaking the Rome Railroad south of the city and passing near Shannon on May 17 and 18. On May 17 McPherson left Calhoun for Barnsley's and camped at McGuire's, where GA 53 and 140 intersect. Shannon is two miles southwest on GA 53.

Evidence of 41–3's importance before the Interstate was built is provided by the old red tile service stations and restaurants that line this route. Note the scenic old concrete bridges over streams beside the main highway and barns with overhangs in front to protect hay entrances. Andrews covered the nine-mile distance between Calhoun and Adairsville in seven and one-half minutes, an unheard of time; Fuller followed at a leisurely, but still suicidal, mile a minute.

At 8.8 miles turn right onto GA 140, left at .1 onto Main Street, and right at .6 onto Public Square Road .1 to downtown Adairsville.

The region surrounding Adairsville was an important breadbasket to the Confederacy, and the town was also of vital railroad interest as it had been designated a terminus of the Western and Atlantic and machine shops and a roundhouse had been constructed, in addition to a gun and gunpowder factory. Each October the community sponsors a Great Locomotive Chase festival. For information, call (404) 773-3451.

Adairsville is a perfectly preserved example of a small Georgia town. On the left is a row of old-fashioned stores, most of them still open. Inside are traditional wooden floors and broad counters, and the clerks use crank cash registers and manual adding machines. To the right of the square, which boasts a gazebo, is an antique store converted from the depot and an old warehouse. Clustered in the downtown area are pretty churches and old homes, and nearby are recreational facilities. Adairsville is alive.

Johnston temporarily established a defensive line just north of town and skirmished with Sherman before setting his trap. Most of the Confederate army retired directly to Cassville along the modern route of 41-3. Hardee, with Thomas and McPherson following, went to Kingston along the railroad. So will we.

Drive west beside the old warehouse on Park Street .4 to Hall Station Road and turn left. At 1.7 turn right onto Rock Fence Road.

You are traveling through scenic Snow Valley along the route followed by McPherson to Barnsley's Gardens, an antebellum plantation where he camped the night of May 18 before moving into Kingston. Thomas marched straight to Kingston along Hall Station Road, but this route is infinitely more attractive.

Travel this winding road slowly so you will have time to appreciate the beauty of this secluded valley. Wooded ridges rise all around, and creeks babble beside the road. Cows graze in the lush fields and in summer submerge all but their heads in the streams and ponds, separated from the road by old wire strung on decaying timber posts. Behind tree-lined fence-rows are fields littered with wonderfully weathered farm buildings, outhouses, wells, and old homes with tin roofs and double chimneys.

Bear left at the next three branches to a stop sign at 4.6. Turn right onto 106 and left at .4 onto Barnsley Church Road. Barnsley Church is at .7.

Barnsley Church is on what once was an extensive plantation. The quaint little church has twin outhouses and a wonderful covered picnic area for dinner on the grounds.

From the church, return to 106 and turn right, passing Rock Fence Road. At 1.0, to your right, is the entrance to Barnsley's Gardens.

Godfrey Barnsley arrived in Savannah from Great Britain and made his fortune in cotton and shipping. In 1840 he purchased thirty-six hundred acres in Cass County halfway between Rome and Marietta, hoping the mountain air would help his wife's tuberculosis. He began building a grand three-story twenty-eight-room brick Italianate manor, named Woodlands, which remained under construction for several decades. The grounds were as magnificent as the mansion, featuring acres of gardens, goldfish ponds, and exotic trees from around the world.

In late May 1864 the Army of the Tennessee passed Barnsley's. As the Federals approached, Confederate Col. Richard G. Earle, a personal friend, raced to warn Barnsley of the threat. While riding away, Earle was killed by Yankee soldiers. He is buried on the grounds, and the grave is a prominent landmark.

Barnsley flew the British flag and claimed neutrality, despite the fact that most of his assets were invested in Confederate war bonds and his two sons fought in Rebel armies. McPherson, who called the plantation "a little piece of heaven itself," issued orders that Woodlands should not be harmed. Unfortunately, after camping on the grounds May 18, the general and the main Federal body continued on south, and stragglers broke into the cellar where they consumed a reported two thousand bottles of wine. The drunken men then started a large bonfire, fueling it with exquisite furnishings, while objects of marble and porcelain were smashed. What survived, along with all the food, was looted.

Barnsley filed a claim for $155,000 in damages against the Federal government through the British consulate in Washington. He collected nothing.

Barnsley lost his fortune in the Civil War. His bonds were rendered worthless, and two of his ships were sunk attempting to run the blockade. His sons refused to take the oath of allegiance to the United States and emigrated to the famed Confederate colony in Brazil. Two children died, and when Barnsley died in New Orleans, a surviving daughter buried him at Woodlands and operated the plantation. Heirs were forced to sell off land, and a tornado in 1906 ripped off the roof and forced the family to live in the detached kitchen.

The plantation house and grounds fell into decay, kudzu covering outbuildings and trees taking root in the manor. In 1988, however, German investors purchased sixteen hundred acres and have spent several million dollars clearing the land, stabilizing the striking three-story ruin, restoring the extensive gardens with tens of thousands of plants, and opening a café, gift shop, and theater. A museum displays Civil War artifacts excavated on the grounds, and regular programs are sponsored, including a Confederate ball and Civil War days.

After McPherson had camped overnight, he continued on to Wooley's Plantation, just west of Kingston and south of GA 293 on a county road loop. A few buildings remain there, but they are not accessible to the public. The Army of the Tennessee crossed the Etowah River there on a covered bridge, advancing on Dallas by way of Macedonia Church, while the remainder crossed the Etowah at Gillem's Bridge and a pontoon bridge at Milam's Bridge.

Continue east to Hall Station Road at 2.5 and turn right.

To your left are the low Cassville Mountains, which separated Thomas and McPherson from Schofield.

At 4.7 stop at the sign and turn left onto GA 297 into Kingston. At .5 turn right beside the store/gas station onto Shaw Street .1 to the stop sign.

To either side are rows of old stores, eleven buildings in all on Railroad Street, which face the tracks and park. Most are closed.

To your front is a large, well-kept park that has witnessed a great deal of southern history. It was to Kingston that Sherman retired after the near battle at Cassville to plan his advance on Dallas. He returned here in October after chasing Hood north to plot his infamous March to the Sea.

The original business district, constructed in the 1830s, stood across the tracks, but Sherman burned it when he left for the coast. Rebuilt on the north side after the war, the buildings, except the brick two-story DeSoto Hotel on your right, now on the National Register, were destroyed in a second devastating fire in 1911. Built in 1890, the DeSoto was a favored stop for salesmen. Its food was renowned throughout the region.

On May 12, 1865, Confederate Gen. William T. Wofford surrendered the last Confederate troops in the state, and the last east of the Mississippi River—most of the four thousand men were Georgians—to Federal Gen. Henry M. Judah in this park. Judah generously issued the hungry Rebels rations and released them to return home and work their farms.

Several street signs in Kingston are confusing, identifying portions of different streets as Main, Park, and Church; so ignore the signs and follow these directions. From the stop sign at Shaw and Railroad streets, drive across the railroad tracks to the street nearly opposite and continue to the end of the park at .1. The Confederate Memorial Museum is in the small building in the park to the left. It contains a collection of Civil War artifacts—weapons, munitions, money—and is open on special occasions.

In the facing yard is a monument recognizing Kingston as the site of eight Confederate hospitals that treated ten thousand men from 1862 until the spring of 1864. Then the wounded and sick were evacuated to Atlanta out of the path of the contending armies. The monument also honors local women who cared for the men. Once captured, the hospitals were used by Union troops until the war ended. Fuller was able to close the distance on Andrews's raiders as the *Federal* was de-

layed here an hour by several passing trains. Faint remains of the depot and spur lines can be found near the railroad tracks to your right. Eight skirmishes occurred around Kingston between May and September 1864, including several Confederate raids.

Turn right a short distance to the four-way stop and left on Johnson Street at .3 to the Confederate portion of the city cemetery.

Here 249 unknown Confederate dead, one known, and two unknown Federal soldiers who died in the hospitals are buried. The only identified warrior here is Sterling F. Chandler, a twenty-nine-year-old private in the Georgia infantry. The sight of these blank headstones is a chilling reminder of the true cost of war.

Inside the enclosure is a small monument to the unknown soldiers and an obelisk erected to honor the Confederate dead. For more than 120 years women from the United Daughters of the Confederacy have laid wreaths at the obelisk and small Confederate flags at each grave; descendants of original Kingston families keep the tradition alive. Confederate Memorial Day (or Decoration Day, which is held to remember Southern men who died in the Civil War) was held in Kingston in April 1864, the first observance in the United States and a continuous one. When ladies requested permission from Judah to decorate Confederate graves, he agreed if they would also grace Federal graves with flowers. They did.

Kingston is one of many sites claimed to be the spot where Sherman planned or began his march to the sea, and this community has a better claim to that honor than most. Sherman established headquarters here on May 19 and again in late November after chasing Hood into Alabama. Here he received permission from Grant to campaign against Savannah. Sherman was quartered in the Thomas Van Buren Hargin House, which burned in 1947.

Across the small parking area is a monument to Kingston's Confederate veterans, all of whom lived rich lives following the Civil War. From this hillside cemetery is an impressive view of hills to the north.

Return to the four-way stop and turn right at .1 to the Methodist Church.

Built in 1854, it is the only original church left from the time that Sherman occupied the town. For several years it hosted all denominations, served as the local school, was the scene of the first Confederate Memorial Day services, and was later the site of temperance rallies. A pastor of the church was Confederate general and noted author Clement A. Evans, and the famed evangelist Sam Jones preached from its pulpit. A superbly crafted bell that hangs in the tower was a gift from John Pendleton King, president of the Western and Atlantic Railroad, a U.S. Senator, for whom the town was named. The bell, audible for four miles, saw use as the town fire alarm and was rung to announce peace following four wars.

Continue to the notable Baptist Church and turn left opposite it and right at .3 for the short drive to Cassville on GA 293.

Sherman's affection for the Etowah Valley can be understood by the beauty seen along this stretch. In 1975 the U.S. Department of Agriculture designated the Etowah Valley as Georgia's largest historic district, forty thousand acres. The highway winds gently beside creeks, rolling hills, beautiful green fields, and farms. Thomas and McPherson raced across this land when they realized the threat to Schofield, who had found Johnston entrenched before Cassville.

At 5.7 turn left onto Spur 293–C .4 to the stop sign at the intersection with U.S. 41–GA 3. Cross the four-lane highway to the Cassville–White Road. Immediately on your left is the fourth Atlanta campaign interpretive pavilion.

This station is the largest of the five, but is in terrible condition. Some of the long, curving walls are crumbling, the relief map has disappeared, and maintenance has been dismal. The marker remains to describe the action that took place at Cassville just east of this spot. Relax at one of the picnic tables here and reflect on the tragedy that occurred around you.

Cassville was the seat of Cass County and one of the most prosperous cities in northern Georgia before the Civil War. The courthouse was surrounded by stores, four churches, four hotels, separate colleges for men and women, and many fine homes. In 1861 the Georgia legislature changed the county name to Bartow to honor Georgia Gen. Francis B. Bartow, who died at Manassas (Bull Run for those of the Northern persuasion), and the town was renamed Manassas.

Two months after Atlanta fell, Union soldiers marched into town on November 5, 1864, with orders to raze it. The two thousand people of Cassville were given little time to evacuate homes and businesses and only managed to save a minimum of belongings. The town soon blazed fiercely and by sundown only smoking timbers and charred chimneys were left to mark the site of the formerly thriving city. The people were left to shift for themselves in a cold rain with no shelter, and many died of exposure and malnutrition during the hard winter. Only three churches and three homes, used to house the sick, were spared destruction. Cassville was never rebuilt, and the county seat, most of the people, and all the businesses were relocated in Cartersville, just north on the Western and Atlantic.

The reason for Cassville's destruction remained a mystery for over a hundred years, but a diary entry by a Federal officer explains Sherman's action. The area surrounding Cassville was a center of guerrilla activity, and in early November 1864 the men of a Union patrol were found dead. The grisly scene suggested that they had surrendered to guerrillas and had then been executed. To retaliate, Sherman in an apparently unrecorded order, directed every structure within five miles of the murders to be razed. Cassville lay within that range.

Proceed east on Cassville–White Road. The Baptist Church to your left at .8 is on the original location of a former sanctuary that was spared the conflagration of November 1864. At .1 on your right is the old Presbyterian Church, the same that survived the fire. Just down the road at .2 is a sign indicating the historic Methodist Church to the right on Church Street. Follow that narrow road .1 between cornfields to the beautiful church, which has been slightly altered but is the original building.

Continue on Church Street around the curve, down a straight stretch, through an intersection, and around another curve; at .4 the old Cassville Cemetery is directly in front of you. Turn right and enter the second drive on your left and circle the cemetery to the Confederate section on the eastern slope of the hill.

Eight large Confederate hospitals were established in Cassville from late 1861 until May 1864, treating thousands of soldiers before being evacuated south.

Of the five hundred Confederates who died in those hospitals, three hundred were buried here. Only one, W. M. Barrow, a twenty-year-old from Louisiana, is identified. In May 1899, the Cassville Chapter of the United Daughters of the Confederacy honored these men by placing headstones over each grave. Towering above the Confederate graves is an obelisk, dedicated on April 26, 1878, by the Ladies Memorial Association to pay homage to the bravery and sacrifice of these men. The obelisk carries messages such as, "Is it death to fall for freedom's cause?" "It is better to have fought and died than not to have fought at all," "You loved liberty more than life," "Rest in peace, our own Southern heroes." Above the fallen flies a Confederate flag, and ancient cedar trees shade their resting place.

Gen. W. T. Wofford, a Cassville native, is also buried here. Wofford, a cavalry captain in the Mexican War, rose to the rank of general in the Confederate army. He fought bravely at Manassas, South Mountain, Antietam, Fredericksburg, Chancellorsville, and the Wilderness. After Thomas R. R. Cobb was killed at Fredericksburg, Wofford assumed command of his Georgia troops until January 1865, when the War Department in Richmond dispatched him to his native north Georgia. Wofford's assignment was to protect the citizens from marauding bushwhackers who terrorized the region after the collapse of organized government that inevitably followed Sherman's destructive visit. In May 1865 it was his duty to surrender surviving Confederate soldiers in the region at Kingston.

The second Confederate line at Cassville skirted the cemetery to the south. The Federal line occupied the northern ridge, extending through the Female College and just north of the Male College. The city lay in the valley between the lines.

From the cemetery drive back the way you came, round the curve, and at .2 turn right at the intersection onto Cassville–White Road. After .2 on your left is a large park area that marks the old courthouse square.

In 1936 the WPA erected a monument here in memory of vanished Cassville. All that remains of Cassville today are the churches, the cemetery, one store, a post office, and a new fire station across the street from the empty courthouse grounds.

On May 24, 1864, Wheeler's cavalry made a daring dash around the Federal left to Cassville, where they intercepted a Federal supply train. After driving off the Union cavalry guard, they burned 180 wagons and brought 70, loaded with supplies, and 250 teams of mules, 200 prisoners, and many head of cattle back to Confederate lines below the Etowah River, where they were gratefully received.

At nearby Cass Station, .1 off GA 293 on Burnt Hickory Road, the abandoned depot and a boarded-up store remain where Andrews and Fuller thundered past surprised and disappointed travelers in the Great Locomotive Chase.

Drive west .5 and turn left onto Mack Johnson Road. At .3 you pass through the ridge that was Johnston's second line.

Polk's headquarters, where he and Hood dissuaded Johnston from attacking and thereby ignited the Cassville Controversy, stood just south of the ridge.

Continue 1.5 through this lovely tree-lined valley with a stream flowing beside the road. Turn left onto 41–3 to drive south on the four-lane highway into Cartersville. If you are continuing with the next portion of the tour, at 7 miles turn right off the highway where the signs call attention to Cooper's Furnace, and then left on River Road (360).

Curiously enough, following the Civil War Sherman's son Tom marched to Cartersville in a demonstration for peace.

There are many interesting things to see in and around Cartersville, including the Etowah Indian Mounds, which impressed Sherman, and Roselawn, home of nineteenth-century evangelist Sam Jones. At the Weimann Mineral Museum is a replica of a cave used to mine niter for gunpowder during the war. The Bartow History Center displays relics, documents, and photographs related to Bartow County's Civil War involvement, including a plan of the Allatoona battle. The Cartersville Railroad depot is the original, dating to 1864. By the time Sherman left, the wooden roof and floor had been burned and large holes were punched into the brick walls. It was repaired in 1865, sections were later added to each end, and in 1975 the structure was partly demolished. In 1985 the depot was restored to its original appearance and the tourist and visitors center hopes to eventually relocate in it. At Cass Station, beside US 41–GA 3 south of Cassville, stands the shell of the original depot. If you have the time, visit these attractions or return later; to continue the Civil War tour, drive south through Cartersville. Below the city, enjoy the lovely green peaks that are scattered about, many of them bearing mining scars.

CHAPTER 5

Desperate Fighting in a Georgia Wilderness

After pursuing Johnston's forces to ensure they retreated south of the Etowah River, Sherman decided his men deserved a break from three weeks of continuous fighting and marching. He returned north to the pleasant town of Kingston on May 20 and remained there until the 24th planning the next phase of his campaign. Sherman was satisfied with the progress his army had made; but the Confederate force remained intact, and Atlanta was still distant, separated from him by considerable rough country and many determined men. One of Sherman's officers confided in a letter home, "We will have some bloody work before that place."

Sherman allowed his troops three days of rest in Kingston, Cassville, and around Cartersville on the north bank of the Etowah. When the railroad was repaired into town, the officers' luggage arrived on the first train, along with tons of mail for all ranks and supplies that refreshed the men. The wounded were tended, and time was taken to gather the dead from a half-dozen battlefields and give them decent burials.

The Northern soldiers were enchanted by the beauty of the Etowah Valley. Howard described it as "a country picturesque with its natural features, with farms and woodlands as quiet and peaceful as if there had been no war." Sherman was fond of this region and took time to revisit the "remarkable Indian mounds" (Etowah Mounds) to which he had taken a fancy on an earlier tour of the area.

The Confederates dug earthworks and rested south of the river, watching for Sherman's next move. Pickets glared at their counterparts across the river; but exchanges of fire were rare, and many friendly insults and commodities were traded when officers were absent.

Sherman realized that if he chased Johnston's army along the railroad, he would be forced to fight through a rugged country known as the Allatoona Range. As a young lieutenant in 1844, Sherman had been stationed briefly at Marietta. Horseback rides across the region had given him an intimate knowledge of the terrain, and he knew the natural strength of Allatoona Pass and assumed that Johnston had fortified it heavily. It would be suicidal

Earthworks guard the north bank of the Etowah River downstream from the railroad bridge. [GEORGE N. BARNARD, LIBRARY OF CONGRESS]

to attack the gap, and so Sherman abandoned that possibility. If somehow the strongpoint could be avoided, he mused, then Johnston would be forced to abandon the fortress.

The steep Allatoona Mountains protrude 1,000 feet above the surrounding countryside several miles south of the Etowah River. The railroad passed through a narrow defile in the mountains, a forbidding 65-foot-deep gap with high rock ledges to either side that were studded with cannon and riflemen. The position was far stronger than Dalton, and Johnston hoped Sherman would attempt to storm Allatoona to follow the railroad to Acworth, Big Shanty, Marietta, and Atlanta. Since an attack would result in a slaughter of the Federal horde, Johnston sensed that Sherman would not follow that potentially disastrous course. As a precaution, he stationed cavalry along the Etowah River to detect the Union direction of advance.

Sherman finally decided to execute a long flanking movement by swinging twenty miles southeast of Kingston and following a network of rough country roads that converged at Dallas, southwest of Johnston's Allatoona citadel. From Dallas his armies would advance over other primitive roads to the Chattahoochee River and Atlanta, hopefully before Johnston could oppose the movement. If the advance achieved surprise, Sherman could trap Johnston north of him, destroy the Confederate army, and march unopposed into the city. At worst, Sherman felt Johnston might recover to meet him in battle close to Atlanta.

Sherman severed his railroad supply line and ordered the men to carry all

The railroad bridge over the Etowah River was supported by these stone piers. After Johnston burned the span, Sherman rebuilt it, then dismantled and stored the timbers when he marched to Savannah.

the provisions and munitions they would need for several days. On May 23 the Union army began crossing the Etowah River across fords, covered bridges left unburned by Rebel cavalry, and pontoon spans.

"The Etowah is the Rubicon of Georgia," Sherman recorded in his diary. "We are now all in motion like a vast hive of bees and expect to swarm along the Chattahoochee in a few days." After crossing the Etowah, his troops converged on Euharlee and Stilesboro, then split into the three separate armies.

McPherson composed Sherman's right wing on the advance to Dallas. He veered far to the west from Stilesboro to Taylorsville, Aragon, and Van Wert. Returning from Rome, Davis followed McPherson's route a day later. On May 24 McPherson turned east toward Dallas, marching over Dugdown Mountain at York, and camped for the night at Pumpkinvine Church, two miles southeast of Dallas. On May 25 he broke camp before dawn, drove Confederate cavalry out of Dallas, and occupied the town by 2:00 P.M. His progress was abruptly halted just east of town when he unexpectedly ran into the resolute defense of Hardee. McPherson was stunned that the Confederates had reacted so swiftly. He would have been further surprised had he known his men would be locked in desperate combat here for the next two weeks.

From Stilesboro, Thomas and Schofield—Sherman's left wing—continued directly south over several poor rural lanes. They marched just east of the Allatoona Range, staying close enough to support each other in case

Johnston lashed out from his mountain redoubt. Sherman had learned a valuable lesson from his near disaster at Cassville and was being more cautious. The Federals skirmished with Southern cavalry at Raccoon Creek, then stopped to rest for 24 hours at the tiny community of Burnt Hickory to give McPherson, who was wheeling far to the west, time to reach Dallas. On the afternoon of May 25, they continued the march and approached New Hope Church, a crossroads settlement five miles northeast of Dallas.

The entire Union army, from Sherman to the lowliest infantryman, soon regretted this foray into what they felt was the worst region in Georgia. Their admiration for the Etowah Valley turned to disgust at the terrible conditions around Dallas, fourteen miles south of the Etowah River. They found the countryside desolate, a Georgia wilderness broken by a few scattered farm clearings. No accurate maps of the area, one of the wildest in northern Georgia, existed. Rolling hills were choked by thick forests and underbrush that pickets found impossible to penetrate. Tangled hogbacks fell into deep ravines, then ran into steep ridges. The soil was loose and sandy, the lowlands swampy, with quicksand common. Sherman tersely noted, "The country was almost in a state of nature."

The heat was intolerable, and the torrential rain that began to fall continued for a month. Roads were turned into quagmires, adding to the misery of the men engaged in this deadly game. It was the wettest spring on

Union troops crossed the Etowah River over covered bridges similar to this one at Euharlee.

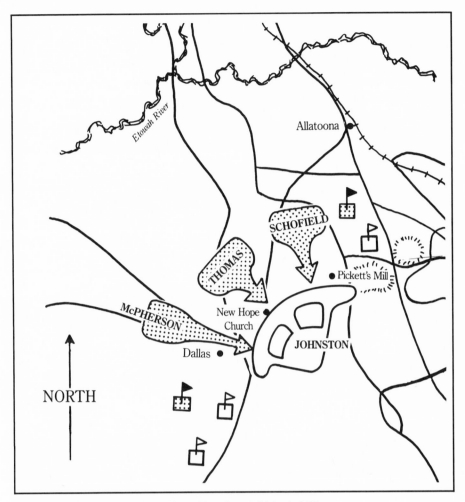

Map 11: The Battle of New Hope Church and Pickett's Mill.

record, resulting in epidemic levels of colds, flu, and pneumonia among the soldiers. Sickness felled more men than battle wounds. Road conditions impeded resupply efforts, and the men went hungry.

Adding to the problems caused by nature were the Confederates. Sherman was shocked to discover he had to contend with the complete Army of Tennessee. He had hoped to pass through Dallas in a few days; but the terrain, weather, and Johnston's skillful maneuvers would force the Federal commander to waste his strength in weeks of furious fighting under wretched conditions.

Sherman had barely broken camp on May 23 when Wheeler's cavalry detected the direction of his movement and sent word to Johnston, who promptly shifted his forces west to counter the advance. Hardee was immediately dispatched from Allatoona to Dallas, where he stopped McPherson's march and anchored Johnston's left. Hood remained a day longer at Alla-toona in case one of the three Yankee armies abruptly moved back to the railroad, then followed Hardee in time to intercept the Federals at New Hope Church. There he became the center of the Confederate line. Polk was ordered to Lost Mountain, a point halfway between Dallas and Alla-toona, so he could provide support to either position that Sherman might threaten. When it became obvious that the entire Federal army was moving through Dallas, Polk was directed to form Johnston's right near Pickett's Mill Creek. All the Confederate forces would find plenty of action in this phase of the campaign.

Hood rushed to New Hope Church and hastily erected log and earth breastworks along a ridge. Some of his men found shelter behind grave-stones in the Methodist Church cemetery, and a unit of sharpshooters was sent forward to act as skirmishers. To support his 5,000 infantrymen, Hood unlimbered sixteen cannon that gave the position extra power. Just hours after he arrived, Hooker's command emerged from the woods directly in front of the Confederate works.

Federal cavalry scouts informed Hooker that a large force of entrenched Rebels held New Hope Church. He sent Geary's division to drive in the Confederate skirmishers, then energetically attacked what he assumed was a weakly held line. Surprised to find a well-manned defense, Geary fell back, began throwing up works of his own, and sent word to Sherman that caution was indicated. Sherman, drawn to the scene by booming artillery fire, re-fused to believe that Johnston was blocking his path. Surely this obstacle was nothing more than pesky Confederate cavalry. He admonished Hooker's hesitancy, swearing there had not been more than twenty Rebels there all day. Rejecting the advice of Hooker and Geary, Sherman ordered a quick assault to brush aside this nuisance so the advance could continue.

At 4:00 P.M. Geary, reinforced by Hooker's other two divisions, marched out of the forest on a narrow lane in a line only six men wide. The foolish attack on Hood's barricades was handily repulsed with heavy Federal losses. The Union ranks were decimated as hundreds of soldiers were felled within minutes by what one Federal officer called an "effective and murderous fire."

The Federal troops courageously regrouped and repeatedly battered the Confederate works, slogging to within 50 yards of their line. They received fire from three sides as the dead piled up in heaps, forcing the attackers to struggle over bodies of their friends. A heavy storm drenched the troops, and great peals of thunder added voice to the Rebel cannon that belched deadly shot point-blank into the assaulting men. Volleys of musketry disinte-grated whole ranks while canister blew gaping holes in the Federal forma-tion. Three times the Union soldiers charged, and three times they were shattered and thrown back with frightful casualties.

Hood offered his divisional commander additional troops to stem the Federal attacks, but the offer was rejected. There were plenty of men for the target practice at hand. Confederate cannon unleashed 1,500 deadly rounds into the surging Union ranks in three hours, but the artillerymen did

New Hope Church, where Confederate troops turned back a Federal assault on May 25, 1864.

not escape unscathed. In the batteries 54 horses were hit and 47 gunners fell.

Fighting raged into the night. Then the disheartened Federals withdrew and fortified a position. Hooker had lost 1,800 men in the savage fighting and had failed to dent the Confederate line. One of his officers reported that they had met "murderous fire from all sides," while another noted, "We have struck a hornet nest at the business end." Surviving soldiers appropriately called New Hope Church the "Hell Hole."

In the darkness a house behind Federal lines was hastily transformed into a hospital. "Torchlights and candles lighted up dimly the incoming stretchers and the surgeon's tables and instruments," a Union soldier wrote. "The very woods seemed to moan and groan with the voices of sufferers not yet brought in."

During the night Schofield's horse stumbled and threw him, disabling the Army of the Ohio's commander for several days. Scattered skirmishing occurred throughout the next day between entrenched armies, although the soldiers could seldom see a target.

Sherman, who slept behind a log near New Hope Church that night, rose the following morning to find earthworks everywhere. He was mystified to find himself stymied at Dallas and New Hope Church. Determined not to be stalled, he ordered his line extended to the east in another attempt to flank

After a disastrous attack at New Hope Church, Union soldiers built a defensive position.
[*MOUNTAIN CAMPAIGNS IN GEORGIA*]

Johnston. On May 27, thinking he had reached the end of the Confederate defenses, Sherman attacked at Pickett's Mill, several miles southeast of New Hope Church, with hopes of enveloping Johnston's right end and imposing himself between the Confederates and Atlanta.

Johnston had correctly anticipated Sherman again. In extending his right, Johnston occupied a hill near Pickett's Mill and stationed 1,000 dismounted cavalrymen to secure his flank across Pickett's Creek. When skirmishers discovered the advancing Federals, the Southern troops were ready. Sherman massed three brigades for an attack in the center, with smaller diversionary efforts to strike either side. These were designed to hold the Confederates in place and prevent aid from reaching the beleagured center.

At 5:00 P.M. Schofield's infantry advanced slowly over the wild terrain, driving back the cavalry screen, picking their way across a ravine, and pushing through thick woods that covered the slope. The 15,000 troops were as startled as Hooker's men had been at New Hope Church two days earlier to find 5,000 Rebels—Patrick Cleburne's full division—confidently deployed and waiting for action. These troops, considered among the best in the Confederate army, lay on the open ridge with a tremendous field of fire stretching before them. Two cannon the Confederates had wrestled over the muddy roads and fields were poised for support.

Showing little regard for the perilous situation, the Federal soldiers bravely broke into a run toward the Confederate line screaming, "Damn you, we have caught you without your logs now!" It was soon obvious to the attackers that the Rebels did not need their accustomed log-and-earth walls. Cleburne wrote that his men "slaughtered them with deliberate aim." A regimental standard was planted fifteen feet from the rapid-firing Southerners to encourage the failing Federals, but five bearers were shot down before the flag was recovered and borne to the rear. The men were blinded by a solid wall of muzzle flashes that felled 500 charging soldiers in minutes, some at the foot of the Confederate line.

The first brigade was broken, its survivors fleeing in disarray through the second brigade, which pressed a determined charge only to run into a withering crossfire between the two cannon firing grapeshot and dismounted cavalry firing rapidly from the flank. Their ranks were shattered as 700 additional blue-clad bodies fell heavily to earth. The third brigade staged a demonstration so the wounded could be extracted. The supporting attacks to each side had been poorly coordinated in the dense forest, allowing the Rebels to concentrate their fire on the main assault in the center. A Federal participant remarked, "The Rebel fire swept the ground like a hailstorm." Two Union brigades had been destroyed.

During the heat of battle, Confederate soldiers, referring to reports in

At the battlefield of New Hope Church the Georgia wilderness was filled with earth and log breastworks. [LIBRARY OF CONGRESS]

Part of the Confederate trenches that protected New Hope Church.

Northern newspapers that Johnston's army had lost its will to fight because of recent retreats, yelled at the Yankee force, "Come ON! We are demoralized!," as they loaded and fired like men possessed.

Hundreds of Federal soldiers found retreat as deadly as the attack had been. The crashing din of musket volleys and the insidious whine of balls snapping away tree branches chased them to earth. The men hugged every crease in the ground for shelter or crawled into the ravine to wait for dark before filtering back to their own lines. The fighting had petered out by 7:00 P.M.; but at 11:00 the Confederates, envigorated by the easy victory and irritated by the sound of the enemy slithering away, fixed bayonets and swarmed out of their freshly dug works to charge across the darkened field "like a whirlwind, screaming like demons," said one terrified Yankee participant.

The maniacal charge struck fear into the remaining Federals, who fled the field accompanied by a swarm of rabbits flushed by the crazed Johnnies. The exultant Southerners captured 250 prisoners, including many wounded abandoned by the routed Union troops. One Confederate described the charge as a "desperate and reckless thing" that would have been cut to ribbons if the Federals had resisted, but, having exhausted their ammunition, the bluecoats were helpless.

Cleburne lost 35 men killed in the attack, 500 total casualties counting wounded and missing; Union losses were 1,500. The attack cost one unit 203 of 400 men; another lost one-third of its men in an advance measured in yards. In 45 minutes 500 Federals fell, 300 in another half hour. A Federal soldier involved in the assault commented, "This is not war; it is butchery." One Union officer at the scene, writer Ambrose Bierce, later penned an article titled, "The Crime at Pickett's Mill." The battle, he wrote, was "fordoomed to oblivion." It was one of the bloodiest battles in the Atlanta campaign.

Schofield's battered men fell back several hundred yards and established a defensive line parallel to the Confederates, centered on a hill where a four-gun battery was placed to stabilize the position. That night the hillside was littered with many wounded, and flickering campfires illuminated men "with broken limbs or disfigured faces." Howard was counted among the wounded.

Dawn's faint light revealed a ravaged woodland strewn with hundreds of corpses. Confederates observing the scene noted that some of the youthful faces expressed peace; others were fearfully contorted from agonized deaths. Gazing at the grisly sight from the safety of their rifle pits, the men in gray were sickened by the terrible slaughter they had accomplished. The Federal dead were left on the field for several days, creating a stench the burrowing combatants could not escape and would never forget. Burial details later counted 700 bodies of Union soldiers, many in drifts three and four deep. They were gathered for burial in two mass graves that could not be located after the war.

Pickett's Mill marked the low point of Sherman's otherwise brilliant strategy. Although he neglected to mention the disaster in his memoirs, he did term this a "wretched week" that was a "wearisome waste of time and strength."

By the Book ■ William J. Hardee

[LIBRARY OF CONGRESS]

Hardee was a native Georgian who spent the entire year of 1864 desperately defending his homeland—in vain. Born in Camden County, he attended West Point and fought the Indians and Mexicans before the Civil War erupted.

In 1856 he authored *Rifle and Light Infantry Tactics,* popularly known as *Hardee's Tactics,* which was adopted for use in the classrooms of West Point. With the outbreak of the war, many officers in blue and gray used the manual to train hundreds of thousands of civilian soldiers.

Hardee earned the sobriquet "Old Reliable" for his steady leadership in every battle fought by the Army of Tennessee: Shiloh, Perryville, Stones River, Chickamauga, and Chattanooga. With the departure of Braxton Bragg, Hardee refused command of the army, preferring to serve under Johnston.

Following Johnston's departure, Hood blamed Hardee for the series of disastrous defeats suffered by the Confederates; and Hardee demanded a transfer. When Hood marched away to Tennessee, Hardee was assigned to protect Georgia against Sherman's legions. He assembled a scratch force of 10,000 men in Savannah; but when Sherman's 60,000 hardened veterans invested the city at Christmas 1864, Hardee slipped across the Savannah River in an audacious move that caught Sherman completely by surprise.

Hardee ended the Civil War in the same capacity as he started the Atlanta campaign. Johnston had been brought back to command the pitiful remains of the Army of Tennessee; and he rushed to oppose Sherman in North Carolina, where Hardee once again came under his command.

Tragedy struck Hardee in one of the war's final battles. Succumbing to the pleas of his fourteen-year-old son, Hardee allowed the boy to join the Confederate cavalry at Bentonville. Hours after kissing his son goodbye, Willie Hardee was killed in his first combat. ■

In the two battles of New Hope Church and Pickett's Mill, the Federals lost 3,000 men, the Confederates 800. Following these twin defeats, Sherman decided to move far to the east of the Dallas–New Hope–Pickett's Mill line. On May 28 he sent George Stoneman's and Kennar Garrard's cavalries to occupy the abandoned Confederate positions at Allatoona and to seize Acworth, a railroad station to the south.

Sherman planned to shift McPherson from the extreme western end of the Dallas line, behind Thomas and Schofield, to the east toward Acworth, Big Shanty, and Marietta. He urgently needed to regain the railroad to resupply his hungry army, and the move would place him in better position for an attack on Atlanta. Sherman had quickly realized that this type of warfare was not to his benefit. Like Grant in Virginia, Sherman knew there would be no decisive battle fought in this wilderness.

Johnston anticipated the move and ordered Hardee to attack McPherson when he was in the vulnerable withdrawal, hoping to destroy the Army of the Tennessee and turn the Union right flank; but the comedy of errors continued, this time at Confederate expense. The theory was faultless, but the timing was catastrophic. McPherson was not withdrawing, and his troops were still strongly entrenched. At 3:45 P.M. on May 28, according to a Union report, "a heavy column of Rebels rose from the brush with a yell the devil ought to copyright," and attacked.

The Confederates surged recklessly forward and carried the first line of Federal works and a three-gun battery by ferocity alone, but punishing salvos from the primary Union trenches decimated their ranks. The Southern boys determinedly fought off McPherson's fierce counterattacks but were overwhelmed after two hours when General John B. Logan leaped his horse over the earthworks and personally led a charge to recapture his guns and works.

Because they found themselves in a hopeless situation, the attacking Confederates did not order waiting units to join the assault. Unfortunately, a Kentucky brigade on the far end of Hardee's line, fearing they had missed the signal to attack, did so alone. They also occupied some works, capturing several guns and some prisoners; but intense Federal artillery and musket fire from the main position halted the advance. When the first wave of attackers retreated, the Kentuckians missed the withdrawal signal and were left to stubbornly fight on alone. After suffering frightful losses to struggle within twenty yards of the Federal line, the Kentucky commander seized his brigade's flag and started for the rear, forcing his men to abandon the hopeless mission. They had lost half their number. Ironically, these men were already known as the Orphan Brigade because Kentucky had not seceded; this battle would make their name synonymous with heroism and tragedy in the short history of the Confederacy. In the futile Battle of Dallas, the Rebels lost 610 men, the Yankees 380.

In his memoirs, Sherman wrote of this battle, "Fortunately, our men erected good breastworks and gave the enemy a terrible and bloody repulse." Johnston referred to it as a minor affair.

On the night of May 27, Hood was dispatched to execute a long march designed to strike McPherson's left flank by surprise. Then Hardee and Polk would join the assault to destroy the entire Federal army. When the battle was scheduled to begin, Hood sent a message to Johnston stating that the Federals were too strongly emplaced to attack. The bold plan was canceled. For a second time Johnston angrily charged Hood with disobedience of orders, stating that he lacked the will to attack and noting that in a ten-hour march Hood had only moved the distance of a musket shot. This was yet another round in an increasingly contentious relationship.

Johnston continued to extend his works to parallel the Union line and prevent Sherman from outflanking him. Constant deadly skirmishes erupted as the two armies faced off in this Georgia wilderness campaign. Their lines eventually extended ten miles, from the edge of Dallas three miles northeast across the high ridges of Ray's Mountain and Ellsberry Mountain to New Hope Church, and southeast to beyond Pickett's Mill. The heavily wooded ridges, choked with briars and heavy brush, were soon crisscrossed with miles of heavy earthworks.

By May 29, Johnston was certain that Sherman would begin shifting his troops east to sidestep to the railroad and flank him out of this strong position. To counter this move, Johnston ordered a series of night attacks on McPherson to keep the Federals from withdrawing and sliding down the line. Some Union troops reported being attacked seven times in a single night by screaming Rebel phantoms who stormed abruptly out of the darkness. One Federal officer recorded in his diary, "Oh God, what a night!" The attacks continued until June 1, completely frustrating McPherson's efforts to execute an orderly withdrawal.

McPherson finally inched out of his position by developing a new tactic designed for this unique situation. Part of his force would ditch a defensive line behind the main works, then the men would fall back into the new

The Hard Luck Army

In November 1862 Confederate armies were joined to form the Army of Tennessee, the South's second great military force. Made up of strong fighting men from Tennessee, Kentucky, Georgia, Arkansas, Alabama, Louisiana, Mississippi, and Missouri, the army had an impossibly large area to defend, 300 miles wide and 600 miles long.

That this valliant army never matched the exploits of the more famous Army of Northern Virginia can be attributed to leadership. Its first commander, Braxton Bragg, was a brilliant planner; but he seemed to lose his nerve at crucial points. Bragg's health was poor; he was prone to fits of despondency; and he alienated virtually everyone he knew. It is rumored that a soldier tried to kill him in Mexico, and Nathan Bedford Forrest threatened to murder him following Chickamauga.

In the fall of 1862, Bragg launched an invasion of Kentucky. After an inconclusive battle at Perryville, the Confederates retreated to Chattanooga. Advancing to Murfreesboro in central Tennessee, Bragg attacked the Federal army on New Year's Eve 1862, winning an incomplete victory. The contest was later renewed with inconclusive results, and Bragg decided to withdraw. At Chickamauga in October 1863, Bragg routed the Union army but failed to pursue and destroy it. After Grant relieved Bragg's siege of Chattanooga, the Army of Tennessee retreated in disarray to Dalton; and Bragg resigned.

Joseph Johnston restored the army's morale, but led it on a hundred-mile retreat to Atlanta in 1864. There John Hood assumed command and sent the army to four disastrous defeats around Atlanta, then finished its destruction at Franklin and Nashville, Tennessee. Johnston returned to lead the army in one final battle, where his ragged veterans blunted Sherman's drive through North Carolina.

In fighting spirit and ability, the Army of Tennessee equaled its famous Virginia counterpart; but in sacrifice and endurance of adversity, they exceeded their comrades under Robert E. Lee. These men never won a complete victory, but they persevered to the bitter end. ■

trenches. This exhausting process of creeping backward was repeated many times, and Johnston's men scurried to occupy the abandoned trenches and keep up a relentless pressure.

The fighting in the thickets around Dallas introduced a new form of warfare to the campaign: private wars between small groups of soldiers. The combatants were often within conversational range, and the fighting was constant and vicious. Both sides turned hills, ravines, and stands of trees into natural fortresses. A Federal soldier compared the operations around Dallas to "Hell and its awful fires." Another officer paid homage to the courage of the fierce Confederates who were defending their homes. "Braver men never shouldered a musket then those Rebels as they came up to drive us out of our works" charging blindly from the dark, hats pulled down over their eyes, "like men who care only to throw away their lives."

When troops advanced or retreated, they needed no orders to dig in. Making "the dirt fly," as they said, was a simple matter of survival. Skirmishers fanned out in front of the new line to slow enemy advances and protect the main force of soldiers who stacked their guns and broke out shovels to dig trenches. Others grabbed axes and felled trees for logs used to reinforce the parapets; they also cleared deadly fields of fire in front of the breastworks. From such stout fortifications, experienced soldiers could hold off the most determined assaults.

Given an hour, an entire regiment would systematically protect itself against infantry attack and artillery bombardment by digging connecting trenches and placing huge logs on top of the parapet, which were then covered with dirt. The earthworks had a log wall backing, and a log was placed over the ditch to protect the soldiers' heads. The men fired from gaps beneath the head logs. The head log rested in grooves cut into two other logs that extended to level ground behind the trench. If a cannonball hit the head log, it would skitter harmlessly over the soldiers instead of falling into the pit and crushing the defenders. Such works were safe, but uncomfortable; and as the spring rains continued to fall, the works turned into miserable quagmires.

Another mode of defense used extensively since Resaca were gabions, containers of wattle filled with earth—sometimes fifteen feet thick—that could stop artillery fire. On the Dallas and Kennesaw lines, and particularly in forts before Atlanta, Confederate defenders energetically produced chevaux-de-frise, a primitive, but wicked, form of barbed wire made by piercing large logs with long, sharpened stakes, devices that slowed down attackers considerably. In clearing fields of fire, soldiers would leave many trees lying where they fell, creating a natural obstacle of tangled branches.

An intricate trench system like that which would cover France 50 years later in World War I quickly developed. A Federal observer said an area 10 miles by 20 miles looked like an enormous furrowed field. He estimated that 400 to 500 miles of earthworks were constructed in six weeks.

West Point graduates in blue and gray worried that this style of defensive fighting meant the men had lost their nerve for traditional infantry action. Instead of charging across open no-man's-land in suicidal charges, they

Hood suffered severe casualties when he launched an unauthorized attack near the Kolb Farm.

sneaked into enemy trenches at night. Hood, who was particularly disturbed by this new brand of trench warfare, feared the men were losing their offensive edge. Schofield took the side of the men, believing this new form of war to be an all-American endeavor. The soldier was like a civilian in business, Schofield said. "He wanted to see a fair prospect that it is going to pay," payment in this enterprise meaning survival.

During the last week on the Dallas line, the soldiers fought no pitched battles, but there were constant sniping, skirmishing, and volleying. The Army of the Cumberland fired 200,000 rounds of barely replenishable rifle ammunition daily in this disorganized conflict. This type of fighting extracted a heavy toll on the exhausted men. For weeks they endured the strain of constant alarms, living among the screams of the wounded and the stench of the unburied dead. Soldiers were isolated for days with no rations or water, but they fought with a ferocity seldom matched in the Civil War. Unrecorded heroism was a common occurrence.

Sherman had committed a grievous error by advancing into an area that a defensive genius like Johnston could put to deadly advantage. The Confederates had become invisible. In two weeks Sherman saw only a half-dozen Rebels dodging between trees and rocks to snipe at his troops. Severe casualties mounted daily in what the Union commander called a "big Indian war."

It was inevitable that Sherman's superior numbers would gain control of the situation on the Dallas front. To the east, at the extreme left of the Federal line, Schofield's troops closed in on the Dallas–Acworth Road. Hardee, transferred from Dallas to form the Confederate right, stretched his troops to meet the threat; but on June 4 Confederate cavalry protecting the vital road were driven off, and Johnston was forced to abandon Dallas. Sherman had finally broken the deadly stalemate in the wilderness.

Federal cavalry had captured Allatoona on June 1, and on June 6 they occupied the railroad town of Acworth. When the rails were repaired and a bridge over the Etowah River rebuilt, Sherman reestablished his supply line north to Chattanooga. Sliding down the rails, they drove Wheeler's cavalry out of Big Shanty, situated between Acworth and Marietta, on June 9, ending ten days of continuous fighting. Sherman bitterly realized that he was no closer to Atlanta then he had been at Dallas. The destruction of the previous two weeks had been a complete waste.

Within a few days most of the Federal army had reached Big Shanty, and Sherman halted there for several days to rest the men, await reinforcements, and resupply his command. Sherman was itching to continue the offensive, but he was unable to get around Johnston. His adversary had been flanked out of the formidable Dallas position, but the Confederate army was again blocking the path to Atlanta.

A DRIVING TOUR
■ Cartersville to Pickett's Mill ■

This portion of the driving tour begins in Cartersville. Turn off Interstate 75 on exit 123 (Red Top Mountain Road); turn west and at .5 turn right on U.S. 41–GA 3. Immediately after crossing the Etowah River, turn right on horseshoe ramp, then left on River Road (360).

Drive slowly 2.4 miles down the winding road that follows the Etowah River to your right. Beyond the Interstate, trees overhang the road and create a dark, green canopy. The road leads to Cooper's Furnace Historic Site Day Use Area.

Cooper's Furnace, listed in the National Register, is equipped with grills, picnic pavilions, and facilities for children's play. There are two historical trails, one which follows the route of the Civil War railroad. Near Allatoona Dam at the end of the road is an enormous outcropping of stone that should be viewed, but the centerpiece of the park is the enormous furnace.

After Jacob Stroup built an iron foundry here along Allatoona Creek in the 1840s, this became one of the most prosperous areas in northern Georgia before the Civil War. In 1858 the foundry was bought by Mark Anthony Cooper, a lawyer and politician who named the facilities the Etowah Iron Works and established a rolling mill, a flour mill, and factories for the production of guns, the South's first railroad iron, tools, and utensils of all descriptions. England's Queen Victoria once wrote Cooper to praise his fine flour.

The railroad engine *Yonah,* which was involved in the Great Locomotive Chase, was Cooper's yard engine, used to carry his products over a small spur line to the main Western and Atlantic tracks several miles west. His company prospered, particularly when the Civil War broke out and the Confederacy suddenly needed vast quantities of iron no longer available from the North. Cooper sold the works in 1862, and the state commandeered the company in 1863. When Johnston abandoned Cassville, he retreated along the route of 41–3, followed by Schofield. After a skirmish on May 21, Schofield's men destroyed the iron works, then rejoined Sherman at Kingston. Some of the facilities were rebuilt after the war, but they could not compete with cheaper northern production.

At its height, Cooper had several cold-blast iron fur-

naces operating on Allatoona and Story creeks. Iron ore and limestone were mined nearby, and charcoal was created from local timber. Ore, limestone, and charcoal were carried on trestles to the furnaces and dumped in layers. The charcoal was ignited and heat increased by blasts of cold air forced into the furnaces by pumps driven by overshot water wheels. The water was carried to the site by flumes from nearby

Map 12: Cartersville and Allatoona areas.

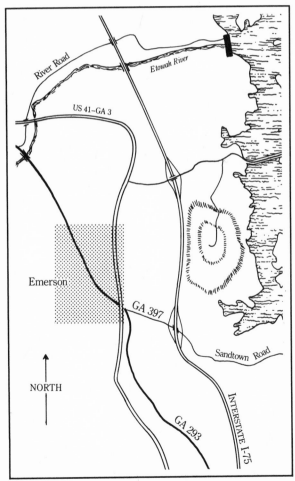

creeks. As the iron ore and limestone melted, the limestone absorbed impurities in the ore and rose to the top to be skimmed off as slag. The molten iron was released from the furnaces through a plug and ran out into casting trenches that resembled pigs eating at a trough, thus the name "pig iron."

This large stone structure is all that remains of Cooper's enterprises, which once stretched for several miles along the Etowah River and employed six hundred people. A large town that housed the employees was situated a mile from the works, but it and other ruins are now beneath Lake Allatoona.

If you have time, obtain directions to the unique Friendship Monument, standing on the opposite side of the dam near a dramatic overlook of the dam and Etowah Valley. Cooper, finding himself $100,000 in debt during the financial panic of 1857, offered to sell his industries to satisfy the debt. Thirty-five friends signed notes for the sum, and by 1860 Cooper was able to repay them. In appreciation, he erected a monument with the names of his friends inscribed on it.

Retrace your route. Just before you reach 41–3, turn into the graveled area on your left and park near the stone piers that are in the Etowah River.

These five piers supported the original bridge when the Western and Atlantic railroad was constructed in the 1840s. Johnston burned the bridge after he crossed, and the railroad was later rebuilt a mile downstream. During the Great Locomotive Chase, Andrews unwisely elected not to destroy the bridge or damage the little engine he found sitting on a siding, and Fuller soon arrived on a handcar to appropriate the *Yonah* and motorize his determined pursuit.

Before leaving the parking area, look up at the high hill immediately across the road to the north. A historical marker indicates that after Sherman passed south, he built a fort on top of this hill and garrisoned it with soldiers whose job was to guard the rebuilt railroad bridge from Confederate cavalry raids. Since there were no raids, the men found the duty boring; so they occupied their time by swimming in the river, hiking the lovely hills, picking blackberries, and playing a newly developed pastime, the first baseball games seen in the region. A few soldiers were captured by Confederates when they left the fort to hunt wild game.

Several hundred yards west was a line of Confederate earthworks built to protect the north bank of the

Sherman took time to revisit the Etowah Indian Mounds near Cartersville. The mound to the left is the second largest in the nation.

Etowah River. They were destroyed by construction of the new railroad and 41–3.

Return to U.S. 41–GA 3, heading south. If you are in no hurry, at .9 you will want to turn left onto Powerhouse Road (294) at the sign for Allatoona Dam. The visitors center interprets the battle of Allatoona, which occurred on October 5, 1864.

A scenic drive along the banks of the Etowah River affords marvelous views of surrounding peaks and the beautiful, green Etowah Valley. At the dam the Etowah is wide and weed-choked, but it becomes narrower and deeper and flows faster farther downstream. Features include camping, picnicking, and fishing areas just before the road dead-ends at the enormous dam. A long flight of stairs invites a strenuous climb to the top of the dam, but the view is worth the exertion. Inside the dam is a visitors center where employees are eager to take you on a guided tour of the mammoth construction and explain how it works.

At 1.1 on 41–3 is a sign for Red Top Mountain to the left, on S1665.

The park offers all the recreational facilities of a state park.

Continue on 41–3 south through the outskirts of Emerson.

Emerson was named in 1889 for Georgia Civil War Governor Joseph Brown's middle name. It was Stegall's Station when Johnston camped here May 20, 1864.

At 1.5 exit right off 41–3 and turn right at the stop sign. A sign in front of you indicates GA 293, which will shortly turn right, but you will continue straight on 397. Cross under Interstate 75 and wind through a gap in the Allatoona Mountains past fields of kudzu. The road turns sharply right and winds down to the tiny village of Allatoona. Drive slowly beside the massive, thirty-foot-high retaining wall of earth and stone that blots out the view of everything opposite the little village of Allatoona, to a spot where the road branches and crosses the railroad. At 2.7, just beyond the railroad tracks, look to the right for a small fenced plot and a sign that reads, "An Unknown Hero."

The railroad originally passed east of town, through part of what is now Allatoona Lake and the retaining wall. The Confederate soldier buried here was killed at the battle of Allatoona and buried in the pass beside

For 125 years railroad workers have cared for the grave of an unidentified Confederate soldier killed at Allatoona.

the original tracks. Later he was disinterred and placed beside the new line so the grave could be tended by railroad maintenance crews. The hill where Confederate artillery was emplaced is just south of this spot. To the east on the lake is a boat ramp, beach, and tent and trailer camping.

Turn around and drive back north .4 to the older buildings and pull off the road to your right in the parking area where a sign indicates no parking. Do not leave your car!

After Johnston was denied the chance to fight a decisive battle at Cassville, he retired across the Etowah River and established an impregnable position in these Allatoona Mountains, where he waited for Sherman to follow. Sherman chose not to. Although Johnston and Sherman did not fight here in May, a desperate battle was waged in the pass above Allatoona in October 1864 after Sherman had occupied Atlanta and Hood attempted to draw him into Tennessee. For an account of this battle, see Appendix B.

The first white, two-story building and the brick structure beside it, which was a store, stood during the Civil War. The large, white house with double porches and a gazebo in front served as a Confederate hospital during the October battle. There are bullet holes in the gables. A marble marker in the yard honors twenty-one unknown Confederate soldiers who died in the unsuccessful assault. Large Federal warehouses were erected south, along the railroad.

The railroad formerly ran to the east of these buildings, along this parking area. The deep railroad cut through Allatoona Pass is still visible north of this spot. To the left of the cut and right of 397 at the curve are the major Civil War fortifications erected by the Confederates and strengthened by the Federals, including the famous "star fort." To the right are lesser works. The eastern redoubt is on public land; the star fort to the west is on private land. Visiting either is difficult. The area is isolated and heavily wooded, and advance permission is required. The Confederates advanced north of 397 and west of Allatoona to attack. The site of a blockhouse captured by the Confederates at the time of the Allatoona battle is now covered by Lake Allatoona.

From Allatoona we pick up Sherman's trail from Kingston, where he retired to rest and plan the remainder of his campaign. He chose to advance on Dallas rather than Allatoona, and Johnston shifted west to Dallas from Allatoona.

Retrace your steps on 397 past I–75 and return north on U.S. 41–GA 3 into Cartersville. Turn left onto GA 113–GA 61. Drive past GA 31 to Dallas for the moment. At 7.2 from the town, you will cross meandering Raccoon Creek and pass scenic Raccoon Creek Church.

Confederate and Federal cavalry clashed at Raccoon Creek Church during Sherman's advance to Dallas.

On this stretch of highway notice the mountains to the right, many of them with large sections cut away. Bartow County is the richest mining region in Georgia, and a great deal of mining activity has occurred here for 130 years. As you approach Stilesboro, Georgia Power's enormous Plant Bowen grows larger in the distance; just before reaching the town you pass under three lines of giant pylons which appear to march across the countryside as they carry generated electricity to much of Georgia.

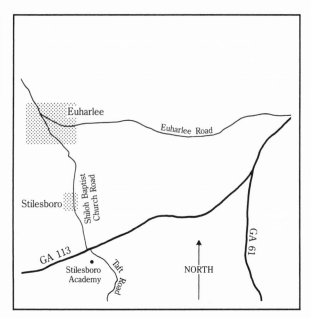

Map 13: Euharlee and Stilesboro.

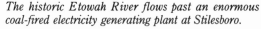

The historic Etowah River flows past an enormous coal-fired electricity generating plant at Stilesboro.

At 1.8 in Stilesboro, turn left onto Taft Road .1 and park on the grounds of the magnificent old wooden building to your right, Stilesboro Academy.

Sitting majestically on a hill, the massive academy is a national treasure. Built in 1859 at a cost of $5,000, it consists of two wings, each containing a single huge classroom forty by forty feet; between is an auditorium–chapel, forty by sixty feet. Broad wooden steps lead to enormous, sixteen-foot-high double doors. The walls of the structure are twenty feet high, and long shuttered windows extend across the rear. The academy possesses a commanding view of the Etowah Valley, as befits such a sentinel of learning, but today that view is dominated by Plant Bowen. Enormous oaks shade the grounds and a sheltered picnic area that is still a center of community life. The academy closed in 1861 when many students went to war or took their fathers' places in the fields, but it was reopened following the war and was used for many more decades.

Sherman's troops moved south from Kingston and Cartersville and crossed the Etowah River at numerous bridges and fords, then converged on Euharlee and Stilesboro. In front of the academy, McPherson marched to swing on Dallas from the west, while

84

Iron bridges like this one near Euharlee once spanned the Etowah River.

Thomas and Schofield moved to the east, camping here for one night.

Return to the highway, turn left onto 113 for .1, and immediately right onto Stilesboro Road and down a straight stretch that leads toward Plant Bowen. When stopped at the first sign at .5, turn left over the railroad tracks and pass the beautiful old Stilesboro Methodist Church and grounds. At .5 turn left onto the gravel road and right .1 at the stop sign onto Covered Bridge Road.

On your left is the settling pond where mountains of burned coal-ash are dissolved, parts of it looking like black tidal pools. To the right are the enormous coal-fired generating plants, four huge cooling towers, and an earthen retaining wall that conceals enormous stores of coal.

This bridge was made during the Depression. These bridges were once numerous along the Etowah, but they are now being replaced. This is the site of Milam's Bridge, a covered structure burned by retreating Confederate cavalry. On their march to

Dallas, Federal troops crossed on a pontoon bridge here, at Gillem's Bridge (now Harden Bridge) on the Kingston-Euharlee road (now Harden Bridge Road), and at Island Ford to the west, which is no longer accessible. McPherson passed Macedonia Church west of here on his way to Van Wert.

After 1.9 to the left in Euharlee Covered Bridge. Because so many structures have been burned by arsonists, a sign directs visitors to check in with the fire department, which is a short distance ahead in Euharlee. The bridge is nestled off the road in a wooded cove with a picnic area.

The Lowery Bridge, which spans Euharlee Creek, is a 116-foot-long single span, town-lattice structure built in 1886 to replace a bridge that was swept downstream by floodwaters. Each piece of wood was numbered before construction, leading historians to believe that it was built in a nearby field to ensure proper assembly, then disassembled and reconstructed over the creek, a common practice at the time. The numbers are still visible. Records indicate that grain mills were established along this creek in 1844; soon after that, a ferry was replaced by another covered bridge, which Federal forces crossed in 1864 on their way to Dallas.

The western entrance to the bridge is long and curved, with two raised tracks in the center like a wide railroad. Inside you can see crossed wooden

Stone ruins at Euharlee mark the location of an old mill.

beams on the sides and the creek below between floor planks. Note the wooden pegs used instead of nails to hold the span together. The bridge is supported twenty feet above the water by concrete piers. Considering its age and the fact that it carried vehicular traffic until a few years ago, the weathered structure is in very good shape. There are remains of a stone mill in the creek and on the east bank between the covered bridge and the new concrete bridge.

The community of 465 was chartered in 1976 to obtain grants necessary for the preservation of the town's pre-Civil War buildings. Guided by experts in historical architecture and preservation, they have restored the 1900-era Militia District Courthouse, where a justice of the peace presided until the 1950s, and have built a calaboose, which was a local jail used for incarcerating minor offenders or public drunks. Behind the courthouse and calaboose are a fifteen-acre park area and picnic grounds used for civic gatherings.

Another landmark is the F&M Grocery, Euharlee's only store, and the post office, a 125-year-old building with a foundation of hand-hewn logs. Near the bridge are a quaint, covered, public well, protected from the elements by a wood-shingled peaked roof, and several attractive wood warehouses. A little farther down the road are two beautiful old churches, Baptist (built in 1853) and Episcopal (1852), and their graveyards. We are fortunate that Sherman was too hurried to devastate Stilesboro and Euharlee the way he did Cassville and other communities in his path.

Between Kingston and Euharlee is Saltpeter Cave, a valuable Confederate resource during the Civil War that the Federals wrecked to impede the South's ability to manufacture gunpowder. It was opened commercially for some time, but has been closed because of damage by vandals and safety concerns.

Across the Etowah River to the east, off Euharlee Road, along Eobert Stiles Road, are three of a number of fine antebellum homes once built on the heights

A series of pavilions interpret the Atlanta Campaign with maps and historical markers. This one is opposite New Hope Church.

overlooking the scenic river. The Stiles house, Malbone-Stiles House, and Valley View survived the passage of Sherman's armies. On May 23, 1864, a Union general wrote, "Wanton destruction of private property and works of art" in this area was commonplace, including the torching of grand homes. Stories of these mansions, present and vanished, can be read in Medora F. Perkerson's *White Columns in Georgia.*

Return to 113 on Covered Bridge Road past Stilesboro and turn left at 3.4, east toward Cartersville. At 5 miles, take GA 61 south (right) to Dallas.

Schofield and Thomas advanced on parallel roads to Dallas, Schofield via Sligh's Mill to Burnt Hickory and Thomas in the center to Burnt Hickory on a more westerly route. Following McPherson's wide sweep to the west toward Dallas can be an interesting side trip. Follow county roads west of Euharlee to Taylorsville and Aragon, GA 101 to Rockmart and Van Wert, U.S. 278–GA 6 to Yorkville atop Dugdown Mountain, and east on 278–6 into Dallas. Thomas passed through Stilesboro on May 23 and 24.

Notice the rough nature of the countryside, rolling hills interspersed with farms. In 1864 the roads were narrow tracks, and Sherman's men suffered miserably trudging through the sparsely settled wilderness.

At 5 miles is the site of Sligh's Tanyard, where Schofield camped for a night, and at 3.3 Burnt Hickory (the present community of Huntsville).

Here Federal armies turned southeast to New Hope Church. That route no longer exists; so continue into Dallas. The site of the Confederate repulse at the battle of Dallas southeast of town is inaccessible, but just south of Dallas, on the east side of Academy Drive off Hardee Street, is the grave of an unknown Confederate soldier. He was probably killed during the futile attempt to turn the Federal flank and was buried in the Morris family cemetery. Sherman's headquarters during operations around Dallas was the Henderson House on East Memorial Drive.

At 7.5 turn left onto GA 6–120. At .3 take a sharp left on 381 to New Hope; the main highway (6–120) curves right.

To your right on the outskirts of town are the peaks of Ray's Mountain and Ellsberry Mountain, part of the long Confederate line at Dallas that was never at-

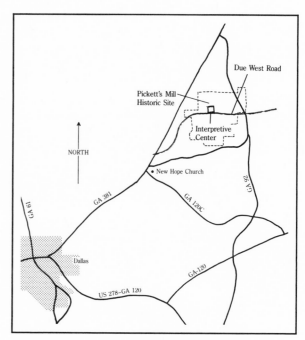

Map 14: New Hope Church and Pickett's Mill areas.

tacked. Johnston maintained his observation station on the peaks. The Confederate works crossed the highway just west of New Hope Church, and again farther east.

At 3.3 to your right is New Hope Church.

Here is where one of the bloodiest battles in the Atlanta campaign was fought. The original New Hope Church, a log structure, stood across the highway at the site of the stone store. The battle occurred just north of the church, and some of Hood's men fired from behind stones in the graveyard. Behind the modern church, shaded by oaks and pine trees and enclosed by a wooden rail fence, is a small Georgia Historical Commission commemorative monument to the battle. A short sidewalk leads to a granite monument and a Confederate flag. The monument honors the Confederate soldiers who fought and died in the trenches at New Hope Church in May 1864. Beside the monument is the grave of Lt. Col. John Herrod of the Mississippi Infantry who died here. Behind the monument are two original trenches used as part of the Confederate defenses. Picture the scene of ten thousand Federal soldiers charging as a fierce thunderstorm raged. Five thousand Confederate muskets and cannon turned the ground into a field of slaughter. Johnston's headquarters was just south of here in the William Wigley home, which no longer stands.

Directly across the side road, behind the Baptist Church, is the last Atlanta campaign station, a small, raised monument. This monument is only a marker and relief map explaining Johnston's interception of Sherman on the Dallas line, the two-week stalemate here, and Sherman's ultimate success in flanking Johnston out of Dallas and regaining the railroad before Johnston's new Kennesaw line. Beside the highway in front of the Baptist Church is a WPA marker erected in 1936 to honor the memory of all soldiers, Northern and Southern, who served at New Hope Church.

Four miles to the north, up 381, at the community of Roxana, was the intersection of the Dallas–Acworth and Burnt Hickory roads. Hood and Hardee marched past here on May 24 to meet Sherman at New Hope and Dallas, and on June 5 McPherson moved from Dallas to outflank the right of the Confederate line and break the stalemate.

Turn right onto 381. After .3, turn right onto Due West Road. After 2.4 turn left onto Mount Tabor Road, at the sign for Pickett's Mill State Park. The parking area for the visitors center is reached after .6.

Pickett's Mill, which is on the National Register, is a unique Georgia historical preserve. It is the only Atlanta campaign battlefield owned by the state and is considered to be the best-preserved Civil War battlefield in the country, the site little disturbed since 1864. The state bought the land in parcels from 1973 until 1981 and presently owns 765 acres. This new visitors center features exhibits and an audiovisual program that explains the battle of Pickett's Mill.

The superintendent has developed a regular living history program, and tours of the site are organized with the assistance of volunteer demonstrators. Authentically garbed men and women demonstrate the daily life of both Union and Confederate troops during the Civil War, featuring the work of surgeons, mess camps and cooking techniques, a sutler's store, firing of artillery, and infantry drills.

The terrain at Pickett's Mill is little changed since the Civil War. The roads used by the troops are still in use, with the addition of a few logging trails, and many well-preserved earthworks are evident, illustrating the use of skirmish lines, reentrant lines, and primary defensive positions. Opposite the Confederate line is Hazen's Hill, where a four-gun earthwork is clearly distinguishable. Three loop trails allow visitors to explore the entire battlefield. The sites of homes and the remains of Pickett's Mill are also seen on the tour, which features the ridge from which the Federals attacked, the deadly ravine where they were slaughtered, and the Confederate line on the next ridge. The staff, with the invaluable help of volunteers and Boy Scout troops, has improved trails, built footbridges, and cleared fields to resemble the landscape of 1864. Visitors are advised to travel light and to wear good walking shoes as the two-mile tour requires two hours of hiking, and the ground is moderate to steep.

From the entrance to Pickett's Mill Historic Site, turn left onto Mount Tabor Road, and at Due West Road turn left. At the stop sign after 1.8 turn left for .1 then right back onto Due West, which was a wartime road.

After crossing Mars Hill Road, Lost Mountain is visible through gaps in the trees to the right, or south. A dirt road runs through the woods along its western base, but the summit is inaccessible. The famed Lost Mountain Store (1881), at the crossroads of the Marietta–Dallas Highway and Mars Hill Road, had been threatened with destruction by the massive development occurring in Cobb County, but the solid brick structure has been moved and incorporated into a shopping center that swallowed its original location. The venerable landmark was once a stagecoach stop.

At the traffic light after 4.9 you will continue straight onto Kennesaw–Due West Road. Immediately on the left are restored earthworks on the former site of the Gilgal Church. This is where the next portion of the tour begins.

CHAPTER 6

Stalemate and Slaughter

Big Shanty would be the Federal supply base for June. Sherman established his headquarters in the top of a cotton gin on the edge of town, from which he could see Kennesaw Mountain, the central peak of a low range of hills that barred his advance to Marietta.

"Kennesaw, the bold and striking twin mountain, lay before me," he wrote. "To our right, Pine Mountain, and behind it in the distance, Lost Mountain. On each of these peaks the enemy had his signal stations. The summits were crowned with batteries, and the spurs were alive with men busy in felling trees, digging pits, and preparing for the grand struggle impending. The scene was enchanting, too beautiful to be disturbed by the harsh clamor of war, but the Chattahoochee lay beyond, and I had to reach it."

Despite heavy fighting in the month-old campaign, troop strength remained stable. Sherman had suffered 10 percent losses since leaving Chattanooga; but on June 8 he received 9,000 men, two infantry divisions and a cavalry brigade under General Francis F. Blair from Alabama. These men were added to McPherson's command, and the Union army now mustered 113,000. Johnston had lost 6 percent of his manpower, but welcomed 6,000 additional men. Soldiers in both armies were much encouraged by the arrival of reinforcements.

Sherman thought Kennesaw Mountain would be the center of a heavily fortified line, and he knew there would be some serious fighting before he reached it. The country before Kennesaw consisted of thickly wooded hills and ridges broken by steep ravines and creeks swollen by three weeks of heavy rain. The few existing roads were impassable muddy tracks, and Johnston's crafty band of veterans had turned the countryside into a fortress. Sherman would probe, feint, and fight his way to Kennesaw Mountain in a series of battles that would last a week.

On June 10 Sherman dispatched his cavalry south to identify the first Confederate line, and his entire army followed close behind. By the next day he had uncovered the Brushy Mountain line, an interconnected maze of infantry trenches and artillery batteries that Johnston prepared after withdrawing from Dallas. The Rebels were again patiently waiting for Sherman to come to them.

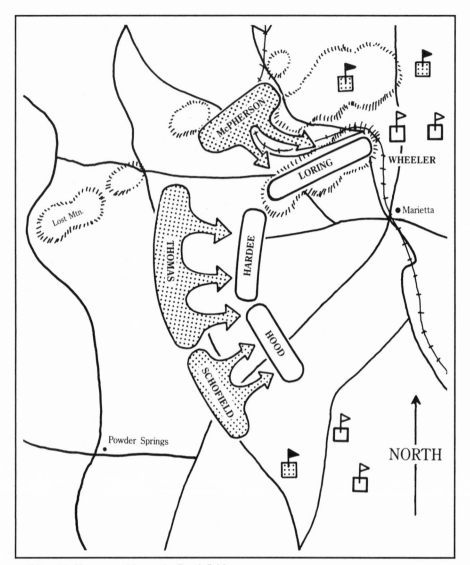

Map 15: Kennesaw Mountain Battlefield.

Johnston's right, defended by Hood, and the flank beyond, protected by
Wheeler's cavalry, lay across the railroad to the east at Brushy Mountain. It
extended west for ten miles across Pine Mountain, which Hardee held in the
center, and ended at Lost Mountain on the western end, Polk's responsibility. Polk's flank was held by William Jackson's cavalry. McPherson slid
down the railroad to oppose Hood; Thomas pressed against the Confederate
center at Pine Mountain; and Schofield closed on Polk around Lost Mountain. This line, anchored by the three hills, was not intended to fend off
Sherman's massive advance permanently. Johnston admitted that it was

"much too long for our strength"; Sherman humorously commented, "I suppose the enemy, with his smaller forces, intends to surround us."

The Confederates benefited from the torrential rains that continued to fall, forcing Sherman to alter his strategy. The ground was too boggy for maneuvering his superior numbers around Johnston, so Sherman determined to press forward and find weak spots where he could break through Johnston's thinly held front. He hoped Johnston would submit to a fair fight on this ground, but his opponent was too wise to allow that. Johnston contracted and strengthened his line in response to Sherman's pressure.

Johnston, the master of defense, had chosen his field perfectly. The heights offered such a sweeping view of the area that Johnston was immediately aware of Sherman's movements and could effectively counter them. The Federals were forced to move slowly and exercise extreme caution, inching forward under successive lines of trenches while engaged in sharp, continuous combat. "Not a day, not an hour, not a minute was there a cessation of fire," Sherman wrote. Conditions required him to convert his cavalry into dismounted infantry for use in what he termed "desultory fighting."

In 1844 Sherman had ridden across this countryside and up to the crest of Kennesaw Mountain several times. Remembering the potential defensive strength of the terrain, he swore, "I will not run head on against his fortifications." Yet the situation continued to aggravate his always volatile emotions; and as each day passed with inconclusive skirmishing, Sherman grew impatient and so evil-tempered that subordinates avoided him to escape his frequently severe rebukes. The Federal commander restlessly paced his lines and smoked one cigar after another in nervous agitation. His troops were equally edgy and depressed by the nerve-wracking forest fighting. Every forward movement became a furious firefight with Confederate sharpshooters sniping from behind rocks and trees. Scurvy plagued the troops, and the dismal weather turned minor wounds gangrenous. A common belief developed that the heavy cannonades had rent the heavens and caused the constant downpours.

The Confederates constructed log-reinforced earthworks as fast as the Federals could root them out of their previous trenches. The bulwarks were so obscured by brush that "we cannot see them until we receive a sudden and deadly fire," Sherman said. The Yankees were forced to protect themselves in like manner, which further slowed their progress. "As he [Johnston] did, so did we," a Federal general claimed. "No regiment was long in front of Johnston's Army without having virtually as good a breastwork as an engineer could plan."

Pine Mountain, a large, conical knoll with a heavy growth of timber on its steep slopes, was the highest point on the Confederate forward line when Thomas advanced from Mars Hill Church on June 10. His initial probes revealed that Pine Mountain was a salient, a formidable redoubt located a mile north of the main Rebel line. The base was ringed with a double row of infantry trenches that protected artillery batteries posted on the summit. The mountain was held by William B. Bates's division of Hardee's corps and supported by the famed Washington Artillery of New Orleans.

The Confederates cleared fields of fire by chopping down countless trees on Pine Mountain, and the logs strengthened their trenches and supplied chevaux-de-frise for defense against assault. As the Federals approached, they felled more trees to use in their protection against the deadly, accurate fire from the mountain. At Dallas and Kennesaw the sound of axes was more common than gunfire.

Rain hampered the Federal advance, and it was not until the morning of June 14 that Union pincers were threatening to isolate Pine Mountain from the Confederate line. Three Federal corps advanced north, south, and west of the salient while artillery softened its works. That day dawned clear; and the ground began to dry somewhat as Johnston, Hardee, and Polk rode to the summit of Pine Mountain to observe the Yankee movements and determine whether the position should be abandoned. Standing above the forward parapets, Hardee pointed out the danger of his post being surrounded, which would cause the loss of valuable infantry and cannon. Johnston, seeing the enemy only half a mile away, was convinced the post should be evacuated after dark.

Ironically, Sherman was at the front prodding his generals when he noticed a cluster of men, obviously officers, watching his operations before "Pine Top." Irked that his maneuvers were being so casually observed— "How saucy they are," was his comment—Sherman ordered a nearby battery to lob a few shells at the crest to force the men to take cover. Howard, the divisional commander, demurred, explaining that Thomas had issued directions to conserve ammunition. "Fire anyway," the irate Sherman snapped.

As the first shot screamed overhead and burrowed into the parapet, Johnston, Hardee, and Bates scurried for cover. The dignified, corpulent Polk walked casually toward the trenches, calmly watching the cannon firing

The Fighting Bishop ■ Leonidas Polk

Polk was born into a prosperous North Carolina family in 1806. He had intended to follow a military career; but only six months after graduating from West Point, he resigned his commission to enter the ministry. He soon became an Episcopal priest and served throughout the South and Southwest, becoming the bishop of Louisiana in 1841 and helping to found the University of the South (Sewanee) in 1861. His duties brought him into contact with Jefferson Davis, and the two men became fast friends.

When the Civil War began, Davis offered Polk the rank of major general and a post in the West, which the Bishop accepted. Polk fought in all the momentous battles of the Army of Tennessee. While his courage was never questioned, his military aptitude was frequently disparaged. After Polk failed to attack at Chickamauga, Braxton Bragg threatened to dismiss him from command and court-martial him. Davis's patronage saved his career and, ironically, sealed the general's doom.

In June 1864, while observing Union movements from Pine Mountain in the company of Johnston and Hardee, Sherman took personal umbrage at their activity and had a battery of cannon fire on the distant fig-ures. The portly, dignified churchman refused to hurry to safety, and a shell passed through his chest, killing him instantly.

Polk had been a stubborn and sometimes even childish general, but he had been greatly loved by the troops. He had imparted a sense of decency and morality to the soldiers, and even the leaders of the army had been favorably affected by his presence. While Polk's loss was less than "irreparable" to the Cause, as Davis lamented, it seemed a symbol of declining Confederate fortunes. ■

Hooker's men assault and occupy Lost Mountain on June 16, 1864. [*LESLIE'S ILLUS-TRATED*]

at him from below. A second shell hit him squarely in the chest, tearing out his lungs and killing him instantly. Johnston and the others raced to the Bishop's side. Weeping, Johnston muttered, "I would rather anything than this." In Polk's pockets he found three books of spiritual guidance that were inscribed as gifts for Johnston, Hood, and Hardee.

Down on the plains, Sherman wondered who he had just killed, a question that was quickly answered. His signal officers had broken the Confederate cipher and could decode messages flashed between Rebel stations. Sherman was soon informed that an intercepted signal from Pine Mountain to Kennesaw Mountain read, "Send an ambulance for Polk's body."

As a religious figure, Polk had aroused controversy in the North for taking up arms; and many felt he had received his due. Sherman's laconic report on the following day read, "We killed General Polk yesterday, and have made good progress today."

During the night, the Confederates withdrew to their main line a mile south. When Federal troops occupied Pine Mountain at daybreak, a northern newspaper reporter found a crudely lettered sign attached to a broken ramrod that contained the accusation, "You Yankee sons of bitches have killed our old General Polk."

To the grieving army Johnston delivered a eulogy for their fallen leader. "You are called upon to mourn your first Captain, your oldest comrade-in-arms. In this distinguished leader we have lost the most courteous of gen-

The Long Arm ■ Artillery

Field artillery had changed very little since early in the 1800s. Most Civil War cannon were bronze Napoleons, muzzle-loading smoothbores of 1840s vintage. There were several types of cannon, but the average range was up to 1,700 yards. Weighing around 2,000 pounds, they were mounted on stout, horse-drawn carriages.

An artillery battery commonly consisted of six guns manned by 40 soldiers. The guns were extremely mobile and could be quickly moved to an area under attack.

The smoothbores were inaccurate at long range, but the guns could throw six- to twelve-pound solid iron balls with deadly effect among advancing infantry. As the enemy approached within 800 yards, gunners fired case shot, hollow balls filled with a small powder charge that exploded and spewed deadly lead shot among the charging troops.

At 300 yards the artillerists switched to cannister, thin-walled tin containers packed with iron balls that spread out like a shotgun blast and cleared lanes through enemy foot soldiers.

When a battery was close to being overrun, bundles of large, solid shot were thrust into the muzzles. Upon firing, the balls immediately sprayed out to destroy any man standing in front of the battery. In times of extreme danger, crews would fire two loads of cannister, or grape, at once. ■

tlemen, the most gallant of soldiers. This Christian patriot has neither lived nor died in vain. His example is before you; his mantle rests with you." Johnston added that "in every battle he had distinguished himself," a genteel misstatement uttered for the troops' benefit.

Polk's body was carried to the Marietta depot for transportation by rail to Atlanta, where on the following day the largest funeral Atlanta witnessed during the war was held at St. Luke's Episcopal Church. The reality and nearness of battle were revealed to the thousands of Atlantans who wept over the coffin.

Polk's death was not a significant military loss to Johnston. The Bishop had been awarded great devotion and respect by his men, who were saddened by his death; but Polk's officers regarded him as a harmless and ineffectual commander. He had given both Bragg and Johnston considerable grief, and his greatest contribution had been influencing many Louisiana men to serve the Confederacy when he joined the Southern cause in 1861.

Johnston appointed William Loring temporary commander of the Army of the Mississippi, and the grinding combat continued unabated. The Federals occupied Pine Mountain, but behind it Kennesaw rose like a fist raised in defiant challenge to the approaching enemy.

With Pine Mountain lost, Johnston began to shorten his line west and north of Kennesaw during the following week. The primary weakness of the position was the proximity of the Chattahoochee River to his rear. Mindful that he might be forced to abandon Kennesaw, Johnston ordered his chief military engineer, Francis Shoup, to prepare two lines of field fortifications between Kennesaw and the river, one at Smyrna, another on the north bank of the river itself. Shoup hired 1,000 slaves from local planters to build the works. If he had to retreat, Johnston would not allow Sherman to trap and destroy him against the Chattahoochee.

The people of Atlanta grew increasingly concerned over the approaching conflict, which seemed to creep closer each day. The mayor declared a day of prayer and fasting, and a newspaper headline proclaimed, OUR CITY IS IN A STATE OF SIEGE.

With the capture of Pine Mountain, the center of the Confederate line was revealed before Thomas; and Schofield began probing the Rebel left, anchored on Lost Mountain. It was a natural bastion that allowed the defenders to observe approaching troops and greet them with damaging fire.

On May 24 Polk had marched past Lost Mountain on his way to Dallas from Allatoona; and on June 4 he had withdrawn from the Dallas line and established a position here, while Jackson's cavalry covered the extreme southern left, southwest of the mountain. On the night of June 9, Johnston transferred Polk to the peaks of Big and Little Kennesaw, and Jackson assumed the defense of Lost Mountain.

On June 15 and 16 Stoneman's cavalry drove off the Confederate cavalry screen in front of the mountain and penetrated between Lost Mountain and the primary Confederate line behind it at Gilgal Church. This action threatened to separate Lost Mountain from the rest of the army; so Jackson was forced to abandon it. He fought a spirited rearguard clash as Johnston's line was again contracted, this time to a position behind Mud Creek. In the skirmishes for this strongpoint, the Federals suffered 300 casualties, the Rebels 150.

While possession of Lost Mountain was being challenged, elements of Schofield's army were assailing the main Confederate works at Gilgal. On June 15 Hardee's men were driven from a line of rifle pits and scampered over several thinly wooded ridges in a running skirmish, then they dropped into prepared deep ditches and log barricades at Gilgal. A determined assault late in the afternoon was decimated by the protected Southern infantry and artillery, leading Schofield to stop and entrench a line parallel to Hardee. Howard reported gallant fighting all along the line that day, which cost the Federals 500 casualties to Hardee's 150.

On June 16 Schofield positioned his artillery on high ground to sweep the Rebel defenses and roads leading to the rear, so Johnston withdrew his men from Gilgal and Lost Mountain that night. The left portion of the Confederate line swung back like a hinged door to a readied position behind Mud Creek, forming an angle to the north at the Latimer Place where it joined the existing Confederate trenches behind Pine Mountain.

Schofield was at his best, alertly observing the Confederate withdrawal and following swiftly. At the new Rebel line, one division of Union soldiers maintained a rapid fire that forced the defenders to keep their heads down while other Federals quickly dug in only 400 yards from the Confederate works. One Union brigade made a reckless charge that carried a Southern skirmish line and captured many prisoners, while a second brigade occupied a Confederate position, lost it to a savage counterattack, then retook it in the wake of a hot barrage from muskets and cannon.

Schofield quickly brought up his heavy guns and placed them on a ridge overlooking the Confederate position across Mud Creek. In the close-range

Pickets atop Lost Mountain contemplate a peaceful dawn. [HARPER'S WEEKLY]

artillery duel that followed, the Federal guns were brilliantly served. Two Confederate cannon were blown over, two disabled, and the crews of the rest scattered. Geary proudly wrote that his men "opened a rapid and accurate fire" that "produced great havoc among the enemy's works and guns."

Cleburne's division suffered a terrible pounding from the massed batteries, and their own cannon were unable to return the fire. One shell seriously injured General Lucius E. Polk, nephew of the Bishop. The wound, his fourth, forced Polk to retire from military service.

On June 18 rain stalled all offensive operations, and Geary's infantry spent a miserable day in the swollen creek bed. That night Cleburne was instructed to fall back, an order he was relieved to obey after holding an untenable position for 48 hours.

Geary recorded that Confederate snipers had hidden in trees across Mud Creek, and his sharpshooters knocked several out of their "elevated hiding place." Other Confederates cut bushes and placed them in their belts, effective camouflage, Geary said, which on a "dark, misty day, rendered them almost indistinguishable." The Confederates had become expert at this Indian fighting.

Just north of Mud Creek was the center of Johnston's original line at the Latimer Place, also know as Hardee's Salient. It was held by French's division against twice as many Federals under Howard's command. The Yankees made a quick thrust on the night of June 17 that forced Confederate pickets to sprint for safety to avoid capture, and Howard occupied the Confederate outer works. The Federals brought up their artillery to the north and west of the line and dropped shells down the length of the Rebel trenches. There was no defense against this brutal enfilading fire that pinned down the Confederate troops. Realizing that a major Union assault would rupture the entire line, Johnston evacuated it and withdrew to another prepared position two miles south: the famous Kennesaw Mountain line.

After successfully crossing Mud Creek, Sherman decided to concentrate on forcing the western end of Johnston's position. Since there had been little action between McPherson and Hood to the east around the railroad and Brushy Mountain, he shifted McPherson west to face Loring opposite Kennesaw Mountain. Thomas moved farther south but remained in the center opposing Hardee, and Schofield and Hooker slid southwest beyond the Confederate line in an attempt to flank Johnston out of Kennesaw Mountain and precipitate a hazardous retreat to the Chattahoochee barrier.

Schofield advanced on the Sandtown Road in a long, muddy march from Lost Mountain against Jackson's stubborn cavalry. The Federals reached flooded Nose's Creek at dark on June 19, forded it the following day, and drove off Rebel skirmishers guarding the opposite bank. On June 21 Schofield rebuilt the bridges and resumed his slow, methodical advance to Olley's Creek.

Seeing this threatening development, Johnston ordered Hood's three divisions to march through the night from Brushy Mountain and establish a line that would stem the dangerous Union sidestep. Arriving from his swing behind Loring and Hardee, Hood initially faced his men in the wrong direc-

Pickets before Kennesaw Mountain exchange shots. [MOUNTAIN CAMPAIGNS IN GEORGIA]

tion. After discovering the error and correcting his deployment, Hood decided to attack and turn the Federal right flank, unaware that he was facing the center of a strongly held line.

On the morning of June 22, Hooker occupied a ridge near Valentine Kolb's farm, with Schofield guarding his right flank. He had 14,000 infantrymen distributed on a one-and-one-half-mile-long line. For support 40 pieces of field artillery were emplaced on high ground with excellent fields of fire. Hooker ordered two regiments to skirmish as far south as possible and warn him of approaching enemy forces. For several hours they chased their Confederate counterparts across creeks, hills, and fields, springing between cover and firing sporadically. The Confederates finally dropped into a line of rifle pits, and the Union advance ground to a halt.

Late in the morning Federal skirmishers captured 30 Rebels and hustled them to the rear for interrogation. Hooker was surprised by Hood's sudden appearance and disturbed to learn the aggressive Confederate was preparing an immediate assault. Familiar with Hood's fearsome reputation from Virginia battlefields, Hooker frantically ordered his troops to dig in. Federal soldiers abandoned their berry-picking in the pleasant summer sunshine and began hurriedly dismantling fences to erect wooden barricades and scooping out shallow holes from which to fight. Artillery crews cleared their batteries for action.

In front of Hooker, the Federal skirmishers watched apprehensively as 11,000 Confederates formed three long lines for battle. When the Rebels advanced, the Northerners ran like foxes for the security of their own lines. Hooker's forces held their fire until the men sped past, then at a range of 500 yards the cannon opened a brutal fire on the steadily approaching Confederate ranks.

At the Battle of Kolb's Farm, the artillery work became legendary. Forty crews served their cannon as if they were part of the guns. Like enormous shotguns, canister spewed dozens of deadly iron balls into the air, shredding men instantly and cutting lanes in their formation; case shells timed to explode in the air above the Confederate ranks sent iron hails of ragged shrapnel raining down onto vulnerable men; solid shot bounced wildly across the uneven ground, smashing chests, breaking limbs, and severing heads from trunks with sickening thuds. The crews fell into a well-trained rhythm—load–fire–load–fire—alternating canister, case, and solid shot, volley after volley, often discharging double loads. When the Confederates drew close to the Federal line, they were exposed to a maelstrom of 90 artillery rounds a minute blazing from front and flank.

When the Federal infantry opened fire at 200 yards, the plucky Southerners reeled from the hurricane of destruction. Hundreds of men fell, but the remainder staggered on through the gale of hissing shot, firing muskets at their antagonists but unable to pause and reload in such a dangerously exposed position. The decimated Confederates courageously charged to

Federal perspective of the Battle of Kennesaw Mountain. [ALFRED WAUD]

Federal infantry and artillery try to cover their attacking troops at Kennesaw Mountain.
[*LESLIE'S ILLUSTRATED*]

within 35 yards of the Union line, then broke under the debilitating fire and ran for the safety of a ravine where they regrouped and gallantly mounted other attacks, each time with fewer men.

The slaughter was so appalling that many Confederates surrendered on the field to escape certain death. Federal officers quickly snapped orders not to fire on Rebels approaching their lines to give up. Stouter Southerners remained pinned down, hugging the ground for the little shelter it offered or huddling behind fence rails, tree stumps, and in pits they hastily scratched out of the earth with bare hands. Withdrawing in the face of such awful fire was tantamount to suicide.

Federal soldiers later declared that if Hooker had taken the initiative and ordered a counterattack, the entire Confederate force would have been destroyed or captured; but Hooker believed he was weathering the brunt of a major assault by the entire Confederate army. Instead of sallying forth to annihilate Hood's weakened corps, Hooker ordered his men to dig in and wait for another attack, which never materialized.

During the night, surviving Confederates crawled to the sanctuary of their lines a mile south, dragging wounded comrades with them. In the dark hours the exhausted Federals were tormented by haunting wails and moans from the dying. Unable to offer assistance until dawn, some imagined they could see the contorted faces of men pleading for their mothers or awaiting the release of death.

At dawn Union burial parties went about their grim work. They discovered Confederate bodies piled like cordwood, up to a dozen corpses huddled in ditches or crouched behind trees, many dismembered by grapeshot. Of the 5,300 men who participated in the assault, 1,100 fell. Federal casualties totaled 300. Hospitals in Marietta were flooded with wounded from this single engagement, and the overflow were treated on the grounds of the courthouse, which was used as an open operating theater. It was considered a miracle that five Southern brothers in the attack not only survived this battle, but returned home safely following the war.

"Fighting Joe" Hooker, as he was known in better times, had won an impressive victory; but since his shattering defeat by Lee and Jackson at Chancellorsville and subsequent removal from command of the Army of the Potomac a year earlier, he had become skittish. Still anticipating another thrust, he sent a message to Sherman informing him of the battle and resultant Rebel losses and expressing apprehension about his right flank, adding, "Three entire corps are in front of us." Sherman, who disliked Hooker and had little confidence in him, was infuriated by the dispatch. He answered that Johnston's entire army consisted of only three corps, so how could they all be massed in front of Hooker? Furthermore, Schofield was conscientiously guarding the flank in question. The inferred criticism invoked Sherman's harshest rebuke, and he severely scolded "Fighting Joe," who sulked. "Hooker was ever after incensed at Sherman" for the reprimand, Howard observed.

When command of an army later opened, Sherman refused to consider Hooker for the assignment, a decision that led Hooker to resign angrily from the army and enter politics. Sherman welcomed his departure. Hooker is primarily remembered today because the freedom given female camp followers in his units is commonly thought to have originated the slang term for prostitutes, *Hookers*.

On the Confederate side, Johnston found considerably stronger reasons for castigating Hood over his blundering part in the action. Hood was censured for launching an impetuous, poorly planned, and hastily organized assault with no reconnaissance and without the knowledge or permission of his commanding officer. Hood also neglected to report the calamitous results of his ill-advised foray to Johnston. Hood had been completely ignorant of the situation at Kolb's farm, lacking any intelligence concerning the enemy's strength or position. The stunning loss was senseless, Johnston argued, a sentiment echoed by one of Hood's brigade commanders who wrote after the battle that Hood was "totally unfit for command of a corps." Hood's contemporaries averred that he was one of the Civil War's great divisional commanders when attacking on the orders of a superior officer; but his rash personality and poor judgment were fatal flaws, rendering him unqualified to lead a corps or army.

After the war, Johnston wrote that the fighting at Kolb's Farm was ended either by "the general's [Hood's] orders or by the discretion of the troops." It probably was the latter.

Union General Thomas's headquarters in front of Kennesaw Mountain on July 4, 1864. Tree branches shade the tents. [LIBRARY OF CONGRESS]

Two lessons were to be learned from Kolb's Farm. The first was that troops advancing in the open against a protected enemy would be slaughtered, and the second concerned the fitness of Hood for command. Tragically, both lessons went unheeded.

Johnston's final line was anchored on Kennesaw Mountain's 1,800-foot-high peak. His men laboriously dragged cannon up the steep, rugged slopes by hand; from the summit those guns guarded the railroad and obstructed Sherman's route to Marietta and Atlanta.

The line began at the railroad and extended west over Kennesaw Mountain, Little Kennesaw, Pigeon Hill, a ridge that would become known as Cheatham Hill, and to the flatlands beyond. Wheeler's cavalry held the railroad, Loring the solid center on Kennesaw, Hardee Cheatham Hill, and Hood the left, with Jackson's cavalry extending that flank. This six-mile-long line took advantage of the natural strength offered by the mountain, ridges, and forests; and it was fortified to the point of impregnability by the addition of extensive earthworks, artillery batteries, forward rifle pits, slashings, and chevaux-de-frise. Union veterans of Gettysburg considered it a stronger position than the one they had held at Cemetery Ridge, a daunting thought.

Three weeks of nearly incessant rain gave immeasurable assistance to the defenders, flooding creek beds, rendering roads impassable, and hampering Sherman's favored offensive technique, the famous flanking march. While Sherman grew increasingly frustrated by the Kennesaw Line, his officers became apprehensive for the future of the campaign; and the men and animals were sick, soggy, filthy, and generally miserable. The situation before Kennesaw had developed into a strategic stalemate, which only favored Johnston; and the weather compounded the problem. Sherman wanted to close with Johnston and force a decisive battle; but he admitted, "The assault would be too dear." Still, there had to be some action he could take. His memory turned to the attacks against invulnerable Lookout Mountain and Missionary Ridge seven months earlier, when his troops had unexpectedly routed the Confederates with inspired charges. Perhaps that success could be repeated.

Of the morass before Kennesaw, Sherman telegraphed Washington, "We continue to press forward on the principal of an advance against a fortified position. The whole country is one vast fortress, and Johnston must have fully 50 miles of connected trenches with abatis. . . . We gain ground daily fighting all the time . . . our lines are now in close contact and the fighting incessant with a good deal of artillery fire. As fast as we gain one position, the enemy has another all ready." He later added, "It was a continuous battle, lasting from June 10 to July 3," 23 days of confused combat on the Kennesaw front.

In this agitated state, Sherman began to suspect his men of having lost their desire for offensive action, a condition he blamed on trench warfare. "A fresh furrow in a ploughed field will stop the whole column, and all begin to entrench," Sherman wrote, aiming particular venom at "Old Slow Trot" Thomas. In this excited condition, Sherman considered abandoning his flanking efforts for a frontal assault on the entrenched Rebels.

"I am inclined to feint on both sides and assault the center," of the Kennesaw Line, he informed Washington. "It may cost us dearly, but in results would surpass any attempt to pass around."

Having consistently stated that he would not attack strong fortifications, Sherman justified the idea by explaining that the roads were too wet to flank. He postulated that Johnston was weary of being flanked out of successive positions and had probably strengthened the ends of his line but left the center relatively unsecured, thinking Sherman would never dare attack the forbidding trenches. By striking the weak center, Sherman believed he would split the thin gray line and destroy the two halves of the Confederate army piecemeal.

Weary of the stalemate and unable to slip around Johnston, Sherman committed his forces to one definitive battle. It would be his only rash decision of the Atlanta campaign. Sherman had previously stated that what occurred before Atlanta "would probably decide the fate of the Union," and he was ready to decide that fate. He also thought his soldiers were tired of the flanking tactics and desired the campaign to be determined in one final clash. The political situation in Washington also influenced Sherman's course. Lincoln desperately needed a victory, and Sherman realized he was expected to supply it.

Sherman had another reason for making the assault, a petty one that would diminish his stature as a great general. Sherman felt he was being denied a rightful share of popular attention. Grant was grabbing the head-

Union fortifications before impregnable Kennesaw Mountain. [GEORGE N. BARNARD, LIBRARY OF CONGRESS]

lines with his meat grinder tactics against Lee in Virginia, and Sherman believed his successes were being unfairly overshadowed. If Sherman won a great victory, the press, which had long been hostile to him, could no longer ignore his exploits; and he would receive the publicity and adoration he rightfully deserved.

For two weeks Sherman had fought a constant heavy skirmish action. Knowing his strength had peaked, he decided that Johnston must be finished here to put an end to the deadly chess game. "We must assail and not defend," Sherman admonished Thomas. The decision was made; the time for offensive action had arrived. The Kennesaw line would be attacked and, hopefully, breached. The Army of Tennessee would be destroyed, and Atlanta shortly captured.

In the days before the attack occurred, Sherman commenced an artillery bombardment all along the line to soften up Confederate positions. Thomas brought 140 guns forward to pound the Rebel center; and the Confederates responded, producing a spirited artillery duel that caused little damage to either side. The Southerners soon ran low on ammunition and were ordered to conserve their fire for a full-scale assault, which Johnston could feel approaching. On the mountain, some Confederate batteries were so well targeted that during the day the positions were pounded smooth. At night the gunners would dig out their protective lunettes, and the process would begin again at dawn. The bombardment cut the forest into kindling; huge slashing splinters produced more casualties than the shelling.

Blue and gray infantry sat on their works to watch the spectacle and cheer their artillery, until an irritated enemy gunner would lob a shell at them. The men tumbled into the trenches until the shot passed, then climbed out to enjoy the show again. For three days shells screamed overhead, while in the valley between the batteries the Federals continued their advance. One soldier compared the sound of constant skirmishing to a "thousand wood choppers."

Sherman was particularly irked by crowds of civilians from Atlanta who climbed Kennesaw Mountain to watch the "burrowing Yankees" approach. After several noncombatants were killed by the shelling, Johnston forbade further casual visits. The citizens of Marietta treated the situation more seriously; their town was overrun by hundreds of wagons loaded with wounded soldiers and supplies, and crowds of refugees passing south.

Sherman spent a week planning the assault, which would consist of two attacks, one by Thomas and a second by McPherson. The army commanders were allowed to choose the men and places to attack. Thomas selected the junction of two Confederate divisions where a salient was formed, manned by B. F. Cheatham. It was enfiladed by Federal artillery that was concentrated to prepare the Rebel line for assault. McPherson chose to attack a gap between Little Kennesaw and Pigeon Hill. Schofield would not participate in the battle, but Sherman directed him to demonstrate against Hood on the day of the assault. That would prevent Hood from sending reinforcements to assist the Confederate center when the real attack opened, and it would convince Johnston his left flank was being threatened.

On June 25 Sherman issued Special Field Order Number 25, which announced that the assault would take place at 8:00 A.M. on June 27. That morning broke with an ominous quiet; birds could be heard chirping in the woods. Then 200 pieces of Federal ordnance opened a thunderous, hour-long bombardment of solid shot and case on the length of the entire Rebel position; and the whole Union army advanced in a giant skirmish formation that kept the Rebels from locating the actual assaults until the last moment. Confederate guns returned fire when Federal infantry appeared, battering the troops in the valley below. Kennesaw Mountain was hammered by Yankee batteries on a ridge opposite, but this time it was gleefully answered by counter battery fire from the Rebels. A Confederate said "the ground seemed to heave" under the weight of the continuous fire, while other soldiers were reminded of volcanic explosions or Niagaras of flaming fire.

The Federal infantry formed a curved line two and one-half miles in length that probed the Southern defenses to hold the Confederates in position so they could not rush troops to the points actually under attack. Finding the Rebels strongly posted all along the front, they withdrew.

When the Yankees fell back at 9:00 A.M., Thomas charged forward with 8,000 men in five brigades to attack Cheatham Hill, three at the salient itself (soon to be called the "Dead Angle") and two a short distance farther east. The Confederates had an equal number of men defending the sector. Thomas chose to attack with a controversial formation known as massed

European infantry tactics, one of the few occasions in the Civil War where it was employed. Thomas advanced on a narrow front only 200 yards wide, instead of the standard 1,500 yards. The men were deployed in twelve closely packed ranks, a tactic designed to batter through the thin Confederate defenses; but instead they presented targets for Confederate infantry and grapeshot-firing artillery. To make matters worse, only the front rank of Union soldiers could return the debilitating fire. One brigade was led by Colonel Daniel McCook, one of fourteen brothers and cousins famous in the Union army as the "Fighting McCook's," who recited "Horatio at the Bridge" as his men formed their columns.

The Federal soldiers scrambled from their works on a ridge opposite Cheatham Hill, and in the oppressive summer heat they bravely swept out of the woods to charge 600 yards without cover across a wheat field. The ground was soon littered with their dead and wounded as artillery fire tore great gaps in the ranks, which closed up and relentlessly continued to advance. Rebel sharpshooters took a slow, steady toll on the Yankees. At a range of 100 yards, Confederate muskets let loose their first volley, a blast of fire and smoke that ripped the front line and stunned the Federals. Trees splintered from the crashing Southern fire, and one Yankee wondered if a single bird could survive a flight across the field. Men fell in appalling numbers, but those standing charged recklessly forward, taking death like "wooden men," a Confederate thought.

A dramatic portrayal of the doomed Federal assault against Cheatham Hill at Kennesaw Mountain [CURRIER & IVES]

Guns emplaced behind these earthworks helped repulse Thomas's determined attack at Cheatham Hill.

The Federals rooted Confederate skirmishers out of a line of rifle pits, paused briefly at the foot of the slope to reform, then pressed up the ridge to the Confederate trenches. There they met a galling fire from infantry standing shoulder-to-shoulder two deep and from ten cannon that smashed the Union column from two sides. Rebel fire reached a deafening crescendo as a few courageous men raced to the crest of the hill and mounted the parapets, planting two flags on the enemy works. For an instant, desperate fighting enveloped the Confederate line as men in butternut savagely defended their position, flinging rocks, timbers, dirt clods, and shovels at the attackers and bayoneting Yankees who tried to leap into the trenches. Union soldiers on the works were shot and fell dead on top of men who had killed them, and some Rebels fell in the hand-to-hand melee.

The raging Southern fire staggered the Federal troops, who reeled and started to fall back. McCook, Sherman's civilian law partner, vainly attempted to rally the troops, dramatically shouting to the tormenting Confederates, "Surrender, you traitors!" He was shot dead only a few feet from the Southern line. Leadership fell to his inspector, who died seconds later; a third commander was killed within five minutes. The attack sputtered, stalled, and began to recede; but the Federals who had survived the ill-fated assault found themselves in a dire situation. The attack had obviously failed, but they could not retreat. They would have been riddled in flight by the deadly, accurate Confederate fire; but 40 yards below the Rebel line on the slope of the ridge was a hollow where enemy fire could not reach, and hundreds of men sheltered there, unable to advance or retire. McCook's brigade had lost 35 percent of its men, and Union casualties at the "Dead Angle" reached 824.

Cheatham proudly reported that his men had delivered a cool, relentless fire, deliberately aiming, firing, and reloading. Some guns grew so hot they discharged when loaded. In one regiment each man killed five enemy soldiers. All that was required was to load and shoot; it was impossible to miss a target. Sam Watkins, a Confederate rifleman, removed ammunition pouches from fallen comrades and fired 120 rounds during the struggle. Cheatham's infantry had been supported by flanking artillery that maintained a murderous crossfire and added to the blazing din of battle that echoed across the hills.

To the east, the other two Union brigades under General Charles G. Harker were led into a more perilous situation. They lost formation climbing over their works and approached the Rebel line in uncoordinated dribbles. Confederate cannon quickly broke the back of the attack, carpeting the ground with broken men. A U.S. flag was briefly planted on the bristling Confederate works; but the Union soldiers rapidly found refuge from the crippling fire and made only occasional half-hearted forays against the enemy. Sherman's carefully orchestrated strategy had degenerated into chaos.

Shell explosions ignited the underbrush in front of the Confederate line,

A hail of Rebel fire staggers the Union advance at Kennesaw Mountain. [MOUNTAIN CAMPAIGNS IN GEORGIA]

putting many Federal wounded in danger of being burned alive. Rebel Colonel William H. Martin of Arkansas courageously leaped atop his trenches waving a white flag and yelling to a Union officer that he was willing to observe a cease-fire so the Yankee wounded could be rescued. "Come and get your dead and wounded," he called. "We won't fire a shot until you do."

The offer was gratefully accepted, and the fighting ceased. Confederates clamored from their trenches and helped the Yankees drag their wounded off the field to safety. Federal Major Luther M. Sabin presented Martin with a brace of Colt revolvers in appreciation of the humane act; then the soldiers reluctantly returned to their positions, and the slaughter resumed.

General Harker's efforts to rally his men from horseback made him an inviting target, and a charge of cannister felled the general only fifteen yards from the Rebel works. Devoted soldiers braved the storm of lead and carried Harker's body from the field. The remainder of his command was shattered by the appalling fire, and the troops promptly ended the assault by acclamation. "Our men rushed back like a herd of infuriated buffalo," said Howard, "running over and trampling each other under foot. I was run over and badly bruised, but glad to get off so well."

"The enemy's fire was terrific," he continued. "Our men did not stop until they gained the edge of the felled trees; a few to fall close to the enemy's parapet, but most sought shelter behind logs and rocks, in rifle holes or depressions," before they vacated the field in inglorious panic. In two hours of combat, 650 of Harker's men fell.

Some Federals later claimed they could have carried the enemy works at Cheatham Hill if they had not been forced to struggle over their own dead and wounded. That their columns had been dispersed before they struck the Confederate line also hampered the assault.

Although the slaughter was less severe at Pigeon Hill, that clash proved even less successful than the one at Cheatham Hill. McPherson chose to attack the gap between Little Kennesaw and Pigeon Hill because it was the junction of two Confederate divisions and there was always the hope of exploiting confusion between two commands. He selected three brigades for the attack; the first would spearhead the effort and bear the brunt of the defenders' fire so the second brigade could overrun the Confederate line, and the third would break into the Rebel rear and roll up the enemy ranks. His 5,500 men would assail 5,000 entrenched troops. The attack, set to begin with the general bombardment of the Kennesaw position, was synchronized with the strike against Cheatham Hill.

The Federals advanced quickly through the forested valley that separated the combatants. They sprinted between the shelter of large boulders and trees and surprised a regiment of Georgians acting as pickets. Rebels were shot and stabbed in rifle pits; in one hole two men of eleven survived. Over 100 skirmishers were captured before the attackers continued their rush and burst onto the center of the Confederate line undetected. Thirty feet from the trenches, McPherson's troops were blasted by murderous salvos from Confederates crouched behind earthworks, rocks, and trees. The brigades were thrown back in confusion by the massed fire; then the broken

Confederate troops hold their fire while wounded Federals are removed from the path of a brush fire. [MOUNTAIN CAMPAIGNS IN GEORGIA]

troops swung to one side and ran into an exposed valley where they were pinned down by Rebel fire from two directions and slain in awful numbers.

These men faced the same hopeless situation as their comrades at the Dead Angle. If they retreated, the Southerners would shoot them down; so hundreds hugged the ground for what poor cover was provided by natural obstacles for over ten hours, unable to return the punishing Rebel fire. Confederates on Little Kennesaw added insult by rolling rocks on them and shouting taunts. After dark the Federals crawled back to the sanctuary of their own lines.

During the attack, other soldiers on Little Kennesaw quickly found positions from which they opened a plunging fire on the enemy attacking the base of the hill. At no point along Pigeon Hill did the Yankees near the Confederate line. They lost 600 men in the brief assault, while Southern losses were 300, mostly pickets captured in the rapid Union advance through the forest.

The Confederate line remained intact, while Sherman had lost heavily and gained nothing. The battle wore out by 11:30 A.M., and the Federals counted losses all out of proportion to their gains or to Confederate casualties. Although brave men pressed their fight to the Confederate works, the Federals had failed to dent the line and died in a tempest of fire on the parapets and in the Rebel trenches.

"The sun beating down on our uncovered heads, the thermometer being 110 degrees in the shade, and a solid line of blazing fire from the muzzles of the Yankee guns poured right into our very faces," was how a cannoneer at Cheatham Hill described the battle, "singeing our hands and clothes, the hot blood of our dead and wounded spurting on us, the blinding smoke and stifling atmosphere filling our eyes and mouths, the awful concussion causing the blood to gush out of our noses and ears, and above all, the roar of battle, made it a perfect pandemonium.

"When the Yankees fell back and the firing ceased," the Rebel continued, "I never saw so many broken down and exhausted men in my life. I was as sick as a horse, and as wet with blood and sweat as I could be, and many of our men were vomiting from excessive fatigue, overexhaustion, and sunstroke; our tongues were parched and cracked for water, and our faces blackened with powder and smoke, and our dead and the wounded were piled indiscriminately in the trenches. There was not a single man in the company who was not wounded."

Colonel Robert Fulton, a Federal involved in the struggle, wrote, "The Rebels fought with a desperation worthy of a better cause. The conduct of our soldiers and officers on this occasion needs no comment; never did men show more gallantry, mounting the works, shooting the enemy, and beating them over the heads with the butts of their guns," in a gallant but futile effort.

General Samuel French had ridden to the crest of Kennesaw Mountain on the morning of June 27 when Union artillery fire indicated an imminent battle, and he was presented with an unobstructed view of the action. "Presently, as if by magic, there sprang from the earth a host of men," he related. "In one long, wavering line of blue the infantry advanced and the Battle of Kennesaw Mountain began." He was awed by the magnificent panorama of 150,000 men "arrayed in the strife of battle on the plains below." As the enemy advanced, several miles of Confederate defenses were marked by tongues of flame and blue musket smoke. Through the resultant haze French observed the struggles at Cheatham Hill and Pigeon Hill develop and dispatched reinforcements, which proved unneeded, then he watched the Union tide recede. He termed the battle "pageantry on a grand scale . . . one of the most magnificent sights ever allotted to man."

Elated by the signal victory, Johnston allowed, "The Northern troops fought very well, as usual," displaying their "characteristic fortitude" which "held them under a close and destructive fire long after reasonable hope of success was gone."

Howard wrote, "We realized now, as never before, the futility of direct assault upon entrenched lines, already well prepared and well manned."

After the attacks had failed, Sherman questioned his generals about renewing the assault. Thomas replied, "We have already lost heavily today without gaining any material advantage. One or two more such assaults would use up the army."

Sherman recognized the attack had been a dismal failure, but he tried to justify the effort. "At times assaults are necessary and inevitable," he said, explaining that some end in victory, others in defeat. He was wrong to think the Kennesaw line could be breached by storm, and later he bitterly reflected that the battle had no effect on the final outcome of the campaign. Federal losses were 3,000, including seven regimental and two brigade commanders; Confederate casualties were 600.

Sherman, who had shown a rare zest for offensive action at Dallas and Kennesaw Mountain, confided in a letter to his wife how the change in tactics had affected his values. "I began to regard the death and mangling of a couple of thousand men as a small affair, a kind of morning dash." But, so reminded of the waste, he returned to the art of maneuver.

Hardee reported that a thousand dead Union soldiers lay unburied in front of his lines for two days. On June 29 a truce was declared, and Confederate and Federal soldiers cooperated in dragging decaying bodies to holes for burial. Tobacco and coffee were traded during the welcome break from combat. Some Yankees, admiring his resolute defense, requested Cheatham's autograph.

The Federals remained pinned down at Cheatham Hill, a hundred yards from the Confederate line, until the Rebels withdrew on July 3. Trenches were dug to connect the isolated men with the main Union line, but they survived for several days without food or water. Some wired mirrors to their rifles so they could aim and fire without exposing themselves. The Confederates caught on to this ruse and extended their hats on sticks over the trenches in a competition to see who could collect the most holes in their headgear and also to encourage the Yankees to waste their ammunition. The Northern soldiers recognized that the Rebels could easily overrun them, but instead the Johnnies contented themselves with pitching rocks into the hollow and calling insults to the trapped men. The Yankees were temporarily down, but their spirit was intact. They started digging a tunnel beneath the Confederate position, intending to blow it up with a large mine; but the Rebels retired before it was completed.

Sherman's desperate gamble had been a bloody failure.

A DRIVING TOUR
■ Kennesaw Mountain ■

This portion of the driving tour begins west of Marietta. From Interstate 75 take the 120-Loop exit. If you are coming from Atlanta, take the south loop exit and follow it to the right until it comes to 120; turn left and follow 120 west through Marietta. If you are coming from the north, take the north loop exit, turn left under I-75, and follow the loop until it comes to 120; turn right and follow 120 west through Marietta. West of Marietta it also is known as Dallas Road.

At approximately 9 miles follow the Acworth-Due West Road as it branches off to the right (north). This is about 3.2 miles east of Lost Mountain. At the traffic light and intersection turn right onto Kennesaw-Due West Road. Immediately to the left are the restored earthworks at Gilgal Church.

The battle of Gilgal Church (the structure was destroyed during the combat), fought on June 15, 1864, was centered here. At this spot Sydney K. Kerksis purchased twenty acres of land and reconstructed a portion of typical Civil War earthworks in a small roadside park open to the public, the only place in Georgia where visitors can view an authentic 1860s fortification. Trenches were dug six feet deep, with the dirt piled in a protective wall facing the enemy. The inner face of the trench was reinforced with large logs held in place by vertical posts driven into the ground. A head log was placed atop the trench wall for protection, and soldiers fired through the gaps between the dirt and head log. Long logs extended from the front trench wall to the rear so that timbers dislodged by cannon fire would roll above the solders rather than crash down on top of them. Trees were cut down in front of the trenches to clear fields of fire and for arranging entangling abatis to slow attackers.

Portions of the Confederate line exist northeast of the clubhouse, but they are rapidly succumbing to residential development. The Federals advanced along this road from the north to attack Johnston's Brushy Mountain Line. Thomas established his headquarters at Mars Hill Church, just south of U.S. 41-GA 3, and crossed Mascon Bridge over Allatoona Creek.

Drive back to 120 and turn left. The road crosses Mud Creek, where Confederates suffered terribly from Federal artillery fire. The Rebels occupied the ridge to the east of the creek, Yankees to the west.

At 2.9 miles turn right on John Ward Road for .6, then turn left on Cheatham Hill Road 2 miles to the intersection with Powder Springs Road. Cross the road, immediately on your right is the Kolb Farm.

This is the original 1836 home of Valentine Kolb, who died in 1859. His son's widow occupied the six-hundred-acre farm when Hood impetuously attacked strong Federal forces here. The home served as Hooker's headquarters, and Federal sharpshooters fired from its windows and fences at the approaching Confederates. Daniel Butterfield, who fought here as one of Hooker's divisional commanders, composed "Taps." The National Park Service has restored the house, which was heavily damaged and is used for staff accommodations, but it is not currently open to the public. However, you can inspect the exterior of the home and view the family graveyard.

On June 22, Sherman established his headquarters here to watch Thomas's five brigades form on this ridge and attack Cheatham Hill, which is directly east.

At 120 turn right .5, then right into the Cheatham Hill section of Kennesaw Mountain National Battlefield Park.

To your right, among the trees facing open fields over which the Federals advanced, are portions of the Confederate trenches. A cannon placed behind a protective lunette appears as it would have during the battle, firing grapeshot to shatter the advancing Union columns. The pink granite memorial was erected in 1964 to honor Texans who fought in the Army of Tennessee. A marker along the road indicates the site where Confederates arranged a truce to rescue Federal soldiers from fires sparked by exploding artillery shells.

At .6 is a parking area and a trail leading to Cheatham Hill.

Near the edge of the parking lot is an artillery position that was instrumental in turning back the eight thousand Federal soldiers who assaulted this line.

As you walk the shaded quarter mile to the Dead Angle, examine the original Confederate trench line on the left. The exact locations of individual units are marked by signs. In 1864 the earthworks were deeper, and Rebel soldiers crouched beneath head logs to coolly aim and fire at the steadily advancing Yankees.

On the path to the Dead Angle notice the trenches that join the main line of defense but run in the other direction. These protected soldiers against enfilading fire that occurred at a salient when the enemy was on either side of the work and fired artillery the length of the main line. It was also a refuge in case a portion of the work was overrun and allowed the wounded to be removed and reinforcements to rush the front.

The Dead Angle, five miles south of Kennesaw Mountain, is the most dramatic spot on the battlefield. Here the full force of the Federal attack peaked and ebbed. A beautifully reproduced painting at a display here shows that some Union troops actually reached the top of the Southern trenches, but were shot and fell dead on their adversaries. Some Confederates threw rocks at the charging Federals, and wounds

were inflicted by bayonets and muskets used as clubs. Near the trenches, Col. Dan McCook, Sherman's former law partner, fell while trying to rally his men. The force of the attack was broken, and the Confederate line remained intact.

The magnificent Illinois Monument, which stands at the crest of Cheatham Hill, was erected by the state of Illinois and dedicated on June 27, 1914, exactly fifty years after the battle occurred, to honor the 480 men from that state who died on this slope. The marble monument is thirty-four feet square at the base, and the shaft rises twenty-five feet. Stairs ascend the monument from the direction of the assault. Atop the monument is a seven-foot-high bronze soldier clutching a rifle and two women in classic Greek garb.

Encouraged by veterans' organizations, Illinois bought sixty acres of the battlefield in 1899, then donated it to the U.S. War Department in 1917, which

Map 16: Kennesaw Mountain and Marietta.

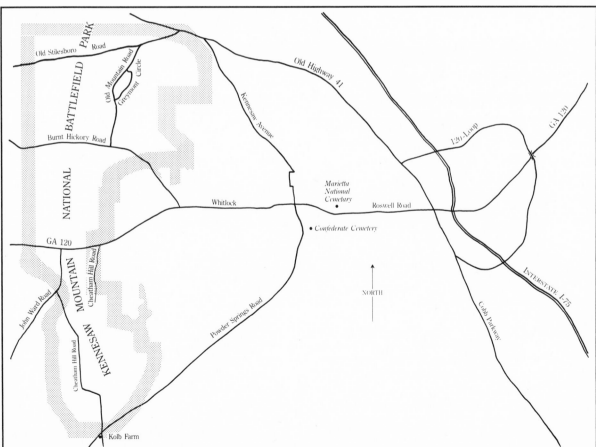

assigned it to the National Park Service in 1933. The federal government felt it could preserve either the battlefield of Kennesaw Mountain or Peachtree Creek to commemorate the Atlanta campaign, and it chose the former. It is significant that Kennesaw Mountain National Battlefield Park was originated by soldiers who had fought here.

At the base of the memorial is the Tunnel Monument, which seals off an excavation started by trapped soldiers who planned to burrow beneath the Confederate line and destroy it with an enormous mine like the one detonated at Petersburg, Virginia. The tunnel was incomplete when the Confederates withdrew. Nearby is the gravestone of an unknown soldier whose remains were discovered in 1934 by CCC workers. It was impossible to determine for whose army he died.

A trail extends across the field, over a stream, and through the woods six hundred yards to the spot where the Federals began their attack. On the wooded slope is a monument to McCook, a two-foot-high granite marker that commemorates the start of the assault.

Return to 120 and turn right. At 1.2 turn left onto Burnt Hickory Road N.W. At 1.2 is Pigeon Hill.

The hill received its name from the thousands of pigeons that paused here on their migratory journeys. It was here that McPherson's brigades attacked and were soundly thrown back. The fields were much more extensive then. Hiking trails lead through the battle area on the right to well-preserved works and continue on to Little Kennesaw and Kennesaw Mountain.

Turn right onto Old Mountain Road and at 1.5 turn right onto Stilesboro Road. At .5 turn into the parking area for the visitors center.

A number of cannon are scattered across the grounds, which offer the best view of the imposing mountain. At the battle of Kennesaw Mountain Illinois troops feinted here and were repulsed by Rebels from Alabama and Arkansas who were concealed in woods at the base of the mountain.

In the visitors center are numerous exhibits that illustrate the history of the Atlanta campaign and the battle that took place at Kennesaw Mountain, plus displays of artifacts, uniforms, and period photographs. A theater regularly screens a fifteen-minute slide show that further explains the importance of this battlefield. Pick up a park brochure in the lobby and examine the Civil War literature available for purchase.

A steep road behind the visitors center winds to the top of Kennesaw Mountain. On weekends and during the summer a tour bus takes visitors to the summit; at other times you may drive yourself up the 1.7-mile road. On the right near the base is a monument that honors Georgia troops who served the Confederacy. There are beautiful views of the surrounding countryside as you drive up the mountain, and from the parking area near the summit is a scenic overlook of the valley below. A long flight of stairs leads to a stone observation platform with markers indicating surrounding points of interest, and a memorial to the fourteen Confederate generals from Georgia who served at Kennesaw. A steep one-mile hike from the visitors center to the summit leads past rifle pits.

A trip to Kennesaw Mountain is not complete without a hike to the summit, which is steep but only one-fourth mile in length. The trail passes several recreated artillery positions situated in original Confederate earthworks. Some of these lunettes were leveled by Federal fire, but few casualties and little actual damage resulted from the spectacular duel. The Confederates cleared the summit for trees used in fortifications and to create fields of fire, and Rebels hauled numerous cannon by hand up the precipitous slopes of Kennesaw Mountain and Little Kennesaw to fire on the Federals below. This position was held by William W. Loring's troops.

The summit contains a number of interesting historical markers that direct visitors to observe Atlanta to the south—vulnerably close on clear days—the Allatoona Mountains to the north, and Little Kennesaw, the second peak of this double mountain, to the west. You have been examining the Kennesaw Line, but Johnston's overextended first barrier, the Brushy Mountain Line, lies to the north and west and can only be appreciated from this vantage point. Lost Mountain, which you passed, is a large hump to the west; Pine Mountain, where Bishop-General Polk was killed, is clearly visible to the north, crowned today by a water tower and lined with homes. A monument marking the spot where Polk was killed lies atop Pine Mountain. To visit it, from the visitors center turn left onto Stilesboro Road, turn left onto Beaumont to the tops of the ridge and park. A short path to the right of the Georgia historical marker commemorating Polk's death leads to the twenty-foot-high marble monument placed by a Marietta Confederate veteran and his wife in 1902. This is private property, so please be considerate. Brushy Mountain to the northeast along the railroad tracks marks the Confederate right, not far from U.S. 41–GA 3. The Brushy Mountain Line is endangered by commercial development. Parts of it may be preserved, perhaps not.

On Gilbert Road a rough gravel track that is off Stilesboro Road west of the visitors center between Stilesboro Road and Old Mountain Road, is the site of a twenty-four-gun Federal battery that pounded Confederate positions on Kennesaw Mountain. From this peak French and other Confederate officers watched the awesome spectacle of one hundred thousand Union soldiers advancing in a three-mile-long line to probe the Southern defenses.

You can combine an interest in history and hiking at Kennesaw Mountain. A sixteen-mile loop trail takes you across the entire twenty-nine hundred acres from the visitors center to Kennesaw Mountain, Little Kennesaw, Pigeon Hill, Cheatham Hill, the Kolb Farm, and back, across mountain peaks, pleasant meadows, wooded creek bottoms, and along eleven and a half miles of earthworks. Shorter hikes are also featured. Ask at the visitors center.

On the trip down pull over into the parking area on the right and walk to the side of the road to observe the beauty of Little Kennesaw and the countryside.

At the park entrance turn right to the stop sign and left onto Old 41 (Kennesaw Avenue). At .3 cross the path of the contested railroad; at 1.7 is U.S. 41–GA 3. Drive straight through the four-lane intersection, and at 1.8 turn right over the railroad tracks. To your left is the Big Shanty Museum.

Established in the 1830s as a shanty camp for railroad workers, residents changed the name of their community from Big Shanty to the more socially acceptable Kennesaw in 1870. Sherman kept his headquarters here during operations against Kennesaw Mountain. When the fighting moved farther south, a Federal occupation force fortified the Lacy Hotel and built a stockade around it as a strongpoint on the Western and Atlantic. It was captured by Hood's forces in October 1864, but when Sherman marched east to Savannah in November, he burned the hotel.

The town is famous as the site where the Great Locomotive Chase began in 1862. Federal raider James J. Andrews and his men boarded a train pulled by the engine *General* in Marietta. When the passengers and crew disembarked for breakfast at the Lacy Hotel, Andrews and his men stole the train and started north to destroy the railroad bridges between Atlanta and Chattanooga. By cutting the railroad, they hoped to aid the Union occupation of Chattanooga, but they were thwarted in this daring attempt by the resolute pursuit of the *General*'s engineer, Captain W. A.

Fuller, who chased his train on foot, with a pole car, and on three different engines, running two of them backward in a harrowing eight-hour journey that covered eighty-seven miles. Fuller forced Andrews to abandon the *General* near Ringgold, and all of the Raiders were captured. Eight were hanged in Atlanta for sabotage, and the rest escaped or were exchanged. All but Andrews, who was a civilian, received Medals of Honor.

The geography of the chase sounds like a reverse forerunner of the Atlanta campaign: Marietta, Kennesaw, Acworth, Allatoona, Cass Station, Kingston, Adairsville, Resaca, Dalton, Tunnel Hill, and Ringgold. Alongside the tracks in Kennesaw is a memorial honoring Fuller's heroic determination, and a stone tablet that marks the site where the adventure began; a similar monument north of Ringgold signifies the end of the chase.

The *General* was damaged but repaired and came under Union artillery fire on June 27, 1864, when it ran a load of ammunition to the Confederate defenders of Kennesaw Mountain. Two months later, on September 1, the *General* and another locomotive, the *Missouri*, labored south on the Macon Railroad with cargoes of munitions and quartermasters stores that Hood evacuated from Atlanta. Federal cannon at Rough and Ready (now Mountain View), where Sherman's troops had cut the railroad, forced the engines to reverse and back into Atlanta. At the Georgia rail yards near Oakland Cemetery, the *Missouri* rammed into a train of ammunition cars, then the *General* and another locomotive and its cars crashed into it and all was set ablaze. The explosion of the five engines and eighty-one ammunition and supply cars could be heard for miles.

The *General* barely survived being scrapped following the war, but was again rescued and refurbished. It was involved in two wrecks near Kingston and was displayed at several reunions of Civil War veterans. Forgotten for years, the *General* was discovered on a siding in Vinings, restored, and featured at the 1893 Chicago World Columbian Exposition, the Atlanta Cotton States Exposition, the 1939 World's Fair in New York, and then placed on permanent display in Chattanooga. At that time the state of Georgia touched off a three-decade struggle for possession of the locomotive by announcing plans to display the *General* at Kennesaw Mountain or in Kennesaw.

The *General* made a centennial run over the route of the chase in 1962, and in two years traveled fourteen hundred miles to appear in 120 cities. When the Louisville and Nashville Railroad, which had obtained the engine on lease from the Western and Atlantic, agreed to return the engine to Georgia in 1967, the city of Chattanooga "captured" the locomotive, this time with a court order. After three years of litigation the *General* was returned by federal court order for the final time to Kennesaw, appropriately to a spot within yards of where it was originally hijacked. It has been housed in the Big Shanty Museum since 1972.

The museum, a restored cotton gin, features a slide show about the Great Locomotive Chase in an upstairs room that is decorated with beautiful stained-glass windows depicting the engine's history. The *General* rests on tracks below, with surroundings that give the illusion of a train station. There are many informative displays, including flags, weapons, dated cross-tie nails, a brick from the tunnel through Chetoogeta Ridge, a Federal axe head used to fell trees before Kennesaw Mountain, and *Gone with the Wind* mementos.

The Lacy Hotel and depot were at one time beside the tracks across Cherokee Street from the museum. North of the hotel was Camp McDonald, established by Gov. Joseph Brown in July 1861 to train Georgia recruits. Georgia veterans held reunions here for decades following the Civil War.

Next door to the Big Shanty Museum is Kennesaw Commons, a collection of restored homes where antiques and crafts are sold, and opposite it is the Kennesaw depot. Another local landmark is Wildman's Civil War Surplus, operated across the tracks from the *General* by colorful Dent Meyers, who offers a wide variety of Civil War literature and artifacts for sale.

Each April, Kennesaw hosts the Big Shanty Festival, celebrating the Great Locomotive Chase. It features reenactments, entertainment, arts and crafts, and good food. Check at the museum or Wildman's for details.

Retrace your route to Kennesaw Mountain and drive past the park. At .3 from the park, turn right onto Kennesaw Avenue.

Here you may observe several impressive and historically important antebellum homes. Oakton, 581 Kennesaw Avenue to your right, was used as headquarters by Confederate Gen. William Loring, and Fair Oaks, at 505, was Johnston's headquarters during the fighting at Kennesaw Mountain. At 435 is the former home of Andrew J. Hansell, a colonel of the state militia and aide to Governor Brown; the Archibald Howell House at 303 was occupied by Federal Gen. Henry M. Judah in late 1864 and early 1865. Judah

received the surrender of Confederate troops at Kingston and distributed food to the civilian population in this area. When Union officers took over Tranquilla, Mrs. Andrew J. Hansell refused to vacate and was allowed to remain in residence. The grounds of the Bostwick-Fraser House were used as a Federal hospital, and Fanny Fraser served as a nurse.

At 2.3 turn right onto Church Street Northwest.

A short distance to the left up this one-way street is the First Presbyterian Church, built in 1852. It was used as a hospital by both armies during 1864, and was so heavily damaged by the Federals that the U.S. government paid three thousand dollars for repairs. Union forces also utilized the Saint James Episcopal Church next door. It burned in 1964, but a small chapel is original and contains an organ that the Federals filled with molasses. In the Episcopal cemetery on Winn Street, between Polk and Whitlock, is the grave of Alfred R. Waud, a noted Civil War artist.

Note the Kennesaw Station complex to your right. On the other side is the old Western and Atlantic passenger depot, built in 1898 on the site of the original that Sherman burned. It is now the Marietta welcome center. To the left is the interesting courthouse square. East of the square was the original Cobb County Courthouse, which Sherman fortified when he advanced toward Atlanta, then ordered burned when the March to the Sea began. Confederate troops had mustered and drilled on the square, which now features a tiny replica of the locomotive, the *General,* on which children now play.

At .4 turn right onto Whitlock for .1.

To your right is the Kennesaw House, built in 1855 as a summer resort hotel, the Fletcher House. Here Andrews's Raiders met the night before they stole the *General* to plan their sabotage, and until 1864 Confederate casualties and refugees from fighting farther north found shelter here. Sherman briefly established his headquarters in the building while chasing Johnston on July 3. It partially burned shortly after the war but was reconstructed; it is now a restaurant.

Available from the welcome center is a comprehensive walking-driving tour guide brochure to fifty-two historic homes, churches, commercial structures, and cemeteries in Marietta. Audio cassette tours can be rented. Also pick up a copy of the Cannonball Trail, prepared by the Cobb landmarks and Historical Society, which lists seventy-one Civil War sites in the city. The welcome center offers guided walking tours and even carriage rides through Marietta. Kennesaw Mountain National Battlefield Park frequently hosts lectures and interpretive programs, and hopes to build a new visitors center or greatly expand the existing one.

At the traffic signal turn left onto South Marietta Parkway, S.W., which becomes Powder Springs Road for .7. Turn left onto West Atlanta Street at the sign for the Confederate Cemetery. After .1 turn left at the sign into the Confederate Cemetery.

The Marietta Confederate Cemetery was originally established on September 24, 1863, on land donated by Mrs. Jane Glover, Ann Moyer, other residents, and the city of Marietta. During two weeks of fighting at Kennesaw Mountain five hundred casualties were buried in the hospital section. In 1866 a project was initiated to move Confederate dead from Chickamauga and battlefields of the Atlanta campaign to this Marietta cemetery. The work, funded by the state of Georgia, was directed by Miss Mary J. Green of Resaca fame, and Mrs. Charles Williams of the Ladies Memorial Association.

The cemetery contains the graves of 3,000 men, representing every state in the Confederacy, and monuments record the number of "heroes" sacrificed by each state. Tennessee has the most, 325, and surprisingly Georgia, with 116, ranked only fourth behind Alabama and Mississippi. The original wooden headboards deteriorated and were replaced in 1902 with marble stones, many of them blank. Magnificent old trees frame the grounds, and from the hillside is a beautiful view of Kennesaw Mountain to the north. A statue to the memory of these men and Cobb County's Confederate veterans has been erected in the park, and a gazebo, erected in 1974, is employed yearly for Confederate Memorial Day observances. In 1911 a ten-foot-high memorial arch was dedicated. A bronze 6-pounder cannon kept on a special platform was used for training by the Georgia Military Institute from 1857 until 1864, then saw combat under the cadets during the March to the Sea. It was abandoned when the Confederates evacuated Savannah, and Sherman sent it north as a trophy of war. It was returned in 1910. Services are held here every Confederate Memorial Day.

Just south of the cemetery and opposite it on Powder Springs Road is the site of the Georgia Military Institute, now a country club, and the surviving home of Arnoldus V. Brumby, superintendent of the institute. The institute had been founded in 1851 in hopes that it would become the Southern West Point.

When Sherman approached, two hundred cadets, aged fifteen to eighteen, marched off to fight for the Confederacy. When Sherman left on the March to the Sea, he torched seventeen buildings of the institute, the courthouse, and every commercial building on the square. A second brass cannon belonging to the cadets was returned in 1928 and now stands in front of the former clubhouse of the Marietta Country Club.

The Kennesaw chapter of the United Daughters of the Confederacy and the Rotary Club of Marietta have published a handy guide to the cemetery. Ask for one at the welcome center.

East of Powder Springs Road on Garrison Drive is the impressive Glover House, now the Planter's Restaurant. A skirmish was fought there on July 3 as the Confederates slowly retreated to Smyrna.

Continue straight through the Confederate Cemetery to West Atlanta Street to loop back to Cemetery Street and turn right onto Powder Springs Road. After .6 turn right onto Whitlock (GA 120). (Across GA 3–5 West Park Street, Whitlock becomes South Park Street and then Roswell Street N.E.) Stay in the right lane until Waddell is crossed. After .3 turn left onto Haynes Street N.E., then almost immediately right onto Washington Street. At .2 the entrance to the Marietta National Cemetery is on your right.

The cemetery was established in 1866 on twenty-four acres donated by Henry Greene Cole, a local citizen with Unionist sympathies who hoped that Federal and Confederate soldiers could be buried together as a gesture of healing. When his offer was rejected, he donated the land for the burial of Union soldiers. Federal soldiers who fell south of Resaca and the Oostanaula River in the Atlanta campaign were buried here, while the Chattanooga National Cemetery was established for all Union men who died north of that point. After the war 10,132, including 3,000 unidentified casualties from battlefields at Adairsville, Cassville, Dallas, New Hope Church, Pickett's Mill, Kennesaw Mountain, and the Atlanta battles, were exhumed and reinterred here. Local people were employed to construct coffins, fences, and markers, and to landscape the grounds. For many years former slaves from the Atlanta area gathered at the cemetery on Memorial Day to celebrate their emancipation.

A high wall encloses the twenty-four-acre cemetery, and large oaks and magnolia trees shade the graves on a rolling hillside. Monuments from several Northern states honor their dead, and a pavilion for ceremonies is on top of the hill. As the only national cemetery in northern Georgia, impressive services are conducted here each Memorial Day when veterans groups gather to honor the participants of America's wars.

Nothing remains to commemorate the fighting at Smyrna or the race to the Chattahoochee River, but on Concord Road west of Smyrna is a scenic covered bridge spanning Nickajack Creek that replaced one destroyed during the Civil War. This bridge is threatened today by developers. The battle of Ruff's Mill was fought in the area. McPherson raced west of here to reach the left flank of Johnston's River Line, while Schofield advanced in the center with Thomas on the outside to the east.

The river line, constructed by Francis A. Shoup, was four miles in length and up to one mile in depth and extended from present-day Dixie Highway to the Bankhead Highway. The line consisted of forty unique Shoupades with overlapping fields of fire. Each square blockhouse, built at eighty-yard intervals and defended by eighty men, was sixteen feet high and had double log walls with earth fill between. They were twelve feet thick at the base and four feet thick at the top. Between each Shoupade was a two-gun redan, and all were connected with deep trenches and eight-foot-high stockades. Adding further security to the line were lunettes and redoubts containing 20-pounder Parrott rifles transported from Mobile, and the ends of the line at the river were anchored by larger artillery forts. Twelve Shoupades remain, eleven on private property, but one of the artillery forts, a seven-gun battery at the southern end of the river line at the mouth of the Nickajack Creek, will be preserved in a park in the future.

Vinings, named for the man who constructed the Western and Atlantic through the area, was founded by Hardy Pace who arrived in the 1830s, purchased ten thousand acres of land, and built an important ferry across the Chattahoochee River where Pace's Ferry Road is today. Sherman and his staff viewed Atlanta from the top of 1,170-foot-high Vinings Mountain, and while artillery batteries were emplaced opposite Confederate guns across the river, Sherman established headquarters in Pace's home for eleven days before crossing the Chattahoochee River at Power's Ferry just upriver. Throughout the siege of Atlanta, munitions and supplies arrived at a railroad established here as wounded were treated and evacuated north. The mountain was garrisoned through the fall for use as a signal station, but when Sherman started for Savannah Pace's house was destroyed.

Pace had refugeed to Milledgeville, where he shortly died. His widow returned his body for burial at the top of Vinings Mountain and cobbled a new home from three slave cabins. Vinings soon became a resort spa where Gov. Joseph Brown built Pavilion House to encourage rail trips to the springs.

In recent decades Vinings was known for its pleasant taverns, restaurants, and shops, but developers found this refuge north of Chattahoochee and quickly bulldozed the rear of the mountain for three twelve-story office towers and six hundred apartments, and development continues. The second Pace Home may become a museum, and the pavilion and springs remain. Vinings is bordered by the river, U.S. 41–GA 3, and Interstate 285.

Old U.S. 41 crosses the Chattahoochee at Bolton, where Johnston retreated across the river to defend Atlanta when he abandoned the River Line. Artillery exchanges and cavalry clashes were frequent occurrences for weeks, and Sherman defended this same spot to protect the vital railroad bridge when he shifted most of his forces south to Jonesboro. At the Lovett School, just south of Vinings, Thomas crossed the Chattahoochee at Pace's Ferry on July 17. The Second Corps crossed at Power's Ferry the same day.

If you are continuing the driving tour, from the cemetery turn right onto Washington and right again .4 onto the second street, which is Rock, for .1 to Roswell Street (120), and turn left. Stay on this road across U.S. 41–GA 3 at the famous Big Chicken and continue on 120 under I–75 for 11.8 miles into Roswell. At 3.8 in this drive note the Marietta Campground to your right.

South of this route, at the point where Papermill Road crosses Sope Creek at a sharp curve, are extensive stone ruins, with the most impressive remains found on the western bank. This was the Marietta Paper Mill, established in 1859 and burned by Garrard's cavalry. On July 7, 1864, Schofield's men effected the first passage of the Chattahoochee River there, forcing Johnston's withdrawal from the river line. The mill was rebuilt, burned in 1870, brought back into production, and closed permanently in 1902.

The city of Atlanta and a private foundation plan to build a nine-mile-long urban and historical park along the Fulton County side (the southern and Confederate bank) of the Chattahoochee from Peachtree Creek to Camp Creek. It is part of a 112-mile-long trail system to be developed throughout Atlanta. On the northern, Cobb County and Union side of the river is the Chattahoochee National Recreational Area that preserves forty-eight miles of riverfront. It consists of foot trails with interpretive exhibits that explain the historic and natural features of the area.

CHAPTER 7

The Final Barrier

After the disaster at Kennesaw, Sherman became convinced that further attempts to smash through the Confederate lines would be futile, wasteful exercises. However, he was heartened by a dramatic change in the weather when the rain ceased for several days and the countryside began to dry. With direct assault unwise and the roads finally passable, Sherman decided to resume his masterful flanking movements. He would cut loose from the railroad again for a swing to the west around Johnston's left and devour the remaining country before Atlanta. His men were instructed to carry all the munitions and rations they would need for several weeks, and the advance was set in motion.

On the day of the Kennesaw assault, while Thomas and McPherson valiantly attacked the Confederate positions, Schofield feinted around Hood, who occupied the extreme left of the Rebel front, successfully lodging his men behind Johnston by reaching the Sandtown Road and threatening the Confederate flank. Sherman called this the "only advantage of the day." Schofield, with McPherson following, would sweep around the Southern line and force Johnston to abandon Kennesaw Mountain. Thomas would play his usual role, remaining before the Rebels and exerting pressure on the center of their works.

On July 2 Johnston was alarmed to discover Schofield and McPherson closer to Atlanta than he was; but his human resources were exhausted, and he lacked the manpower to extend his line to the west and meet Sherman's new threat. Withdrawal to a more defensible position seemed his only choice; so during the night Johnston executed another of his legendary disappearances by extricating his command en masse. A weary Confederate soldier recognized Sherman's premier skill by remarking that the Union general would surely escape hell by flanking his way into heaven.

Dawn on July 3 revealed no trace of the Confederate army on the mountain or in the lengthy trenches west of the citadel. Sherman watched anxiously through his glasses as Federal pickets cautiously crept up the cratered slopes to examine the powerful works atop the battered crest. The Kennesaw Line was completely vacant, and Sherman assumed his nemesis was in total retreat beyond the Chattahoochee River and would occupy the trenches that guarded the outskirts of Atlanta, "for no general, such as he,"

A Note on Casualties

When Sherman marched into Georgia, his strength was 98,800 soldiers. The number of Union troops peaked in early June at 112,819, but the siege took a toll; and after the action at Jonesboro, Sherman counted 81,758 men in the ranks. During the campaign, Federal losses totaled 4,400 killed, 23,000 wounded, and 4,500 captured or missing.

Johnston started with 42,900 men, peaking at 64,600 after Polk's corps joined him. Most of the Confederate casualties—3,000 killed, 19,000 wounded, and an incredible 13,000 captured, missing, or deserted—occurred after Hood took command and opened his offensive battles. When Atlanta was evacuated, the thin gray ranks of the Army of Tennessee numbered only 35,000 soldiers. ■

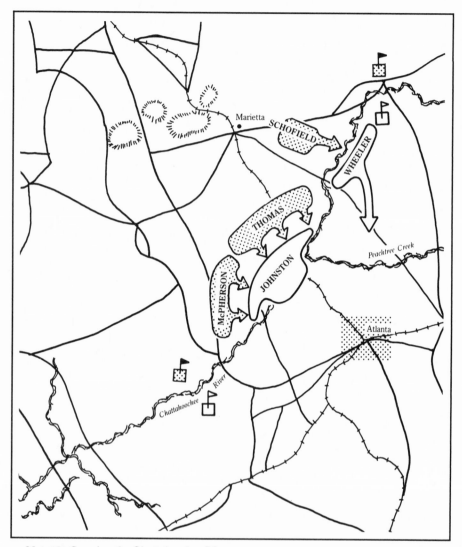

Map 17: Crossing the Chattahoochee River.

Sherman wrote, "would invite battle with the Chattahoochee behind him." Sherman intended to pursue Johnston hotly and destroy the Confederates as they attempted to cross the river; but Johnston would baffle Sherman again, making two audacious stands before slipping over the final barrier.

The race to the Chattahoochee would be a close contest, with the winner controlling the bridges, ferries, and fords across the river. If Johnston prevailed, he would be able to defend Atlanta; but if Sherman won, then Atlanta and the Army of Tennessee would likely be destroyed.

Sherman and his staff quickly rode into Marietta early on the morning of July 3, but his anger was kindled by the absence of Garrard's cavalry and

"Old Slow Trot" Thomas and his ponderous Army of the Cumberland. Garrard and Thomas eventually arrived, but the vanguard only covered five miles south of Marietta before it was rudely halted at Smyrna. Instead of fleeing for the protection of Atlanta, the Southern army had occupied a line of strong fieldworks constructed on a ridge behind Nickajack Creek that commanded the railroad and turned to face its pursuers. Johnston was inviting Sherman to attack, but this time the offer was declined.

At first light on July 4, Sherman rode to the front of Thomas's column, reluctant to believe that Johnston had stopped with the Chattahoochee at his back. Thomas explained that the Confederates were entrenched in force at Smyrna, but Sherman dismissed that possibility. "There is no force in your front," Sherman admonished Thomas. "They are laughing at you."

"We will see," Thomas replied, sending forward a line of skirmishers to probe the Rebel works. Batteries of concealed guns and ranks of invisible infantry on the wooded hill hurled a murderous storm of shot at the troops, which rapidly withdrew. Sherman decided against jeopardizing his men with a frontal assault against the stout line and instructed Thomas to keep the Confederates busy while Johnston was flanked out of this position. Then, the frustrated Sherman thought, we will certainly catch him in a perilous withdrawal across the river.

Thomas opened what a Confederate called a "furious shelling" of the Rebel works, and Union troops made demonstrations against two points of Johnston's defenses. A division assaulted the left of the Confederate line, held by Hood at Ruff's Mill, and was repulsed. A second effort carried Hood's first line of works, but the Rebel front remained intact. A second Federal force had a try against Hardee's trenches at Smyrna, on the Confederate right, but found it impregnable.

Sherman wrote, "We celebrated our Fourth of July by a noisy but not desperate battle to hold the enemy there [at Smyrna] till Generals McPherson and Schofield could get well into position below him near the Chattahoochee crossings."

Events were progressing more to Sherman's taste to the west, where Schofield's and McPherson's forces faced only Jackson's cavalry and some newly arrived Georgia militia.

In late June Georgia's intransigent Governor Joseph Brown had unexpectedly dispatched 3,000 Georgia militia to join Johnston's command, on condition that he could withdraw the men from Confederate service whenever the state required them. Most of these soldiers were raw and poorly trained, untried young boys and old men, led by Gustavus W. Smith; but Johnston nonetheless welcomed their presence. Smith resourcefully appropriated a battery of guns that were being refitted in Atlanta and reported his pitiful force for duty. Smith's cavalry deployed to patrol Chattahoochee River crossings, and the infantry filed into place on Johnston's left flank at Kennesaw.

When Sherman initiated his latest flanking effort, Smith and Jackson were ordered to impede the Federal march, a task the militia performed well. They skirmished aggressively with the Federals, then withdrew in good order to keep the enemy at their front. As Smith admitted, his principal response was to "get out of the way" when the two Yankee armies advanced. Faced with such overwhelming odds, the blocking force was thrown back several miles on July 3, took up a new position for the night, and on July 4 was hit hard and forced to retreat to Johnston's final line of defense on the northern bank of the Chattahoochee. There the Yankees formed a heavy skirmish line, and Smith awaited the inevitable assault by half the Federal army. Fortunately, his battery was expertly tended. The Confederates peppered the Union ranks with a deadly fire that kept the enemy at a respectful distance. In return, his own position received a destructive artillery fire.

Smith felt lonely when darkness fell. He was outnumbered ten to one, his flanks were dangerously exposed, and his troops had never known serious combat. Most troubling was the absence of the Confederate army. Smith dispatched a note informing Johnston that the undermanned works would be occupied by massive numbers of Union troops when they attacked at daybreak. If he did not receive a reply from Johnston by dawn, Smith intended to retreat across the Chattahoochee and save his command from certain ruin.

During the night the Army of Tennessee appeared, an unruffled Joe Johnston at its head. He commended Smith for accomplishing a difficult mission. The Georgia militia had proven themselves under fire, bravely holding off a superior force until the regulars could arrive to resume the fight.

When Johnston abandoned Smyrna, Sherman was hard on his heels, convinced that the Confederates would hurriedly cross the river this time. But the resourceful Johnston quickly occupied the formidable works on the north side of the river, and Sherman was brought up short for a second time. Johnston had won the race by a hair, again frightening his own officers but managing to make the maneuver appear simple, to Sherman's continued mystification.

An exasperated Sherman could hardly believe the sight that greeted him. Instead of a vulnerable army feverishly attempting to span the wide river, he found Johnston's "River Line," as it became known, an extremely heavy perimeter of artillery forts and infantry trenches that Sherman called the "best line of field entrenchments I have ever seen." The bastions, log and earth works with walls twelve feet thick, were located at 80-yard intervals and linked by log stockades. Augmenting Johnston's field guns were huge siege cannon requisitioned from the defenses of Mobile, Alabama. The line was six miles long and one mile deep, occupying high ground from a ridge overlooking Nickajack Creek on the left to the Chattahoochee River on the right. The massive defenses forbade attack. The fortifications covered the railroad bridge over the river, a major wagon bridge, and three pontoon avenues that Johnston installed to ensure a safe passage if he were forced to withdraw quickly. There was adequate space for his entire army, with Loring occupying the right, Hood the left, and Hardee the center.

On July 5 Sherman probed the Confederate line, which he compared to a hornet's nest that released a hail of bullets and cannon fire. "I came very close to being shot myself," he remarked.

These Federal pickets felt out Confederate resistance near Atlanta. [LIBRARY OF CON-GRESS]

With cavalry screening the river crossings north and south of the line, Johnston waited for Sherman's reaction, which he hoped would include a debilitating assault. But Sherman, scanning the extensive works, remembered the slaughter at Kennesaw Mountain and rejected that rash action. He was astonished that Johnston had twice violated the rules of military strategy and invited combat with a wide river behind him, but such things made Johnston a worthy adversary.

On July 5 the rapidly advancing Federals chased the Confederate wagon train, which was shielded by Wheeler's cavalry, to the Chattahoochee. Under artillery fire, the wagons crossed safely at Pace's Ferry on pontoon bridges, which were cut loose to float to the southern side. One bridge swung the wrong direction in the current and was captured by jubilant Union forces, who considered it a consolation prize for having let the vital wagon train slip from their grasp yet again.

Late that day the Federals occupied Vinings on the north bank of the river; and from the heights of Vinings Mountain, Sherman and Thomas first viewed the river and the prize beyond. "Atlanta is in plain view," Sherman wrote, giving the city little attention as he promptly began casting about for the most viable location to cross the barrier and flank Johnston from the river line.

Accompanying Sherman was Major James Connolly, who was moved by the sight to write poetically, "Mine eyes have beheld the promised land. The 'domes and minarets and spires' of Atlanta are glittering in the sun before us, only eight miles distant." Vinings became a temporary railroad depot as Sherman built up his munitions and rations for the impending siege of Atlanta, and his wounded were carried there for evacuation north.

Sherman lost little time securing the remainder of the north bank. He sent Kenner Garrard's cavalry dashing north sixteen miles to occupy the important manufacturing center of Roswell and probe for a crossing point. Garrard dispatched a detachment to burn the Sope Creek Paper Mills, which had manufactured newsprint, stationery, and wrapping paper since 1857.

At Roswell, Garrard drove Confederate cavalry over the Chattahoochee bridge, which was burned. Then he destroyed three factories that made cotton and wool used for Confederate uniforms. The owner of one mill raised a French flag in hopes of convincing the Federals the factory was foreign owned, but that stratagem failed. The mills were burned, and Sherman, angered by the connivance, granted advance permission to hang the next man who attempted such a device.

The Federal troops were in high spirits. After six long weeks they had finally emerged from the wilderness of Dallas and Kennesaw. The soldiers were fighting in open country with room to maneuver, the weather was pleasant, and scouting along the banks of the Chattahoochee they could believe the end of the campaign was near.

For Sherman, the first order of business was crossing the river in good order. He had devised a strategy for accomplishing this before leaving Chattanooga: feint south and cross north. The militia and Johnston's cavalry were responsible for holding the fords above and below the river line, and McPherson briefly demonstrated below Atlanta to deceive Confederate scouts and initiate false reports that a Federal penetration was imminent there.

Then, on July 6 Sherman sent McPherson on a long march behind Schofield and Thomas—through the Smyrna battlefield—to the north, where he formed the extreme left of the Union line at Roswell. Schofield followed a day later, swinging around Thomas and camping at Sope Creek on July 8 to form the Federal center. Thomas had his accustomed mission: demonstrate against the River Line to keep the Confederates occupied and prevent them from recognizing the dangerous operations being carried out upstream.

Schofield was the first to locate a chink in the Chattahoochee armor, exploiting it on July 8 at the mouth of Sope Creek, five miles north of the river line. A keen-eyed soldier found the submerged remains of an old stone fish dam; and a few men waded across, seized, and held the bank as twenty pontoon boats ferried across an additional regiment. Schofield rapidly threw a pontoon bridge, which had been hidden from Confederate view behind a ridge, across the river and passed over additional elements of his 3rd Division. With Jacob Cox's regiment acting as skirmishers, additional men quickly joined them to establish a bridgehead on the south bank. They raced up a high ridge 300 yards beyond the river, routed a small camp of surprised Confederates, captured a cannon, and entrenched. Schofield rushed a second division across before Johnston was informed of the development. Without sustaining a single casualty, Sherman had breached the last barrier remaining in his path to Atlanta.

At Roswell on the following day, Garrard made up for the time he lost in Marietta by forcing a crossing at Shallowford. On July 10 Federal army engineers constructed two bridges across the river there.

Also on July 9, Union cavalry made a third crossing just south of Sope Creek. These cavalrymen dismounted, carried their guns over their heads, and waded nude—except for hats—across the river to establish another Federal position south of the Chattahoochee.

These splendid strategic maneuvers, brilliantly conceived and flawlessly executed, accomplished their purpose. Finding himself outflanked on July 8, Johnston was forced to abandon the impregnable River Line and withdraw across the Chattahoochee during the night of July 9. Once more the sound of marching feet, horse hooves, and creaking artillery crossing the wooden bridge and pontoon spans were muffled with straw and cornstalks. When all traffic had passed, the bridge was burned. The Confederates occupied the outer defenses of Atlanta, located several miles north of the city on a ridge overlooking Peachtree Creek. Behind it was only the inner ring of fortifications that protected the city.

Future Presidents Served in Georgia

Among the Federal forces that invaded Georgia in 1864 was a colonel of the green 70th Indiana, who would later make history. Benjamin Harrison, grandson of President William Henry Harrison, first led his 400 men into combat at Resaca. They charged Hood's exposed battery with Harrison shouting, "Cheer, men, for Indiana! Forward!" The Confederate artillerists crammed cannister into their guns and punished the Hoosiers, who sought safety on the ground near the cannon.

When Harrison saw the Rebels' supporting infantry re-treat, he stood up and led his men over the Confederate earthworks with a sword in one hand and a pistol in the other. After desperate hand-to-hand combat, the guns were captured and Harrison's troops had been bloodied.

At Peachtree Creek, when George Thomas's line was bent by a savage Confederate charge, Harrison led a spirited counterattack. His soldiers crashed into the advancing Rebels and slowly drove them back, saving the day for the Union.

Harrison left the army later that fall to occupy a seat in the U.S. House of Representatives, and in 1888 he became president. Although he lost the popular vote, Harrison managed to take the electoral count.

A year earlier, Brigadier General James Garfield had entered Georgia as William Rosecrans's chief of staff. He fled the field at Chickamauga with Rosecrans but returned to deliver instructions to Thomas, who had remained to blunt the Confederate pursuit. That act saved his reputation, and in 1880 Garfield won the presidency by a scant 10,000 votes. A disturbed and disappointed seeker of a government job shot Garfield, and he died seven months after taking office.

In May 1865, Confederate President Jefferson Davis and Vice President Alexander Stephens were captured in Georgia and transferred to Augusta, where they boarded a ship that took them to prison in the North. As the captives rode through the city, nine-year-old Woodrow Wilson, whose father was a Presbyterian minister, peered at the sight through a window of his house. Wilson became president in 1912 and brought the country through World War I. ■

The next week saw little activity along the Chattahoochee front. Sherman marked time on the north bank and in his beachheads on the south side resting his men, rebuilding the railroad and wagon bridge, and waiting for supplies and reinforcements to arrive at Vinings. Sherman's reconstruction of the Chattahoochee railroad bridge is still considered a significant engineering feat. In four and one-half days his engineers built a 900-foot-long, 90-foot-high bridge; and every stick of wood used in its construction was a tree when they started.

Federal and Confederate pickets watched each other warily across the river, but casualties were rare during this interlude. The men—Sherman included—bathed in the Chattahoochee, the first time many had been clean in two months. Enemies swam together, and at night Rebel and Yankee choirs and bands competed with each other and often performed together. A good deal of fraternization and trading occurred, practices that angered McPherson to such an extent he issued 100 rounds to each man in the Army of the Tennessee and threatened to punish those who did not fire the ammunition. His soldiers threw the bullets into the river, and the unofficial truce between enlisted men continued. They realized the time for killing would arrive soon enough.

Johnston was surprisingly quiet during this period of inactivity. He did not attempt to destroy the northern bridgeheads, nor did he attack the Federal armies as they crossed the Chattahoochee in force. Historians have questioned his acquiescence at these lost opportunities, but Johnston felt it was more important to destroy Sherman's capacity to fight in one great battle.

The lull ended when Thomas began passing his enormous army over Power's Ferry and Pace's Ferry on July 16. He and Schofield were across the following day, advancing directly on Atlanta toward Peachtree Creek. McPherson crossed the Chattahoochee at Roswell on July 17, his mission to swing east in a wide arc to occupy Decatur and destroy the Georgia Railroad that ran to Augusta, the Carolinas, and Virginia. This move would prevent Lee from reinforcing Johnston, a lesson learned with fearful loss at Chickamauga. McPherson would pivot at Decatur and attack Atlanta from the east.

Sherman was relieved, but disturbed, that Johnston did not oppose his crossing. The Union commander correctly supposed an unpleasant surprise was being prepared for him. Johnston would certainly not allow Atlanta to be surrendered without a major effort to prevent its fall.

Johnston deployed his entire army in strong works behind Peachtree Creek, and waited. Hardee held the center of the line, Hood the right, and Alexander P. Stewart, who had been appointed permanent commander of Polk's corps, secured the left. Wheeler's cavalry was sent to obstruct McPherson in Decatur while Johnston dispatched the remainder of Sherman's forces. Jackson's cavalry watched for movement south of the Chattahoochee, and the inner fortifications were occupied by the militia.

Johnston's strategy was to destroy the enemy forces as they crossed Peachtree Creek on the march to Atlanta. He would strike the seam between Schofield and Thomas, where a half-mile-wide gap beckoned, rupture

A Federal wagon train crosses the Chattahoochee River on a pontoon bridge. [*HARPER'S WEEKLY*]

the Federal line, and roll it up. At the least, he thought the attack would send Thomas and Schofield stumbling north of the Chattahoochee in disarray with serious casualties. Perhaps he could trap and destroy them against the river or send the Yankees reeling all the way back to Chattanooga; then Johnston would turn on McPherson. If the assault failed, Johnston planned to withdraw into Atlanta's defenses, which he felt could be held forever.

Johnston was ready for the showdown that had been postponed for three months. He had suffered relatively few losses, while Sherman's numerical superiority was daily reduced. Sherman was equally prepared for a climactic battle. Although satisfied with his territorial gains, he was impatient to close the campaign. In two and one-half months Sherman had forced Johnston to abandon four strong positions and had occupied 100 miles of valuable enemy territory; but the opposing army was intact, even stronger than it had been when the fighting began. Sherman was dependent on a single railroad to supply 100,000 men and 25,000 animals, and some of the supplies came from far away Louisville over 500 miles of rickety rail that could be cut by marauding Confederate cavalry at any time.

Lincoln was also pressing Sherman. The offensive in the east had proven inconclusive as Grant and Lee fought desperate battles to a draw in Virginia's Wilderness, Spotsylvania, and Cold Harbor. Grant's butcher bill was mounting, and the Northern people demanded some assurance of ultimate victory. During the summer of 1864, Lincoln faced strong opposition in a grim election campaign, leading him for a time to believe he would be defeated in November. Lincoln needed a military victory in the field to ensure his reelection over a candidate who might make peace with the Confederacy and leave the nation permanently divided. He needed the symbol of a captured Atlanta. For both the United States and the Confederate States, the coming battles would be decisive.

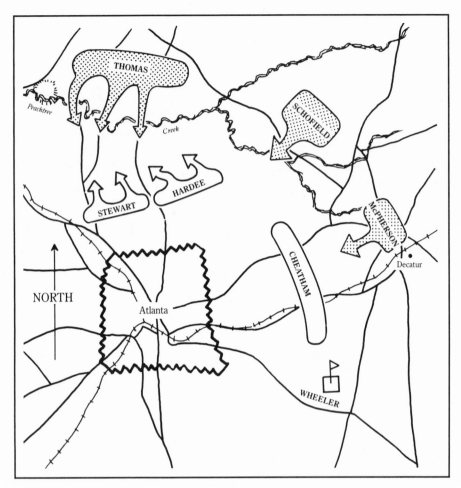

Map 18: The Battle of Peachtree Creek.

Johnston's trap was baited, and Thomas and Schofield were slowly advancing into it when disaster struck the Confederacy. Joseph Johnston was relieved of his command.

At his headquarters late on the evening of July 17, Johnston received a telegram from the War Department in Richmond. Since Johnston had failed to stop Sherman's advance to Atlanta, and because he refused to express supreme confidence in his chances of stopping the enemy, Confederate President Jefferson Davis removed him. "You are hereby relieved from the command of the Army and Department of Tennessee," the message read. Hood was to assume immediate control of the army. It was Davis's greatest blunder.

Johnston replied to the telegram early the following morning: orders received and complied with, command has been transferred to Hood. Johnston briefly defended his actions, adding, "Confident language by a military commander is not regarded as evidence of competence."

Davis had long been dissatisfied with the way the reticent Johnston conducted the campaign. He and the Cabinet had expected Johnston to regain Tennessee, or at least whip Sherman's army; but in ten weeks the Federals had advanced to the outskirts of Atlanta, and Johnston would not swear he could hold the city. The rancorous Davis–Johnston feud that had ignited over rank in 1861 gained momentum over strategy and personal clashes in 1862 and 1863, and it culminated in this critical year. Davis promoted Johnston's officers without consulting him, and Johnston maneuvered across northern Georgia without telegraphing Davis of his moves or future plans. Davis only knew Johnston had relinquished a great deal of territory without fighting any major battles to hold it, and he seemed likely to surrender more.

Johnston had no friends to represent him at the Confederate court. Davis's Secretary of State, Benjamin Judah, stated his belief that Johnston would not fight; and the Cabinet advised Johnston's removal. Davis relied heavily on Braxton Bragg, the disgraced former commander of the Army of Tennessee, for military advice. Bragg harbored deep misgivings about Johnston, believing he should have taken an aggressive offensive stance to defeat Sherman before now and ridiculing his caution and defensive strategy. Davis seemed to forget that Bragg had retreated from central Kentucky to middle Tennessee, and from there to northern Georgia, without fighting.

On July 9 Davis sent Bragg to snoop around Atlanta. Johnston resented his presence, and the reserved general refused to disclose his plans; so Bragg reported that Johnston apparently would not defend the city but would abandon Atlanta and continue to retreat. Bragg also met repeatedly with Hood, who reinforced the advisor's prejudices.

The Fiercest Fighter in the Army: ■ John B. Hood

[LIBRARY OF CONGRESS]

If ever a soldier was promoted beyond his capabilities, it was John Bell Hood. What made his career a greater tragedy is that he was one of the most ferocious fighters in the Confederate army. If he had remained in divisional command, history would have recorded him as an excellent subordinate officer.

Born in Kentucky in 1831, Hood graduated near the bottom of his West Point class in 1853 and was sent to the western frontier, where Indians had the first opportunity to wound the unfortunate fellow. Hood soon began his Confederate service at the retreat from Yorktown, Virginia; and he gallantly led a Texas brigade during the savage Seven Days' Battle, Second Manassas, and Antietam. His conspicuous heroism brought him command of a division, which he fought at Fredericksburg and Gettysburg, where a severe wound cost him the use of his left arm.

Two months later, Hood accompanied James Longstreet to Georgia. While leading his men into the bloodbath that was Chickamauga, Hood suffered a wound that forced the amputation of his right leg. He remained in Georgia and was given a corps under Joseph Johnston; but during the Atlanta campaign, Hood undermined Johnston's position with poison-pen letters to President Davis. When the young general was appointed commander of the Army of Tennessee, he lost Atlanta by launching four determined, but unsupervised, strikes against Sherman's superior army. Abandoning Georgia, Hood nearly destroyed the army with a suicidal strike into Tennessee.

Following the war, Hood entered business in New Orleans; but ill fortune followed him even there. The business failed; and Hood and his wife died from yellow fever, leaving a large family of small children to be divided among various foster homes. ■

On July 17, after receiving Bragg's report, Davis telegraphed Johnston, "I wish to hear from you as to present situation and your plan of operations so specifically as to enable me to anticipate events."

Johnston replied on the same day, "As the enemy has double our numbers, we must be on the defensive. My plan of operations, therefore, depend upon that of the enemy. It is mainly to watch for an opportunity to fight to advantage. We are trying to put Atlanta into condition to be held for a day or two by the Georgia militia, that army movements may be freer. . . ." Davis was not satisfied with this answer, which only convinced him Johnston would not fight for the city.

When Hood arrived to take command early on July 18, Johnston outlined his plan of attack at Peachtree Creek. In a curious turn of events, Hood and the other corps commanders urged Johnston to ignore the telegram and fight the battle, but Johnston had never disobeyed an order.

Before departing, Johnston penned a brief farewell to his troops:

> I cannot leave this noble army without expressing my admiration of the high military qualities it has displayed. A long and arduous campaign has made conspicuous every soldierly virtue, endurance of toil, obedience to orders, brilliant courage. The enemy has never attacked but to be repulsed and severely punished. You, soldiers, have never argued but from your courage, and never counted your foe. No longer your leader, I will still watch your career, and will rejoice in your victories. To one and all I offer assurances of my friendship, and bid an affectionate farewell.

"We lifted our hats," wrote one Georgian of Johnston's farewell. "There was no cheering. We simply passed silently, with heads uncovered. Some of the officers broke ranks and grasped his hand, as the tears poured down their cheeks."

Johnston boarded a train, and by nightfall he was in Macon with his wife. His anger and disappointment must have been intensified by the knowledge that it was Hood who had written Davis and Bragg to question his strategy and lack of offensive action, and it was Hood who had frequently thwarted his aggressive efforts. The crippled general would now determine the fate of Atlanta.

The Federal command was universally joyous over the change. "At this critical moment," Sherman wrote, "the Confederate Government rendered us most vital service. . . . The character of a leader is a large factor in the game of war and I confess I was pleased with the change."

"Much to our comfort and surprise, Johnston was removed," recorded another of Sherman's officers. The dismissal was "received by our officers with universal rejoycing [sic]," he continued. Johnston's "patient skill and watchful intelligence and courage" had stymied the Union army, he continued, and the change was seen "as equivalent to victory for us."

Sherman quickly took counsel of his officers, asking what he could expect from Hood, whom he knew by reputation to be a fighting man. McPherson and Schofield, Hood's West Point classmates, were well acquainted with the

Sherman refused to storm strong Confederate works like these that surrounded Atlanta.
[GEORGE N. BARNARD, LIBRARY OF CONGRESS]

new commander. McPherson had graduated first in the class; Schofield third; Hood, at forty-fourth, near the bottom. Hood confessed he was "more wedded to boyish sports than academics," and the intellectual Schofield tutored Hood in his studies. Schofield now told Sherman, "He'll hit you like hell, now, before you know it."

Sherman, pleased by the information, wondered for years why Johnston was removed. He had been baffled by Johnston's skillful defensive posture and welcomed an attack by Hood's inferior numbers. Sherman characterized Hood as "bold, even to rashness and courageous in the extreme." That attitude was shared by Confederate officers who considered him reckless and impetuous.

Davis had asked Lee's advice about replacing Johnston with Hood, who had been one of Lee's finest divisional commanders. Lee replied that the timing was bad for a change in command, and he feared it would lead to the loss of Atlanta and the army. He said Hood was a tremendous fighter, but personally reckless. He recommended Hardee, who had far more experience, for the job. Lee, as usual, proved correct.

The Confederate army was heartbroken by the change in command. They held Johnston in great confidence, and their love for the general was palpable. The venerated Johnston inspired their loyalty, and they fought like demons for him because they knew he would never waste a single life in senseless combat. The soldiers were optimistic, even when the odds were overwhelmingly against them. Hardee noted Johnston was one of those rare commanders who was trusted by both his officers and enlisted men.

A Confederate captain recorded the scene after Johnston's removal was announced to the men:

> Every man looked sad and disheartened at this information, and felt that evil would result from the removal of Johnston, whom they esteem and love above any previous commander. His address touched every heart, and every man thought that his favorite General had been grievously wronged. . . . General Hood is a gallant man, but Johnston has been tried and won the confidence of the soldiery.

Another infantryman said it was "the most terrible and disastrous blow the South ever received. I saw thousands of men cry like babies—regular old fashioned boo–hoos." A sergeant wrote, "all moan the loss of our grate [*sic*] Leader he would have been retained in preferance to anyone else. Gen Hood now commands us & I hope he will be successful but the releaving [*sic*] of Gen Joe is dampening to his troops."

"Old Joe was our idol," added another Rebel. "Gaunt, stalwart, sunburned soldiers by the thousands would be seen falling out of line, squatting down by a tree or in a fence corner weeping like children." The diminished spirit of the army never fully recovered, although for a time they continued to fight with accustomed ferocity. Gloom permeated the Confederate ranks, leading hundreds of men to desert because they felt the cause was now lost. Personal duels were fought between Rebel pickets and Yankees who taunted Johnston's dismissal.

A cloud of fear and confusion enveloped Atlanta. The city was daily inundated with tattered refugees from the north, pathetic families clutching a few personal possessions. Trains transported more Confederate wounded, who were treated in improvised hospitals set up in schools, homes, and parks. The people of Atlanta tended the wounded and brought them all the food and bandages they could scrounge. The city was deluged by traveling morticians who opened shop in tents, and carpenters turned to making coffins. Atlanta's population doubled, reaching 75,000, and martial law was declared in an effort to curb lawlessness and apprehend deserters. The city government, newspapers, businesses, and many people were removed to Macon and other points south to escape the impending conflict. Those who remained started constructing bombproofs, dugout shelters in their basements and gardens. They remembered with dread published accounts of Vicksburg, and they intended to be prepared for a siege.

A DRIVING TOUR
■ Roswell to Peachtree Creek ■

This portion of the driving tour begins at the intersection of 120 and U.S. 19–GA 9 in Roswell. If you are coming from the north on Interstate–75, turn off on 120–Loop, turn left under I–75, and follow 120–Loop to 120 and exit. Turn left on 120 and follow to the intersection with U.S. 19–GA 9. If you are coming from the south, take 400 North from Interstate–285. Exit on Northridge Road, turn right to 19–9, turn right and follow to the intersection of 120 and 19–9.

From the intersection of 120 (Atlanta Street) and U.S. 19–GA 9 turn left through a restored business district; at .1 turn right on Sloan.

Note the Bricks to your right, quarters erected in 1839 to house workers in the Roswell mills. They were used as a Federal hospital in 1864 and operated by the city as a library in the 1950s. The Bricks are considered the oldest apartments in the United States.

Turn right at .1 on Mill Street to the stop sign; park in the large lot before you.

Below this spot is a cotton mill converted into a shopping complex. In the creek are falls, a dam, and the remains of an old mill.

This is the beautiful, historic city of Roswell. It was named for Roswell King, an officer of the Darien Bank who traveled to north Georgia in the 1830s to open a branch. Enchanted by this spot on the Chattahoochee River, he bought vast acreage and offered his friends on the Georgia–South Carolina coast ten acres each if they would settle here. Many took advantage of the offer and built fine homes that still stand. Roswell and his son Barrington established a cotton mill in a steep gorge along Vickery Creek, and other mills and factories were soon attracted to the area.

The Kings laid out their town with a square and wide streets and gave lots for the building of Presbyterian and Methodist churches, both still in existence, and a school. Roswell was a prosperous city when Garrard and McPherson arrived in July 1864 with orders from Sherman to burn all manufacturing facilities.

Long, sturdy sets of stairs descend from the park-

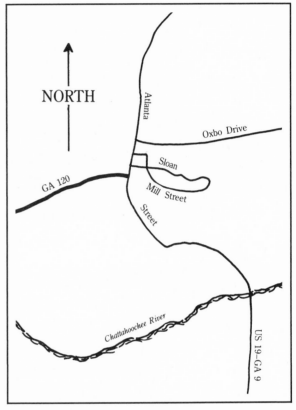

Map 19: Roswell area.

ing lot into Vickery Creek Gorge, where King built his two-story Ivy Woolen Mill that was destroyed during the Civil War. The mill produced Confederate uniforms. When Federal cavalry arrived on July 6, manager Theophil Roche ran up a French flag and claimed protection as a foreign neutral. Sherman ordered the buildings destroyed, and Roche was sent north up the rails.

The factory was rebuilt here in 1882 as the Laurel Mills, but it burned after a lightning strike in 1926. Large sections of thirteen-inch-thick stone walls and a single building remain from the mills, and a path leads to the old dam that channeled water to turn the water wheels, in turn providing power for the mills. It also

Ruins of factory buildings are all that remain at Sope Creek, near the Chattahoochee River.

them to Marietta and then up north to deny their skills to the Confederacy. His orders were to "arrest all those people, male and female, connected with those factories, no matter what the clamor, and let them foot it, under guard, to Marietta, where I will send them by cars to the North. Destroy and make the same disposition of all mills. . . . The poor women will make a howl. Let them take along their children and clothing."

The ladies were rounded up and sent on railroad cars to Chattanooga, Nashville, Lexington, and into Indiana. Contrary to legend, some women returned to Georgia following the war.

Visiting all the historic sites in Roswell would be a profitable day's outing. Attractions include Barrington Hall, which Barrington King built in 1842. Ancient oaks frame this magnificent Greek Revival home that took five years to build. Bulloch Hall, a beautiful home built in a similar style at the same time, was the girlhood home of President Theodore Roosevelt's mother, Mittie; it saw service as a Federal barracks. It is owned by the city and can be rented for special events. Bulloch Hall can be toured, and the Archibald Smith Plantation (1845), with thirteen outbuildings, is also open. Naylor Hall, heavily damaged during the war, may be rented for occasions. Great Oaks (1842) has eighteen-inch-thick walls and was Garrard's headquarters. Mimosa Hall, built by John Dunwoody, is ac-

Bulloch Hall in Roswell is a Greek Revival structure built in 1840. Teddy Roosevelt's parents were married here in 1853.

creates a lovely waterfall that can be heard for a considerable distance.

Above the ruins is the only remaining mill building in Roswell, built in 1929 to replace the second mill and operated until 1975. Previously ravaged by vandals and vagrants, a nine-million-dollar renovation project has transformed the cotton mill into an upscale retail establishment featuring shops and restaurants, and a large amphitheater has been constructed on the banks of the creek.

Just west on Mimosa Avenue is historic Roswell Presbyterian Church. Built in 1840, it retains the original box pews, high center pulpit, and slave balcony. In the belfry is a bronze ship's bell that was cast in Philadelphia. Following Sunday services, a mini-museum is open in the rear of the church where artifacts of church history are preserved, including the original silver communion service hidden in a barrel by Miss Fannie Whitemore until the war was over to prevent its theft by Federal troops, and a checkerboard carved on the back of a cabinet door by bored Union soldiers who used the church as a hospital.

Sherman burned Roswell's factories and mills, but he fortunately spared the city and its fine homes. However, he committed his most dastardly act here: the removal of the Roswell women. Noting the mill labor force was female, he directed Garrard to send tually a reproduction; his first home burned during a house-warming party immediately after it was completed. Allenbrook, a two-story saltbox built of handmade brick in 1840 to house the Laurel Mills manager, is currently headquarters of the Roswell Historical Society and can be toured. Primrose Cottage (1830) was the first building erected in Roswell, a gift from King to his widowed daughter. There is also the home of Francis B. Goulding, minister, author of *Young Marooners* and *Marooners Island,* and inventor of the first sewing machine—but he failed to obtain a patent!

The charming business district dates from 1839. The town square, where Teddy Roosevelt spoke in 1905, was laid out in 1840 and landscaped during the Depression as a WPA project. At the end of Sloan Street is Founders Cemetery, which contains the graves of Roswell King, John Bulloch, John Dunwoody, and other founders of the city. Other early settlers are

buried in the Presbyterian Church Cemetery—established in 1841—and the Methodist Church Cemetery (1850).

The Roswell Historical Society, the Chattahoochee Nature Center, and the city of Roswell regularly sponsor tours of the homes and the mill ruins, raft floats down the river, and re-creations of 1840s life in Roswell. A walking tour featuring twenty-seven sites—mansions, cemeteries, churches, commercial buildings, and mill ruins—has been prepared by the Roswell Historical Society and is available from the society or the convention and visitors bureau. Guided walks are also offered from the bureau.

Return to 19–9 (Atlanta Road) via Mill Street at the top of the mill parking area and turn left (Allenbrook will soon be on your left) to cross the Chattahoochee River at 1.1.

This is the approximate site of the original bridge at Shallowford. The Confederates burned it when Garrard's cavalry galloped into town, but the spans were quickly rebuilt by Union engineers who tore down mill buildings to use the timber in the bridges. In sixty hours they threw up twin spans 710 feet long, 18 feet wide, and 14 feet high. While the Federals were crossing the river, a horrible thunderstorm erupted, and lightning killed a dozen men, split ninety-foot-tall oak trees, and discharged muskets.

On July 10 McPherson crossed here and advanced on Decatur to cut the Augusta railroad and descend on Atlanta from the east, while Thomas crossed from Vinings at Pace's and Power's ferries and proceeded south along Howell Mill Road and Northside Drive, and Schofield crossed at Sope Creek, between Power's Ferry and Johnson's Ferry west of this point, and marched toward Buckhead.

Brave the Atlanta traffic 12.6 miles and take a right on West Paces Ferry Road. At .5 turn left onto Andrews Drive for .1 to the Atlanta History Center and Museum.

The society has created a fascinating complex that can occupy a full day of exploration. It hosts a wide variety of activities and programs. On its thirty-two wooded acres are gardens, the 1840 Tullie Smith House (one of Atlanta's oldest surviving structures), and the Swan House (an Italian-style mansion of the 1920s). The Atlanta Historical Society has recently constructed an eleven-million-dollar facility that hosts various exhibits. A permanent exhibit will explore the Atlanta

Map 20: Peachtree Creek area.

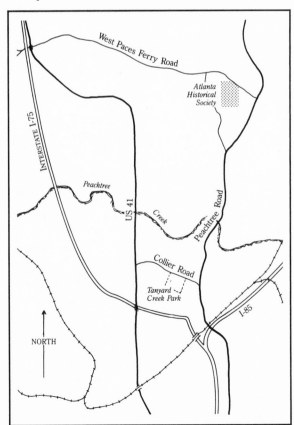

A monument in Atlanta marks the site where Johnston received word of his dismissal.

campaign, drawing on the ordnance collections of Thomas S. Dickey and Beverly M. Dubose Jr.

Every July, on a weekend near the anniversary of the battle of Atlanta, the Atlanta history center sponsors an encampment, featuring Confederate and Federal camps and illustrating everyday soldiering through troop drills, maneuvers, weapons displays, period music, medical practices, lectures, films, and documentaries. Call (404) 814-4000 for information.

From the entrance of the Atlanta Historical Society, return to U.S. 19–GA 9 (which immediately becomes Peachtree Street), turn right, and proceed 2.5 to Piedmont Hospital on the right.

In front is a stone monument that commemorates the battle of Peachtree Creek. South of the hospital along the sidewalk is an older WPA monument marking the spot where Confederate troops opened the assault.

At .1 turn right onto Collier Road; at .5 to your right are the stones from Collier's Mill. Turn left at .1 into Tanyard Creek Park.

This preserve is Atlanta's memorial to Peachtree Creek. Created during the centennial celebration of the Civil War in 1964, nine plaques were set on cement stands to describe the action that occurred in this area, but several have been stolen.

Unfortunately for the Confederate effort, the Federals had crossed Peachtree Creek and set up defensive positions on a ridge just north of here when Hood launched his ferocious assault. The Confederates attacked from the south, crossing at this spot. Their battle line extended through the area of Piedmont Hospital north of Collier and up Northside Drive west of the park. The Confederates made two thrusts, Hardee to the east and Stewart to the west. Confederate Gen. C. H. Stevens was killed at the intersection of Twenty-eighth Street and Wycliff. Collier's Mill was upstream on Tanyard Branch, which flows through the park and is the site where Federals concentrated several artillery batteries that were instrumental in turning back the Confederate drive. Commanding the Federals was Col. Benjamin Harrison, a future president.

Return to Collier, continuing west .3 to U.S. 41 (Northside Drive), and turn left for .5. If you are continuing the driving tour, cross the bridge over the interstate and turn right to enter I–75 South. After 5 miles leave I–75 to get on I–20 East (to Augusta); pay close attention to instructions at the interchange. After 4 miles take exit 30 at Glenwood Avenue. Turn left from the ramp .1 to Walker Monument on the left.

CHAPTER 8

The Siege of Atlanta

Hood had been given command of the Army of Tennessee to take the offensive and destroy the Union forces. His eyes flashing with an indescribable light at thought of the assignment—one subordinate remarked—Hood set out immediately to accomplish that mission. Generally following Johnston's original plan for an assault at Peachtree Creek, Hood positioned Stewart and Hardee, who was angry for not being chosen Johnston's successor, to attack Thomas and Schofield as they crossed the stream. Cheatham, who had taken Hood's corps, was posted to block McPherson from coming to the assistance of Thomas and Schofield, who would be trapped in a pocket between Peachtree Creek and the Chattahoochee River and crushed. Then Hood would turn and dispatch McPherson.

The Confederate attack appeared doomed from the start. Scheduled to begin at 1:00 P.M. on July 20, action was postponed until 4:00 P.M. when Hood was forced to shift his line. This gave Thomas precious time to bring nearly his entire army across Peachtree Creek and entrench on elevated ground. Five Confederate divisions would be assaulting seven Federal divisions, perilous odds at best.

The Confederate advance was hampered by heavy woods, thickets, and ravines; for a time an entire division was lost in the wilderness. Once organized, the lank, tattered Rebels launched a series of furious, but uncoordinated, attacks on the Federal line that accomplished several shallow penetrations; but they finally were murderously repulsed by punishing volleys of cannon and musketry. The most serious Confederate thrust was parried by a counterattack led by Colonel Benjamin Harrison, the future president. Some Southern units took fire from several directions at once. After two hours of persistent fighting in which the Confederates gained nothing, they withdrew, having suffered 4,800 casualties while inflicting only 1,780 on the enemy.

Hood blamed the setback on Hardee for not pressing the assault with enough vigor, but Hood was responsible for much of the disaster. Absent from the scene of battle, he had chosen to direct the action from Atlanta, where he would remain throughout the fighting around the beleaguered city.

While the tempest of battle raged at Peachtree Creek, the first Federal

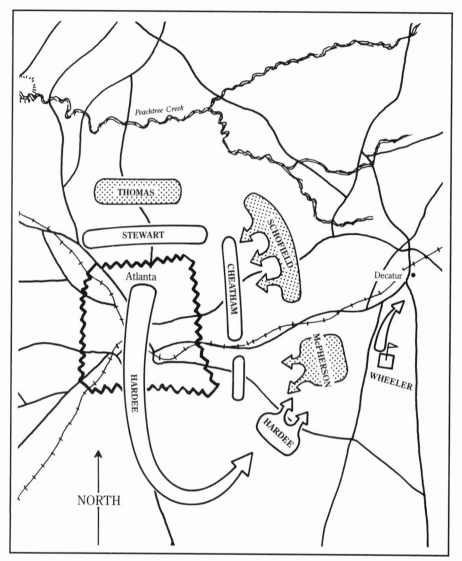

Map 21: The Battle of Atlanta.

shell dropped on Atlanta, killing a little girl. The siege had begun, a fact made clear to Atlantans by the thousands of Confederate wounded who suddenly flooded into the city, the debris of Hood's first combat.

After Hood's attack failed, he withdrew his army into Atlanta's inner defenses and contracted his lines to stave off Thomas. His new strategy involved holding the city's trenches and striking out at Sherman's armies whenever he saw an opportunity. For his part, Sherman had no intention of storming the stout fortifications that surrounded Atlanta. He intended to make a circuit of the city and destroy the four railroads that supplied Hood.

Sherman had already broken two, the W & A and the Augusta roads; and he expected to entice Hood out of Atlanta to protect his two remaining rail lifelines. While accomplishing this mission, Sherman welcomed fights in the open with the considerably outnumbered Confederate forces, instructing his generals to remain vigilant for Rebel sallies. Sherman believed this strategy would be time consuming, but ultimately successful.

Hood refused to allow the bloody reversal at Peachtree Creek to deter him from continuing the offensive. He immediately turned his attention to McPherson, who was dangerously isolated to the east of Atlanta and advancing on the city from Decatur. On July 21 McPherson had told Mortimer Leggett to capture Bald Hill, a strategic post east of Atlanta. The assignment was almost suicidal, but in a brilliant strike his men swarmed over the Rebel parapets to subdue the defenders. The elevation would afterward be known as Leggett's Hill. The Federals suffered 750 casualties in what Cleburne called the most bitter fighting of his career. The loss of the important ridge placed Atlanta under Yankee artillery, and McPherson would have to be thrown back to prevent a bombardment of the city.

Without allowing his men to rest from the exertions of battle and retreat on July 20, Hood set a second full-scale attack into motion on the following day. Hood intended to imitate the successful tactics of the incomparable

Sherman and his staff discuss strategy during the long stalemate before Atlanta. [*HARPER'S WEEKLY*]

Robert E. Lee and Stonewall Jackson in Virginia by dividing his army and sending Hardee on a grand flanking march around McPherson's left, a move Jackson executed to perfection against Hooker at Chancellorsville.

Hood's plan called for Hardee to withdraw from the northeastern lines of Atlanta on the night of July 21, march through the city to the south, and be in place to attack the Federal left at dawn. When Hardee turned the flank, Cheatham was to hit McPherson's front; and the Army of the Tennessee would be crushed. Stewart and the Georgia militia would hold the city's defenses against Thomas and Schofield, preventing them from rescuing McPherson or marching into Atlanta during the battle. Wheeler was instructed to strike McPherson's rear and burn the extensive Union wagon train. Hood believed that, if properly executed, this audacious plan would send the entire Federal army reeling north of the Chattahoochee River in disorganized retreat.

Unfortunately, Atlanta was not Chancellorsville, Hood was not Lee, Hardee was not Jackson, and McPherson was not Hooker. The Confederates were exhausted from the previous battle and withdrawal, and in executing a grueling fifteen-mile march in the dark that would consume twelve hours, they would be sacrificing a second night's sleep. Then they would be expected to fight again.

Confederate high tide at Atlanta: overrunning a Union battery. [MOUNTAIN CAMPAIGNS IN GEORGIA]

The plan was brilliant, if unrealistic. The heat was oppressive, the primitive roads narrow, twisting, crowded, and choked with dust, and progress was slowed by heavy woods, ravines, and marshes south of Atlanta. The march was further delayed by the tardy arrival of some units, and the men suffered terribly from thirst on the long trek. Hardee's inexperienced guides retarded the advance by leading the columns into a pond, which forced a lengthy detour. The troops waited impatiently as cavalry, artillery, and ammunition wagons passed, and for stragglers to rejoin the march.

The people of Atlanta realized a dramatic undertaking was afoot. All day the Confederates raised clouds of dust as troops tramped south through Atlanta. Many feared Hood was evacuating the city and made preparations for occupation by Federal troops.

As the Confederates finally arrayed their battle lines, General William Walker was shot and killed by Federal pickets. It proved an ill omen.

After all the delays, the attack was launched six hours late; it initiated the fiercest combat of the Atlanta campaign. Hardee's men bravely surged forward, screaming like demons through the woods in furious assault on McPherson's men. A Yankee said the enemy "came tearing wildly through the woods with the yells of demons." The determined attack was marked by savage fighting; but the delay had given McPherson time to extend and fortify his position, and the attack did not fall on the vulnerable flank. Hardee's initial lunge was riddled by twelve Union cannon that fired 1,000 rounds at the charging Rebels.

Hardee's attack degenerated into an inconclusive charge and countercharge until Cleburne's dynamic division burst the Federal line, capturing eight guns and 700 prisoners and threatening Union troops from two sides; but a battery of ten Northern artillery pieces beat back the assault, and the hole was sealed. Cleburne sacrificed 40 percent of his men in the effort, including thirty out of sixty officers.

The Intellectual General: ■ John M. Schofield

[LIBRARY OF CONGRESS]

Schofield was perhaps the least physically imposing general involved in the Atlanta campaign. He was short and plump, balding, and sported a long beard; but he had shown competence in organizing Federal forces in Missouri.

Schofield was given command of the tiny Army of the Ohio, which had earlier captured Knoxville and held it against siege by James Longstreet. The Ohioan performed well; and when the Atlanta campaign was successfully concluded, his force was dispatched to help deal with Hood in Tennessee.

When Hood skillfully slipped around the Federal flank at Spring Hill, Tennessee, Schofield should have been destroyed; but in one of the Civil War's greatest controversies, Schofield tip-toed past the sleeping Confederate army. Enraged, Hood launched a foolish assault against the Army of the Ohio at Franklin, a battle which left six Rebel generals dead and his army crippled. At Nashville Schofield helped Thomas destroy the Army of Tennessee, then rejoined Sherman in North Carolina before the war ended.

Schofield's real talents lay in the academic and administration arenas. Before the Civil War, he had taught physics at Washington University in St. Louis. Following the Great Rebellion, he became Andrew Johnson's Secretary of War, served as commandant of the Military Academy at West Point, and finally became Commander-in-Chief of the United States Army. ■

Gen. James B. McPherson is shot by Confederate pickets as he tries to avoid capture.
[*MOUNTAIN CAMPAIGNS IN GEORGIA*]

Several hours after Hardee initiated the battle, Cheatham hit McPherson's center, ruptured the Union line, and captured ten guns, an entire regiment of Yankees, and thirteen stands of colors. As one Confederate said, "We charged with an awful yell, but few Yankees staid [*sic*] to see the racket." The Confederates broke into the Union rear and routed four regiments as they steadily advanced down the line, catching the Federals from behind. The battered Federals received fire from two directions and jumped from one side of their works to the other to blunt successive waves of attackers. McPherson's army was severely distressed, and the entire Union line was in danger of being irretrievably shattered.

McPherson had met with his corps commanders earlier in the morning and was returning to his headquarters when the melee erupted. He quickly galloped toward a ridge where he could observe the scene and direct a defense, but he rode into an unsuspected gap in his lines just as Cleburne's men penetrated. Charging Rebels called for him to surrender; but McPherson wheeled his horse to escape, waving gallantly at the Confederate soldiers. A rattling volley knocked McPherson from his mount, dead with a ball through his lungs. He would never return to Baltimore to marry.

McPherson's body was recovered as the ground changed hands repeatedly, and the general was brought to Sherman's headquarters and laid on a door. The Union commander wept at the sight. He ordered the corpse covered with the flag for which McPherson died and sent the body to Marietta for transportation north. Sherman personally wrote McPherson's fiancee, who was tormented by intemperate comments made by Secessionist family members, describing McPherson as an eclipsed "bright star" and expressing the fear that he would meet the same fate.

Sherman temporarily pushed his grief aside when he recognized the dangerous hole that Cheatham had ripped in McPherson's front. Moving quickly to seal the ruptured line, he ordered Schofield to train twenty massed guns on the gap. Sherman was in his element when crisis beckoned. A staff officer said his "eyes flashed, he did not speak," but exhibited a "concentrated fierceness" in his face.

John "Blackjack" Logan assumed McPherson's command and received this order from Sherman: "Fight 'em, fight 'em, fight 'em like hell!" Logan complied, rallying his stunned men with the cry, "For McPherson and revenge!" In a fury the Army of the Tennessee relentlessly attacked into a maelstrom of fire to restore the broken line, which is the dramatic scene of battle depicted in the famous Cyclorama.

A gale of shot from concentrated Federal cannon shredded a final Confederate charge through the hole, then Logan's men surged in counterattack to

Union troops establish a line to stem a final Confederate charge at the Battle of Atlanta.
[*BATTLES AND LEADERS OF THE CIVIL WAR*]

Abandoned Confederate artillery fort at Atlanta. [*LESLIE'S ILLUSTRATED*]

seal the gap. Men in blue and gray fought with reckless abandon in hand-to-hand fighting. Officers dueled with swords while infantrymen used bayonets freely and rifles were swung as deadly clubs. A more bitter battle or harder fighting was not witnessed in the war. Whole battalions on each side ceased to exist, and guns and flags were repeatedly captured and lost. In one Confederate division, all the officers became casualties. A thick layer of blood covered the ground, and the groans of wounded and dying men drowned out the crashing sounds of mortal combat.

The Federals jubilantly seized their trenches and mangled three Rebel efforts to recapture them. Union batteries and 17,000 massed muskets opened a scathing fire that completely annihilated one Rebel assault, crumpling men like wheat before a tornado, a participant commented.

The tide of battle had decisively turned. Wheeler had successfully driven the Yankees through Decatur; but before the wagon train could be destroyed, the cavalry was recalled to support Hardee.

After eight hours of continuous battle, darkness enveloped the field; and the fighting was halted by the complete exhaustion of the combatants. During the night the Rebels withdrew into the inner ring of Atlanta's defenses, leaving the Union line intact. They had suffered debilitating casualties as 8,000 men fell; the Federals lost 3,700. It was the largest engagement of the campaign, destined to be remembered as the Battle of Atlanta. The cost crippled the Confederates.

The plan had been a bold, brilliant move that could have destroyed the Army of the Tennessee; but it had failed miserably. Part of the blame could be placed on the piecemeal attacks. Four assaults were launched at four different times against unsuspected works, while a single unified attack might have destroyed the opposition. Hood had also expected too much of his weary men, asking them to destroy twice their number. They tried valiantly, but they could not accomplish the impossible. Hood again placed responsibility for the failure on Hardee because of the tardy attack and poorly conducted assaults; but Hood had been distant from the battlefield, observing the smoke-obscured conflict from the area of Oakland Cemetery.

A humanitarian truce was arranged on July 24; the wounded were collected from the battlefield, and the dead were buried. The number of Confederate casualties blanketing the ground was sickening. Governor Brown's brother was counted among the thousands of Rebel dead. Atlanta streets were crammed with ambulances from the front carrying wounded to hospitals and parks in the city, where the grass soon stained red and buckets overflowed with amputated limbs.

Curiously enough, Hood considered the Battle of Atlanta a partial victory, although it had obviously not accomplished the grandiose objectives he had desired. A considerable number of Federal prisoners had been bagged; McPherson's advance had been halted, however temporarily, and Hood strangely thought he had restored the morale of the Army of Tennessee by

Confederate artillery fort in Atlanta, as seen after Union occupation. [GEORGE N. BARNARD, LIBRARY OF CONGRESS]

reintroducing them to offensive combat. The soldiers knew the truth. They had been savaged.

The siege of Atlanta now began in earnest. Sherman lobbed shells into the city, tumbling some buildings into ruins and setting others on fire. On July 28 he began a general bombardment, but he lacked the troops to establish a complete encirclement. Sherman paid careful heed to Howard's warning, "Hood won't give up."

Sherman shortly decided to move west of Atlanta, intent on destroying the West Point and Macon railroads, which shared five miles of track before branching at East Point. Political considerations led Sherman to appoint Howard permanent commander of the Army of the Tennessee instead of Logan, and on July 26 Howard was dispatched on a wide flanking movement around the city to cut the rails that brought supplies into Atlanta. Howard was also instructed to goad Hood into further battle, if possible.

It was possible. Learning of the threat to his lifelines, Hood sent two corps, commanded by Stewart and Stephen Lee, a former cavalry leader fresh from Mississippi who now commanded Hood's old unit, to intercept Howard on the western edge of the city. Expecting trouble, Howard halted the advance when scouts informed him of the approaching Confederates and deployed his men in a defensive position on high ground near Ezra Methodist Church. His men stripped the church to use benches and planks, supported by their knapsacks, for barricades and waited anxiously for the Southerners to arrive. The Confederates rapidly marched into view, dressed their lines of battle, and mounted several unsynchronized, piecemeal assaults beginning at 12:30 p.m. They were badly mauled as they groped forward through tangled underbrush.

The Rebels made four separate charges in three hours of terrible fighting, the last waves stumbling over dead and wounded comrades. Howard brought up his artillery to enfilade the Southern assaults, and shells rained on the attackers from two directions while bullets pelted their ranks like hail. One unit, the 25th Alabama, lost 125 of 173 men. In the fierce fire Confederate battle flags were shot to pieces, and Stewart and General Loring were wounded. Stewart, who personally led three charges, seemed for a while to be charmed, remaining unscathed for long hours while the entire Federal army seemed to be blazing away at his horsed figure. Litter bearers later said it looked like hogs had been slaughtered on their stretchers.

Hardee, sent to assess the situation, reported to Hood there was no point in continuing the attacks with such demoralized troops. They had lost 5,000 men; the Federals 600. That night, Jacob Cox heard a Federal picket call out, "Well Johnny, how many of you are left?" A despondent Confederate replied, "Oh, about enough for another killing."

When informed of the battle, Sherman was delighted, replying that it was just what he required. "Let 'em beat their own brains out," he said in excitement.

The Battle of Ezra Church broke the back of the Army of Tennessee. Some units had fought courageously, but others balked at advancing into the muzzles of a prepared adversary. After fighting heroically in fruitless contests at Peachtree Creek and Atlanta, many had lost heart. Desertion was soon epidemic in the Confederate ranks.

Although Hood's offenses had failed, Sherman paid homage to the Confederate soldiers. "These fellows fight like Demons and Indians combined, and it calls for all my cunning and strength" to defeat them, he remarked.

After examining the results of the Ezra Church encounter, President Davis dispatched an ironic telegram to Hood. "Stop attacking," he directed, "before you completely destroy the army." Perhaps Davis had finally realized the blunder of placing Hood in command and had come to appreciate the wisdom of Johnston's defensive strategy.

Hood was content for a month to rely on the formidable defenses of Atlanta to foil Sherman's designs. The inner ring of works, located one and one-half miles from the city, was ten miles in length and consisted of infantry

Map 22: The Battle of Ezra Church.

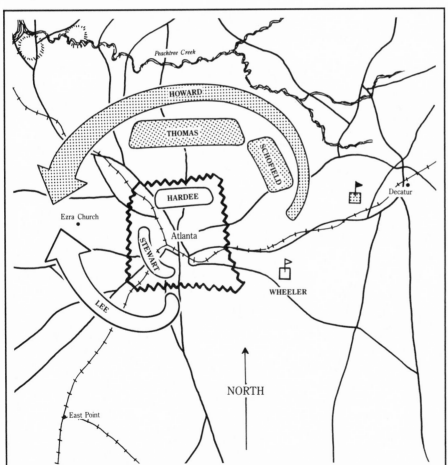

Fighting behind barricades, Union troops repulse Hood's attack at Ezra Church.
[*HARPER'S WEEKLY*]

trenches connected to batteries that provided interlocking fields of fire. The earthworks were further shielded by rows of abatis and four lines of chevaux-de-frise. Thousands of trees were felled, and neighborhoods of houses disappeared as timber was appropriated for the extensive works, which were so vast that they "astonished" the Federals.

Sherman telegraphed Washington that the fortifications were "too strong to assault and too extensive to invest," calling Atlanta "a tough nut to crack." The possibility of attack was dismissed; for "the cost would be too great and success unlikely," and it seemed improbable that Hood would sally forth again. Sherman devised a new strategy to force Hood out of Atlanta, but this plan proved to be one of Sherman's rare mistakes.

Atlanta was receiving urgently needed supplies by the two remaining railroads, one leading to West Point and Mobile, the second to Macon and Savannah. Although Sherman had always considered cavalry useless, he decided to send them on raids deep into Georgia to sever the railroads, make Hood evacuate Atlanta, and, as a bonus, liberate Union prisoners at Andersonville.

Sherman's "Great Raid," which kicked off on July 27, was a disaster from start to finish. Federal cavalry stumbled across western and central Georgia, managing to torch two trains, destroy two miles of track, and lay ruin to a 500-wagon procession. Then, pursued by heavily outnumbered but maniacal Confederate horsemen, each Federal cavalry detachment was annihilated. Stoneman was defeated and captured at Sunshine Church near Macon; Daniel McCook, a first cousin of the colonel killed at Kennesaw Mountain, was shattered at Brown's Mill near Newnan; Capron was scattered at King's Tanyard near Winder. The strategic gamble had completely failed by August 3, and remnants of the isolated commands trickled in for weeks, mainly on foot. Over 4,700 Union cavalrymen began the raid; 1,600 returned. The blunder only served to resupply the depleted Confederate cavalry with captured horses and equipment.

After his cavalry failed to induce Atlanta's surrender, Sherman resumed his tedious flanking maneuvers to cut the railroads. On August 6 Schofield was sent south of the city with his army and another corps under John Palmer, but the two generals' argument over seniority wasted a day. By the time they advanced, Hardee had extended his lines to meet the threat at Utoy Creek. The Federals assaulted the Orphan Brigade, pressing through thickets and brambles to within thirty yards of the Confederate trenches; but fierce resistance caused them to falter, then abandon the attack. During the night the Confederates withdrew closer to Atlanta; and on the following day Schofield flung his troops against the new line, suffering a more savage repulse, which led Sherman to mutter, "The enemy can build parapets faster than we can march." The Federals left 800 men strewn across the valley of Utoy Creek, while the Confederates suffered only 18 casualties and captured large quantities of guns and ammunition.

Union trenches around Atlanta. Soldiers shot from under the head logs, and poles extending across the trenches kept troops from being crushed when a cannonball dislodged the head log. [LIBRARY OF CONGRESS]

With this movement blocked, Sherman commenced a heavy shelling of Atlanta. He telegraphed Chattanooga for two siege guns and 1,000 shells with which he planned to level every building in the city. On August 9, 5,000 rounds thundered down on Atlanta, killing at least six civilians; and Sherman slowly extended a vise-like grip on his objective. As Sherman informed Washington, he intended to "make the inside of Atlanta too hot to endure."

Conditions in the city became critical as Hood struggled to feed his 37,000 soldiers still manning the trenches and 10,000 stubborn citizens and refugees, who Sherman assumed had been evacuated. The Union commander ordered his men to fire every gun that could reach any structure in the city, whether the target was a factory, warehouse, store, church, or private home. Ultimately, over 225 cannon contributed to the "Atlanta Express."

Under a flag of truce, Hood sent a message through the lines to Sherman, criticizing his bombardment of a city filled with defenseless women and children. Sherman replied, "Even Hood must realize that war is the very science of barbarity." "The city is a military target," he continued, "and will be treated as such."

August 10 was the worst day of the bombardment witnessed by Wallace P. Reed. "Ten Confederate and eleven Federal batteries took part in the engagement," he recorded. "Shot and shell rained in every direction. Great volumes of sulphurous smoke rolled over the town, trailing down to the ground; and through this stifling gloom the sun glared like a great red eye peering through a bronze-colored cloud."

One shell crashed into a house, killing a woman and her six-year-old daughter. Another woman was killed by a shell fragment while ironing clothes. A Confederate officer was bidding farewell to his landlady and her son when a shell burst, mortally wounding the soldier and boy. "The two victims were laid side by side on the grass under the trees," Reed wrote, "and in a few minutes both bled to death."

One young family abandoned the inner city for the security of a ridge, but they could still clearly hear "the crash when the houses were struck."

To escape the awful carnage, most families soon dug deep pits in their backyards and gardens to a depth of ten feet, then covered the holes with stout timbers and a heavy layer of earth. Dragging tables, chairs, mattresses, and what provisions were on hand into their improvised "bombproofs," the civilians fled to their dugouts when the shelling became severe or dangerously close. Sometimes a stray shell would fall directly on the tiny entrances and entire families were instantly killed.

Federal General Jacob Cox was horrified by the conditions he found in one shelter, occupied by a large family. "I looked down into the pit and saw there, in the gloom made visible by a candle burning while it was broad day above, women sitting on the floor of loose boards, resting against each other, haggard and wan, trying to sleep away the days of terror, while innocent-looking children, four or five years old, clustered around the air-hole, looking up with pale faces and great staring eyes as they heard the singing of the bullets that were flying thick above their sheltering place."

By offering the starving people a generous meal, Cox coaxed 21 inhabitants of the bombproof into the open, the first time, he was told, they had left its protection in three weeks.

A ten-year-old girl, disappointed by the absence of a cake on her birthday, confided a sentiment to her diary that was doubtlessly shared by thousands of Atlanta citizens. "I hope by my next birthday we will have peace in our land so that I can have a nice dinner."

Civilians were visited day and night by sudden death or mutilation as shells plunged from the sky. Buildings tumbled to the ground or were gutted by flames, and always there was the sound of guns barking and explosions. People still held fast to their homes, even when faced by the specter of starvation.

A second lull descended over the battle front, coinciding with the traditional southern summer doldrums. Goods were traded between the lines, and Union and Confederate songfests filled the sultry nights with music. Cotton bales soaked with turpentine provided illumination, which prevented nighttime assaults; and movement during the day was discouraged by deadly snipers. Sherman considered the siege beneficial to the Rebels. "The enemy hold us by an inferior force," he lamented. "They besiege us." In Washington, Lincoln pondered his future life out of the presidency.

By August 25 the bombardment had apparently accomplished little, so Sherman elected to cut loose from the railroad and his supply base to try one more daring operation. Leaving Henry Slocum's single corps entrenched to guard the railroad bridge over the Chattahoochee River to the north, Sherman evacuated his trenches and sent the entire army, with ten days' rations, wheeling southwest of the city on a six-mile-wide front to cut those two pesky railroads that kept Hood alive. "I have Atlanta as certainly as if it were in my hand," Sherman bragged.

When the shelling abruptly ceased, Confederate pickets crept out of their holes and discovered the enemy works abandoned. For several days Hood believed Sherman had lifted the siege and had returned to Chattanooga in defeat. A victory ball was prepared, with women brought from sanctuary in Macon to help celebrate this fortuitous event. Everyone thought Sherman was scurrying north, tail tucked between legs. Hood's failure to recognize the truth immediately was a result of Wheeler's cavalry raid north to cut the Western & Atlantic railroad that supplied Sherman. Wheeler accomplished little damage, then wandered into eastern Tennessee for a month, leaving Hood with no reconnaissance force.

Hood learned the rude truth of Sherman's location on August 30 when Howard destroyed the West Point railroad. His soldiers did a thorough job, levering up the rails and ties, then piling the ties to form blazing bonfires, heating the rails in the center over the blaze and twisting the iron around trees. Railroad cuts were filled with trees, and armed artillery shells were added to discourage repair crews.

Hood called for Hardee and sent him—accompanied by Lee's corps—to march that night to Jonesboro, fifteen miles south of Atlanta, to protect the Macon railroad and prevent the encirclement of Atlanta. Hardee was bluntly

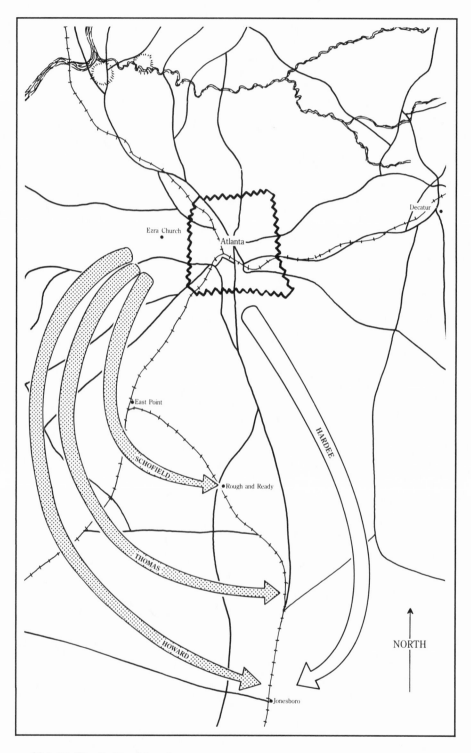

Map 23: The Battle of Jonesboro.

Union infantry destroy the Western & Atlantic railroad through Jonesboro. [*LESLIE'S ILLUSTRATED*]

informed that the fate of Atlanta rested in his hands. Hood believed that only half of Sherman's army was south of the city, and Hardee was expected to drive them back to the Chattahoochee. Stewart and the militia were to remain to protect Atlanta from the remainder of Sherman's troops, and Hood would stay with them again. Hood telegraphed further orders to Hardee, but the wires were soon cut by the rampaging Yankees.

Hardee's 24,000 footsore men were not assembled at Jonesboro until the afternoon of August 31, which afforded Howard's 17,000 infantry time to entrench in a favorable position behind log and fence rail barricades. When Hardee attacked at 3:00 P.M., the two primary assaults were again poorly coordinated. The Confederates overran the Union skirmish line, but at eighty yards they met a "terrible and destructive fire" and were solidly repulsed before the main works. Officers attempting to rally their men found the soldiers had developed a horror of charging breastworks, and many refused to move forward. When a second assault was organized, it was destroyed by a six-gun battery that fired so rapidly that parts of the carriages shattered. The Rebels cowered in a ravine until a Federal counterattack routed them, Yankees calling disparaging remarks in their wake. Hardee broke off the engagement at dark, and the depleted Confederate force retired.

The dismal attack was unlike those previously executed by the Army of Tennessee. Some dispirited men, believing they were already beaten, prayed for capture, despairing of victory or even survival. Those that charged did so timidly. Hardee lost 1,700 men in the debacle; the Federals lost 180.

As Howard fended off Hardee, Schofield cut the Macon railroad at Rough and Ready just after a final train from Atlanta had passed. While the demolition was in progress, a second train approached; but the engineer spotted the troops, reversed his engine, and backed into Atlanta to inform Hood that Atlanta was now isolated. Fearing an imminent attack on the city, Hood ordered Lee's corps to return to Atlanta at 5:00 P.M. The men, who had marched throughout the previous night and had fought a battle during the day, now prepared for a return march into the city that night to reoccupy Atlanta's trenches. Hardee, who had withdrawn to Jonesboro, was alone, dangerously separated from the remainder of the Confederate army.

When morning dawned on September 1, Hardee commanded only one corps consisting of 5,000 men. Many of his troops had deserted or were straggling somewhere between Jonesboro and Atlanta. When Sherman realized Hardee's desperate situation, he directed all six of his corps to converge on Jonesboro in hopes of surrounding and destroying the lone Confederate "army."

Hardee hastily improvised a line of earthworks and was subjected to an artillery bombardment that lasted all day. At 4:00 P.M., he was surrounded

Captured Confederate troops march into captivity after Jonesboro. [HARPER'S WEEKLY]

on three sides. Although one Union corps failed to arrive, Sherman felt it was too late to wait for Hardee to be corralled. He launched a vigorous assault by three divisions that struck the apex of Hardee's curved line. Excited by the knowledge that Atlanta's fall was imminent, the Yankees charged forward with abandon, ignoring holes torn in their ranks by grapeshot and leaving hundreds of their comrades writhing on the ground. They leaped the Confederate parapets and eagerly went to work with bayonets.

The Rebels, languid in attack the previous day, resisted with a ferocity known from their proud past. A battery blew gaping lanes in the surging Federal ranks, but Union counterfire splintered the carriages and forced the artillery crews to abandon their pieces. The angle was smothered by vastly superior numbers, and the line was broken as savage hand-to-hand fighting erupted. Units to either side of the breach valiantly held their positions, and Hardee feverishly rushed in his puny reserves to establish a second line that miraculously firmed and fended off additional Union attacks.

Despite 1,300 casualties suffered in the charge, the Federals were elated, although they quivered in exhaustion. One Union officer called the attack "glorious." Sherman could easily have overwhelmed Hardee if he had bothered to make the effort, but for some unexplained reason he let the opportunity slip away.

Hardee fought off Federal advances until dark, then led his decimated force six miles south along the railroad to Lovejoy Station. In addition to the

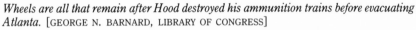

Wheels are all that remain after Hood destroyed his ammunition trains before evacuating Atlanta. [GEORGE N. BARNARD, LIBRARY OF CONGRESS]

eight cannon he had lost, 600 men and a general were captured in the cha-
otic battle. The immortal Orphan Brigade, which counted 1,500 men in
Dalton, now consisted of 500 survivors.

At Lovejoy, Hardee sent a dispatch to Hood, informing him that Jonesboro
had fallen and the last railroad had been severed. Atlanta would have to be
abandoned.

With a band playing "Hail, Columbia," Sherman entered Jonesboro the
next day to find a grisly scene: the dead were unburied and wounded soldiers lay abandoned in hospitals, churches, and virtually every building in
town. The Federals interred 2,000 bodies in mass graves.

Hood placed blame for the defeat at Jonesboro, the loss of the railroad,
and his evacuation of Atlanta on Hardee. The effort at Jonesboro must have
been feeble, he said, if Hardee had only suffered 1,700 casualties on the
first day of battle. Until he died, Hood maintained he was not to blame for
the loss of Atlanta.

Following several days of elation over Sherman's reported departure, Atlanta's citizens were shocked by rumors of a great battle at Jonesboro.
Crowds of stragglers and deserters flocked through the city as government
stores were thrown open to the public. Hood ordered Stewart, Lee, and the
militia to prepare for evacuation south to Lovejoy in the night. The despair-

Union troops march into abandoned Atlanta on September 2, 1864. [CURRIER & IVES]

ing cries of civilians filled the darkness as the remnants of a once feared army filed silently down Peachtree Street to McDonough Road, flags furled.

With the railroads lost, Hood was unable to evacuate his trains, so he ran seven locomotives, eighty-one freight cars filled with ammunition, and thirteen siege guns to the railroad yards, evacuated every building for half a mile around, and a cavalry rear guard set torches to the rolling stock and supplies. Those present called it the most spectacular sight they ever witnessed. For five hours the ground heaved like an earthquake under the detonations, windows were shattered, and nearby buildings were pierced by shells as thousands of explosions rocked the darkness. A fireworks display like the South had never seen lit up this gloomy night. To the north, Slocum wondered if Hood was attacking Sherman. In Jonesboro, Sherman wondered whether Hood was destroying Slocum and his railroad.

In the morning Slocum's pickets found the Confederate trenches empty. Advancing farther, they met a delegation of prominent citizens led by Atlanta's mayor who carried a white flag of truce. "Sir," he said formally to the ranking officer, "the fortunes of war has placed Atlanta in your hands. As mayor of the city I ask protection of non-combatants and private property." Late in the day Slocum's men marched into the city, bands playing as they passed bombed out buildings to hoist the United States flag over city hall.

Sherman probed Hardee's lines at Lovejoy, then marched north to occupy his prize. After 128 days of constant fighting and 35,000 casualties suffered by each side, the Atlanta campaign was over.

On September 3 Sherman wired Washington, "So Atlanta is ours, and fairly won." Lincoln received the message in his study late that night and proclaimed a day of thanksgiving for the capture of Atlanta. Throughout the North 100-gun salutes were fired in celebration of the stunning victory. While Atlanta held out, it remained a symbol of defeat and of Southern resistance. When the city fell, Northerners felt the war could be won. Lincoln was re-elected, and the war continued to a victorious close seven months later.

A DRIVING TOUR
■ Atlanta and Jonesboro ■

This portion of the driving tour begins at the intersection of I–20 East at exit 30 (Glenwood Avenue). If you are on I–75, pay close attention to road signs as you travel through the interchange with I–20 East. Once you are on I–20, it will be 4 miles to Glenwood Avenue.

If you arrive from the west, turn left from the exit ramp to the Walker Monument on the left. If you are coming from the east, the Walker Monument is on your right.

A cannon, its muzzle encased in concrete, marks the spot where Confederate Gen. William T. Walker was killed by Federal pickets at the beginning of the battle of Atlanta. Walker's death in battle surprised no one; he had been severely wounded by Indians and Mexicans and was nicknamed "Shotpouch" for rounds still embedded in his body. Walker had repeatedly resigned from the United States and Confederate armies over perceived slights and had engaged in a newspaper letter war with Jefferson Davis early in the Civil War. His body was returned to Augusta for burial, where his grave rests on the grounds of Augusta College.

Drive back across I–20 on Glenwood .8 and turn right onto Monument. Cross the first street (Metropolitan) to .3, where there is a monument similar to Walker's.

This marks the spot where Federal Gen. James Birdseye McPherson rode into advancing Confederate troops and was shot dead from the saddle.

Turn left on McPherson for .4, right on Moreland for .3, and left onto Memorial.

To launch his flank attack, Hardee marched through the night on Peachtree Street to Five Points and down Capital Avenue almost to the Yellow River. He was joined by Cleburne at Memorial, then turned up Bouldercrest and split his forces on Flat Shoals and Fayetteville Road. Confederate attacks were launched all along the Federal line, which was just north of Glenwood, and farther north up Moreland, at the intersection with DeKalb, which is the focal point of the Cyclorama display. The I–20 exchange you crossed on Moreland is the remains of Leggett's Hill, where the most desperate fighting occurred. The Confederate breakthrough occurred at Moreland and the Georgia Railroad, site of the contested DeGress Battery and Troup Hurt House and current site of a church. It is commemorated by a historical marker. Sherman's headquarters at the Augusta Hurt House, where McPherson's body was carried, was on the grounds of the James Earl Carter Presidential Library. Because of Atlanta's development in this area, a true appreciation of the battle of Atlanta can only be obtained by experiencing the Cyclorama.

At .5 on Memorial notice to your right the old depot, and at 1 mile turn right onto Oakland Avenue; at .1 on Oakland, turn right into Oakland Cemetery.

Map 24: Oakland Cemetery and Grant Park areas.

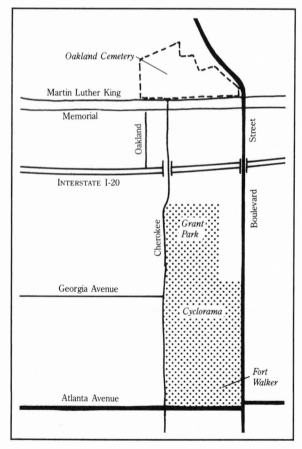

Oakland Cemetery is one of Atlanta's most historic landmarks. It was established 135 years ago, and an estimated forty-five thousand people are buried here, including such Georgia notables as Margaret Mitchell, golfing great Bobby Jones, Georgia Civil War Governor Joseph Brown, five other governors, twenty-three Atlanta mayors, and many founding families of the Atlanta area, including Austells, Vinings, Hapes, and Norcrosses. Confederate Capt. Benjamin Harding Helm, Abraham Lincoln's brother-in-law, was buried at Oakland temporarily after suffering a mortal wound at Chickamauga. It is reported that Lincoln grieved at news of his death. In 1884 Helm was reinterred at the family plot in Elizabethtown, Kentucky. Confederate Vice President Alexander Stephens was temporarily buried at Oakland, a funeral attended by twenty thousand people, but was reinterred at his home in Crawfordville.

More than fifty thousand people wander across Oakland's eighty-eight acres each year, and historical and preservation societies conduct tours. Historic Oakland Cemetery and the city of Atlanta sponsor Sundays in the Park, a celebration of 1900-era picnic excursions and explorations of the cemetery's architecture, art, and history. Information about the ceme-

Hundreds of unknown civilians who were killed in the Federal bombardment of Atlanta rest beneath the grieving Lion of Atlanta.

From this spot in Oakland Cemetery, Hood watched the Battle of Atlanta on July 22, 1864.

tery may be obtained in the visitors center in the bell tower building. An inexpensive, detailed guide to the cemetery may be purchased.

Take the second left at .2 and the Confederate cemetery is on your right. At .1 turn right beside the rows of southern graves and pass the sixty-five-foot-tall Confederate monument in the center of the road.

Here in the Confederate section are buried twenty-four hundred Confederate soldiers. They died of wounds and disease in a complex of forty hospital buildings established at the fairground or in the intense fighting in the battles for Atlanta. More than sixty thousand soldiers were treated in Atlanta. The graves were first marked by wooden headboards, but in 1890 those were replaced with standard government round marble headstones. Some pointed stones were added in 1951. Sixteen Union soldiers rest among the Confederates. A sixty-five-foot-tall obelisk, the tallest structure in the city when it was erected on Confederate Memorial Day 1874, pays homage to the fallen Southerners. A monument to the Real Daughters of the Confederacy is in this section. A number of civilians killed during Sherman's siege of the city are also buried at Oakland.

Under a large magnolia tree to the left is the Lion of

*Union General McPherson was killed here during the
Battle of Atlanta.*

Atlanta, a reproduction of the famed Lion of Lucerne.
The original honors sixteen Swiss guards who died
protecting Marie Antoinette during the French Revolution. The six-foot-high sculpture, carved from a
single piece of Georgia marble, was dedicated on April
26, 1894, to the memory of several hundred unidentified Confederate soldiers who are buried in this plot
without headstones. The grieving creature, clutching
a Confederate flag in one paw, is the most eloquent of
hundreds of Confederate memorials found in Georgia.

Near the lion sculpture, in Block K, are buried three
Confederate generals: John B. Gordon, who rose to
prominence late in the war as one of Lee's great com-
manders, Clement A. Evans, who became a noted
Confederate historian, and Alfred Iverson Jr., a cav-
alry leader whose unit defeated Sherman's troopers at
Sunshine Church during an Atlanta campaign raid.
Their tombs are specially marked. In family plots are
the graves of Gen. Lucius J. Gartrell, William S.
Walker, and Georgia's Civil War governor, Joseph
Brown. Ceremonies honoring the Southern dead have
been held at Oakland since 1866 and continue today.

*At .3 take a sharp right onto the rough brick pave-
ment and a very tight right at .1 beside the south
wall. At .1 to your left is a bronze plaque.*

The plaque indicates that seven of Andrews's Raiders
were executed in what are now cemetery grounds and
buried here in June 1862. Andrews was hanged from a
scaffold at the corner of Juniper and Third and buried
nearby. The seven were reinterred in Chattanooga
National Cemetery in 1866, but Andrews's remains
were not discovered and moved until 1887. Their
white marble headstones surround an impressive
stone monument topped by a bronze replica of the
General, which was dedicated in 1891 before a crowd
of ten thousand. This marker was placed by descendants of the men in Ohio. Ironically, also buried in
Oakland are the three men who lost and then heroically recaptured the locomotive: Engineer William
Fuller, Jeff Cain, and Anthony Murphy.

Beside the railroad tracks near the cemetery, at the
industrial complex, was a rolling mill that supplied armor for Confederate ironclads. Here, at the home of
Mayor James E. Williams, Hood watched the battle of
Atlanta. When the city was abandoned, Hood ordered
the destruction of eighty box cars of ammunition. The
explosion could be heard, felt, and seen for twenty
miles.

*Take the next sharp right and the first left to exit the
cemetery. Oakland Avenue is one-way; so drive
straight on Martin Luther King Jr. Drive and turn
left on Grant Street at .1 to Memorial. Turn left onto
Memorial for .2 and right onto Cherokee for .7 to the
traffic light where Georgia Avenue intersects Cherokee. Then turn left into Grant Park, and the
Cyclorama is directly in front of you.*

Cycloramas, first developed in the late 1700s, saw a
resurgence in popularity following the American Civil
War and Franco-Prussian War, when victors commissioned stirring portrayals of climactic battles. The
Battle of Atlanta Cyclorama has been an Atlanta landmark for decades. The canvas, which is 42 feet high,
358 feet in circumference, and weighs eighteen thousand pounds, is the largest painting in the world. Commissioned by Gen. John A. Logan to support his
campaign for the vice presidency in 1884 (which was
unsuccessful), it was created between 1885 and 1886
by German artists who came to Atlanta from Mil-
waukee. They erected a forty-foot-high tower to examine the battlefield terrain and scrutinized the
battle's history, including interviews with veterans of

the conflict. The painting was exhibited around the country until 1892, when philanthropist George V. Green purchased it. The Cyclorama was eventually given to the city of Atlanta and housed in the present structure in 1926.

The figures in the foreground, called a diorama, were added by WPA workers during the 1930s. The diorama blends perfectly with the painting to create a three-dimensional effect with terrain features like hills, ravines, shell-blasted stumps, wagons, and fighting men, including a dead Clark Gable figure lying on the field of battle.

Unfortunately, storms damaged the roof of the building, and leaks developed that stained the canvas and threatened to destroy the artwork. Real Georgia clay used in the diorama attracted insects and rats, and in 1979 the Cyclorama was closed for a badly needed restoration. The canvas was repaired, the terrain and figures were replaced with lightweight, durable fiberglass, and the entire building was renovated. Eight million dollars later, the Cyclorama has never looked better, and it is still impossible to determine where the painting ends and the diorama begins.

In the entrance to the Cyclorama is a Civil War cannon, and in the lobby is the *Texas,* the last engine used to catch Andrews's Raiders and the *General.* The *Texas* was almost scrapped in 1907, but Atlanta Mayor Courtland S. Winn bought it four years later. It was first displayed on rails at Fort Walker, and in 1936 it was restored and moved to the Cyclorama's basement. There are a gift shop and other Civil War displays, and on the second floor is a Civil War museum. It features artifacts, large photographs of the generals who participated in the Atlanta campaign, a computer that reports the action on any given day of the war, and an exhibit honoring the contributions of minorities to the war.

The next stop on the tour is a theater where a short film describes the events leading up to the battle of Atlanta; then visitors proceed to the Cyclorama. In earlier days a guide illuminated points of interest with a flashlight, and visitors shuffled around to examine the marvel. Today, a 182-seat theater slowly revolves as each segment of the canvas is automatically spotlighted and a taped narrative, backed by appropriately stirring music, describes the action depicted on the canvas. After the taped tour concludes, a guide describes other interesting details in a second viewing of the work.

Nowhere can the true drama of battle be more appreciated than at the Cyclorama. The death, destruc-

Fort Walker, in Grant Park near the Cyclorama, helped the Confederates resist a month-long siege.

tion, and heroism of soldiers fighting bravely for causes they believe in are starkly portrayed as the painting, foreground figures, music, and narrative combine to awe the viewer. The thrilling Cyclorama convinces visitors that they are on the scene of the battle of Atlanta.

Return to the traffic light at Cherokee and Georgia; turn left onto Cherokee for .4, left on Atlanta Avenue for .3, and left onto Boulevard Street. Here, at the southeastern corner of Grant Park, is the bastion named Fort Walker.

Fort Walker is one of the last remaining portions of the Confederate fortifications that once ringed Atlanta. The fort was designed by Col. Lemuel P. Grant, a pioneer citizen from Maine and railroad engineer who later donated over 135 acres for this park. The fort is named for Gen. W. T. Walker, who was killed at the battle of Atlanta.

The earthworks are massive. Visualize them with timber reinforcement, rows of chevaux-de-frise in front, cannon bristling over the ramparts, and lines of supporting infantry trenches extending to either side; imagine ten miles of these defenses. The works were so formidable that Sherman elected not to attack Atlanta. Instead, he cut the rail lines into the city and forced Hood to evacuate after Fort Walker had withstood a month-long siege.

Fort Walker once contained a restored battery of cannon mounted on wooden carriages and caissons, but vandals repeatedly destroyed the woodwork. Two of the cannon are now on display inside the Cyclorama. Missing from Fort Walker is a half-size replica of Oakland Cemetery's Lion of Lucerne. The observation tower that dominated the scene here for decades has been demolished. Before leaving, enjoy the beautiful view of Atlanta's skyline from this vantage point.

Atlanta emerged as one of the South's most important cities during the Civil War. Its location deep in the Confederacy and its rail connections with most points in the struggling nation attracted numerous war industries and made the city a significant military target. On February 16, 1861, Jefferson Davis stopped at the depot at Marietta and Union on his way from Washington, D.C., to Montgomery, Alabama, and spoke to an enthusiastic crowd. He was then entertained at a reception held at the Trent House, which stood at the corner of Decatur and Pryor. Soon afterward, the Confederate flag was first raised at the State Square. Ironically, in 1844 Sherman had been aboard one of the first trains to pass through Atlanta, when it was known as Marthasville.

When fighting erupted in Tennessee in 1862, wounded soldiers from both armies were funneled down the railroad to hospitals established in Atlanta. A general hospital was built at the Fair Grounds, now Memorial and Flat Shoals, and a convalescent camp was situated at Marietta and Ponder. The Gate City Hotel, between Marietta and Ponder, was turned into a distributing hospital.

Atlanta was fortified following the debacle at Chattanooga, and those defenses soon rivaled any in the Confederacy. They consisted of infantry trenches and artillery forts ten miles in length, an average of one and one-half miles from the center of the city. One strongpoint was at what is now the Georgian Terrace Hotel. The Georgia Railroad Roundhouse, famous from postdestruction photographs, was between the Washington Street Bridge and Piedmont Avenue.

Near here is the Grant Mansion, once the center of a six-hundred-acre estate and one of only fifteen antebellum structures surviving in Atlanta. Lemuel P. Grant built the twenty-room house in 1858, and it resisted Sherman's destruction of the city. Today it is a crumbling hulk with a questionable future.

Each July, Grant Park hosts a retrospective on the battle of Atlanta, which includes a Confederate camp and other interesting events.

Return to the Cyclorama's Georgia Avenue entrance and turn left onto Georgia for .8, then right onto Capitol.

On your left is Atlanta Stadium and the statue of Hank Aaron, baseball's home-run king.

At .6 on your right is the Georgia Department of Archives and History. This is the repository of many valuable historic documents.

Formerly housed in the archives were three famed Tiffany stained glass windows which trace the history of the Confederacy. These beautiful windows represent the Confederate Secession Congress at Montgomery, the battle of Bull Run, and Lee's surrender at Appomattox. Commissioned by Amos Giles Rhodes in 1904 at a cost of forty thousand dollars, they were originally placed on a magnificent staircase in the Rhodes Mansion, which housed the state's archives until 1965. When the new building was constructed, the stairs and windows were moved here and faithfully restored. The Rhodes Mansion has since been repaired and serves as headquarters for the Georgia Trust for Historic Preservation, and the windows have been returned to 1516 Peachtree Street N.E.

Continue on and the Georgia State Capitol is on your left at .3. The roads around the Capitol are one-way; so bear left beside the Capitol at .1 onto Martin Luther King Jr. Boulevard (MLK hereafter).

This simple monument in east Atlanta was erected in memory of the Battle of Ezra Church.

The grounds of the Capitol sport several statues and monuments of Civil War interest. There is a statue of Georgia's Civil War governor, Joseph E. Brown and his seated wife, a rare husband and wife combination, and an equestrian statue of John Brown Gordon. Gordon is famous for organizing the Raccoon Roughs in northern Georgia and leading them to Virginia, where he became one of Lee's most prominent lieutenants. After the war Gordon was twice elected governor, and thrice to the U.S. Senate. The statue, erected in 1907, was executed by Solom Borglum, brother of Gutzon, who started the Stone Mountain memorial and created Mount Rushmore, shows Gordon astride Marye, a Yankee horse captured at Chancellorsville. In front of the Capitol are several mounted tablets that describe the battle of Atlanta, the siege of the city, and its evacuation.

The Georgia Museum of Industry and Trade is on the first and fourth floors of the Capitol and features exhibits of Georgia history, including a large collection of Civil War flags that were carried by numerous Georgia units into battle. Some remain torn from shot and shell, and a few were captured in battle by Federal forces and later returned. Unit names and battles in which they fought are proudly stitched on the flags.

Also on display is a statue of Benjamin Hill, an able supporter of Jefferson Davis. The statue was originally erected amid great ceremony at an Atlanta intersection in 1886, where newspaperman Henry Grady introduced Jefferson Davis; the dedication was one of his last public appearances. The former president of the Confederacy was joined by the great Confederate Gen. James Longstreet, who arrived from his home in Gainesville. John B. Gordon was also present. The sight of Davis, Longstreet, and Gordon together inspired the thousands of Confederate veterans present to organize a movement that launched Gordon's political career. In the Governor's Gallery are large portraits of Gordon and Allen Daniel Candler, who lost an eye in the Civil War.

Opposite the western side of the Capitol is Atlanta City Hall, site of the John Neal home where Sherman maintained his headquarters during Atlanta's occupation. From here Sherman later launched the March to the Sea. In September 1864 the grounds of the Capitol were covered by tents of the Twenty-second Massachusetts Infantry. During the war the Fulton County courthouse and Atlanta city hall (1854) occupied Capitol Square. They survived Sherman but were demolished for the Capitol just a few years later. Thomas was quartered in the Austin Leydon house, which was on Peachtree; Schofield and Slocum roomed nearby. At the southeastern corner of City Hall is a monument

Map 25: Westview Cemetery area.

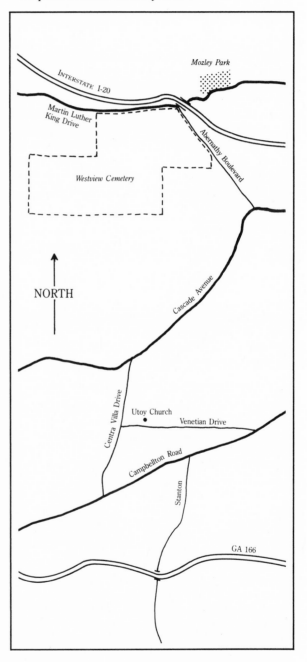

to Thomas Patrick O'Reilly, pastor of Shrine of the Immaculate Conception when the Federals conquered Atlanta. O'Reilly convinced Slocum to spare city hall, the courthouse, and four churches when the city was burned in November 1864. Immaculate Conception, constructed in 1848, survived the war but was demolished for a new church in 1873. Father O'Reilly's tomb is in the basement.

After visiting the Capitol, continue on MLK past the Gordon Statue. At .4 go straight on MLK; do not bear left through the tunnel. You will cross a bridge, and at .3 the Omni and the Georgia Dome is on your right. At .6 pass through Atlanta University.

In this area was the westernmost extension of Atlanta's fortifications. South of MLK, at Ashby and Fair, is the site of Whitehall Fort, a major position on Atlanta's defensive perimeter. Another fort occupied the campus of Georgia Tech.

At 1.8 Mozley Park is on your right.

Many of Atlanta's Confederate veterans requested that they be buried together in Westview Cemetery.

After the battle of Atlanta, Sherman shifted his pressure to the southwest in an effort to destroy the remaining railroads that connected Atlanta with Macon and West Point, and to lure Hood into another costly battle. He succeeded in the latter at the battle of Ezra Church, which occurred in Mozley Park, where historical markers describe the Confederate defeat and mark the site of the church. The Federals advanced from the north and formed a horseshoe-shaped defensive line. Confederate troops marched to Ezra Church along Ralph David Abernathy Boulevard, which was then known as the Lickskillet Road, and attacked both sides of the Federal angle. The assault was a disgraceful failure and resulted in fearful Southern losses.

Pass under I–20 and at .8 turn left into Westview Cemetery, where some of the fighting at Ezra Church occurred. A fountain is directly in front of you; at .1 turn right, then left, and circle around the Ezra Church Battle Monument. Note the impressive mausoleum nearby.

Return to the cemetery entrance and turn right onto MLK. At .4 turn right onto Ralph David Abernathy Boulevard (GA 139), and at .3 turn right into the main entrance of the cemetery. The office is on your left, and on your right is the old gatehouse.

The gatehouse retains its original bell, once tolled to announce funerals. It occupies a battlefield landmark, the Almshouse, where Civil War refugees gathered.

Drive straight past the office, turning left at .2 to leave the white-lined road, left at .1, left at .05, left at .3 where a sign indicates Section 70 on the corner, and straight ahead on the left is a single headstone.

This marks the grave of Lt. Edward Clingman, who died at the battle of Ezra Church. Behind the trees is a section of Confederate trenches that were occupied following the battle. Federal troops later captured the position and brought up a battery of guns to shell Atlanta during the siege.

Drive straight ahead, turning right at .1 in Section 26, right again at .05 at Section 26, and return the way you came, turning right at .3 and right at .1. Turn left at .1 beside the turret-shaped water tower; at .2 on your right is a large Confederate monument.

The monument was erected after the war by Fulton County veterans to honor their comrades. One hundred men are buried around the statue, including some veterans of the Ezra Church clash. On the north side of the monument are two Confederate mortars.

When Jefferson Davis died in New Orleans in 1889, Georgia offered a permanent grave at Westview, but Davis's widow, Varina, selected Richmond as his final resting place. As Davis's body was slowly transported to Virginia, memorial services were held in the Georgia Capitol. Also buried here is Joel Chandler Harris, who, as a boy, witnessed Sherman's passage through central Georgia and was a noted author.

Take the next right at .1, and at the intersection turn left to the Ralph David Abernathy Boulevard cemetery entrance and take a right onto Ralph David Abernathy Boulevard. At .8 turn right onto Cascade (GA 154) and turn left onto Centra Villa at 1.6, left at .5 onto Venetian, and at .3 turn left onto Cabaha. On the corner is Utoy Church.

The battle of Utoy Creek occurred west of here in what is now the Cascade Springs Nature Preserve, which is closed to the public. The Confederate line was south of Cascade (the old Sandtown Road) on either side of Willis Mill Road. Utoy Church, built in 1828, is one of the oldest in Fulton County. During the Utoy Creek fighting, it served as a Confederate hospital. Walk into the adjacent cemetery, and near the northwestern corner are the graves of the eighteen Confederates who died successfully defending the Utoy position. Several feet north is a portion of the Rebel defensive line. This historic cemetery also contains the graves of four Revolutionary War soldiers, a number of Indians, and thousands of slaves who died during a smallpox epidemic.

On the golf course in Adams Park just east of here is a historical marker that draws attention to a shallow depression, which is another part of the Southern defensive line. During the final phase of the Atlanta campaign, Sherman's armies marched south through this area toward Jonesboro.

Return to Centra Villa, turn left, and at .5 is Campbellton Road. Turn left for .8 and right on Stanton 1 mile, then left onto East Woodbury immediately after the underpass at the sign for GA 166 for .1; then bear left onto the Lakewood Freeway (East GA 166).

You are passing just north of Fort McPherson, which was established before the Civil War as a militia drilling ground. During the war, Confederate recruits received their training there. Barracks and a cartridge factory were constructed, then burned by Hood's retreating forces. During postwar Federal occupation, the facility was named for Union Gen. James B. McPherson, killed at Atlanta. It was headquarters for the Third Militia District, whose officers included such Civil War notables as George Meade and John Pope. To the south is East Point, where the southernmost portion of Atlanta's fortifications ended.

At 2.2 follow the I–75 sign right, and at .1 follow the I–75 (to Macon) sign. Exit I–75 at 10 miles onto GA 54, which is the Southlake Mall exit; then turn right.

Historical markers describing Hardee's march to Jonesboro line the highway.

At 3.1 on Mimosa to your right is the Warren House.

The Warren House (1859) was used during the battle of Jonesboro as a Confederate hospital, then as a Union headquarters and hospital on September 2 after the Fifty-second Illinois overran it. Graffiti left by Union soldiers is still visible on the walls.

The Jonesboro Confederate Cemetery is on your left at .2, but you cannot turn here. Drive straight onto GA 138 to the first traffic signal at .3, turn left over the tracks, and immediately left on McDonough Road, which parallels the railroad. At .4 turn right onto Johnston Street, and on the corner to your left is the Confederate Cemetery.

The Patrick Cleburne Confederate Cemetery, named for a renowned Confederate general killed during the battle of Franklin in Tennessee, occupies a site of heavy fighting. The cemetery is on the northern edge of the city. In the entrance arch are embedded twelve cannonballs, and a monument in the center of the cemetery honors the men who died in two days of fighting at Jonesboro and were buried here. Individual markers have been erected for the fallen, although they were actually buried in two mass graves. Blank individual markers were authorized in 1872 by the state legislature when it ordered the reinterment of eight hundred to one thousand soldiers from the battlefield. The stones form the Confederate battle flag.

When Sherman shifted most of his forces southwest of Atlanta, he sent Howard west through Campbellton and Fairburn to Jonesboro, Thomas in the center through Ben Hill to Red Oak, where the West Point railroad was severed, and Schofield inside through Red Oak to Rough and Ready (Mountain View).

Hardee had marched through the night to Jonesboro

via East Point and Rough and Ready. He attacked Howard on the first day of battle in a vain attempt to prevent the destruction of this last rail link with Atlanta. He assaulted the Federal line just west of Jonesboro, across U.S. 41 on both sides of GA 138 near the Flint River, and suffered a severe repulse. On the second day Sherman massed most of his army and mauled Hardee, who had hastily thrown up works on the western and northern fringes of town along the railroad near this cemetery.

During the night Hardee slipped away south to Lovejoy, while Hood evacuated Atlanta and the remains of the Army of Tennessee joined Hardee. After confronting Hood at Lovejoy's for several days, Sherman returned north to occupy his prize. The Atlanta campaign was over.

On McDonough Street one-half mile south of the cemetery and to the left is the Dickson Funeral Home, where the hearse that carried Confederate Vice President Alexander Stephens to his grave in 1883 is housed. Also to the left is the new-old courthouse (1892), and behind it is the old courthouse (1869) on the original foundation. Behind it on MLK is the jail, and just south on the opposite side of the tracks is the depot, all built in 1869 to replace those destroyed in August 1864 by Kilpatrick's cavalry raid. The original depot stood near the Confederate cemetery. The entire business area, which included thirteen taverns, was torched by the Federals. But the wooden interiors were all that were lost to the fire. The brick exteriors survived the war. Two-thirds of Jonesboro, however, was destroyed.

Clustered in the area are other antebellum structures, including the Stephen Carnes House (1850s, whose owner manufactured wagons and caskets for the Confederacy), the Elliott-Morrow Cottage, and the John-Blalock House (used as a Confederate commissary where supplies were stored during 1864 and whose owner, Col. James F. Johnson, signed the Georgia secession ordinance), all of which were used as hospitals following the battle. The Waldrop-Brown-

Edwards House (1860) suffered extensive damage. East and south of Jonesboro are several interesting plantations. Stately Oaks Mansion was a landmark to the invading Union armies; the Allen-Carnes Plantation (1820s) and Camp Plantation sheltered Jonesboro citizens for the two days during which their homes were enveloped in carnage; and Crawford–Talmadge Plantation (Lovejoy Plantation, 1835) at Lovejoy is the spot where Hood gathered the tattered remnants of his shattered force after Atlanta was evacuated.

Of all the Georgia mansions that claim to be the inspiration for the mansions described in Margaret Mitchell's classic novel, *Gone with the Wind,* Tara and Twelve Oaks, Lovejoy seems to have the strongest claim. Mitchell spent many summers in this area with her grandmother and heard numerous stories of the antebellum South from the elderly residents who had survived the war. She returned to research the book in the Clayton County Courthouse records and local historical societies. Jonesboro's association with *Gone with the Wind* is heavily promoted, and plans are regularly floated to construct a GWTW recreational complex in the area. The movie's facade of Tara is owned by Lovejoy's mistress.

Just north of Lovejoy, in a landscaped park beside U.S. 41, is the Sigma Chi Monument, a one-hundred-ton cross-shaped marble marker. After the fall of Atlanta, five Mississippi cavalrymen gathered here to discuss the potential dissolution of their fraternity if the Confederacy was defeated. To ensure its survival, they established the Constantine Chapter. In 1939 this monument was erected to honor their devotion.

Historic Jonesboro sponsors an annual Civil War battle reenactment (call [404] 473-0197) and a Tara ball. A wonderful self-driving tour to thirty-two sites in the area is available from the convention and visitors bureau—the emphasis is on the Civil War and *Gone with the Wind.* Historic Jonesboro plans to open a museum of local history in the old jail at 125 King Street. Stately Oaks and Ashley Oaks are available for tours.

Conclusion
The Importance of the Atlanta Campaign

"This morning, as for some days past, it seems exceedingly probable that this administration will not be reelected."

That was how Abraham Lincoln evaluated his future on August 28, 1864. After reflecting on the year's war news, the President expected the Democrats to win the White House in three months and, as one of their first acts, to sign a peace treaty with the Confederate States of America.

The year had begun on a hopeful note when U. S. Grant, newly appointed General in Chief of the Armies of the United States, devised a three-part offensive that would strike Rebel forces across the country. In the South he would send Sherman to strike a death blow against Atlanta. Sherman rapidly reached the outskirts of the city with miminal losses, but as the war dragged on and each hot summer day passed, citizens of the North became discouraged at the fruitless siege.

In the far western theater of operations, Grant sent Nathaniel Banks to invade the Red River region of Louisiana with a substantial force. After allowing the Federals to penetrate the region deeply, the Confederates savagely turned on Banks. In May Union forces stumbled to safety, having lost 8,000 men, 9 ships, and 51 cannon. Northerners had been thoroughly disgusted at the debacle.

The hopes of most Northerners for a quick end to the war were pinned on U. S. Grant when he led the massive Army of the Potomac into Virginia's wilderness in May. Robert E. Lee gave Grant a typical welcome, lashing out against a vastly superior force and inflicting 17,000 Union casualties.

Earlier Federal generals would have taken this as an invitation to retreat, but Grant bore in relentlessly. He shifted east to Spotsylvania and launched one of the war's largest assaults. He nearly succeeded in splitting Lee's army in half, but the attack failed and cost him 18,000 additional troops.

Undaunted, the tenacious Union commander again shifted east, this time to Cold Harbor. Lee had anticipated the move and had established a labyrinth of concealed works. There Grant believed the works were vulnerable to attack, but his infantrymen obviously disagreed, sewing their names on their coats on July 2 so their bodies could be identified and sent home for burial following the upcoming battle. The attack on June 3, one day later, lasted ten minutes and cost 8,000 men.

The Deaths of Two Noble Warriors

An accidental meeting aboard a cruise ship following the Civil War sparked a long friendship between William T. Sherman and Joseph E. Johnston. The former adversaries visited each other and corresponded; and at U. S. Grant's funeral in 1885, they stood shoulder-to-shoulder.

Sherman had just turned 71 when he died of asthma on February 14, 1891. The North was plunged into mourning as New York City prepared for the funeral, which was attended by over 30,000 soldiers. President Benjamin Harrison, a veteran of the Atlanta Campaign, was present; and so were two former presidents and many other government officials.

Also present was one Confederate who was capable of forgiving wartime unpleasantness, Joseph Johnston, who served as an honorary pallbearer. As Sherman's coffin was placed aboard a caisson, Johnston stood beside it, bareheaded in a freezing rain.

"General," someone pleaded, "please put on your hat. You'll get sick."

"If I were in there," Johnston replied solemnly, "and he were standing here, he would not be wearing his hat."

Johnston fell ill and died a month later at the age of eighty-four. ∎

Grant managed to elude Lee and appeared at Petersburg, south of Richmond; but he had wasted his advantage, and the Confederates blocked him again. The war in Virginia settled into a brutal, ten-month-long siege that was a forerunner to the trench warfare of World War I.

Newspapers in the North labeled Grant the "Butcher," and people clamored for Lincoln to remove him. The President stood firm, realizing that Grant had inflicted crippling losses on Lee. The public could only see three seemingly bungled campaigns—a disgusting continuation to three years of bungled war—and growing lists of men killed, mangled, and missing.

War weariness had settled over the North, seriously weakening the public's resolve to continue the seemingly endless struggle. The human loss—sons, fathers, husbands, and brothers—was a horrible burden to bear. To that were laid crushing taxes to pay for the continuation of the war and the abandonment of long cherished freedoms in an attempt to crush criticism of the war's conduct. In 1863 there had been massive riots in Northern cities to protest a draft, nasty disturbances that saw blacks hung from lampposts and soldiers firing on civilians in the streets. Most people believed the war, with its attendant evils on the battlefield and at home, would continue for several years.

Citizens wondered aloud if the war's goals justified the price that was being paid. Preserving the Union and ending slavery were sound moral causes, but the individual Northerner would not suffer materially if the Confederacy was allowed its independence. It would be much easier to set the South free and end the suffering.

The impending election could stop the long struggle. The Democratic party offered George McClellan as the only man who could save the country. McClellan was still a war hero in the eyes of many Americans, despite a crushing defeat by Lee at the Seven Days' Battle and the stigma of having allowed Lee to escape following Antietam. The Democrats protested that the Federal government had vastly increased its powers and accused Lincoln of usurping the rights of states. They claimed that Lincoln wanted to be a dictator and that the long, costly war was a failure. At the ballot box people would have a chance to change what they believed had gone wrong with America.

While the Democratic party was resurgent, the Republicans were deeply divided. Lincoln's renomination had been bitterly opposed, and throughout the summer the Republicans had attempted to replace him with another candidate.

Then Atlanta fell. "Atlanta is ours, and fairly won." That simple telegraphic message struck the North like a thunderbolt. Victory! The war could be—indeed, was even now being—won. The Union could be preserved. With that now established as a certainty, a negotiated settlement seemed cowardly, and the Democratic claim was made a lie. One of the South's great armies had been soundly whipped and her second most important city conquered.

Five days after Lincoln's spirits had struck their lowest point, his leadership was vindicated. Exactly two months later, Americans voted. Lincoln won 55 percent of the popular vote, gaining 212 electoral votes to McClellan's 21. The public had regained its commitment to continue the war, retaining the man who would prosecute it to a victorious conclusion.

The presidential election of 1864 had been of paramount importance to Southerners, who realized the significance of a potential McClellan victory. After three years of war, the Confederacy had been seriously weakened, but it remained a dangerous adversary. However, the South had suffered far greater casualties, relative to its population, than had its Northern enemy. Even the most optimistic did not believe the Confederacy could survive four more years of war against so determined a foe as Lincoln.

Atlanta's loss proved to be a deathblow to the Confederacy. Lee, hopelessly entangled at Petersburg, could never hope to regain the offensive. Southern fortunes could only be redeemed in Georgia, and that hope had been crushed.

Atlanta had become a symbol of Southern resistance. With its loss and Lincoln's reelection, Confederate morale plummetted. As Northern hopes soared, Southerners lost heart, and their armies suffered an epidemic of desertions.

Political consequences aside, the military effects of the Atlanta campaign dealt a crushing blow to Rebel fortunes. Sherman had inflicted 35,000 irreplaceable casualties on the Army of Tennessee. That once great army would fight valiantly until the end of the Civil War, but its thin, ragged ranks would never again pose a serious threat to Union forces.

The loss of Atlanta's manufacturing facilities was immediately felt throughout the Confederacy. The South had always suffered shortages of cannon, rifles, munitions, uniforms, boots, and dozens of other vital items. Now those things were virtually unobtainable.

The destruction of Atlanta's railroad connections spelled doom to Lee in Virginia. On those rails had been channeled the agricultural bounty of Mississippi, Alabama, and Georgia through the Carolinas to feed the Army of Northern Virginia. Lee's men would starve at Petersburg until the war ended.

Strategically, the Confederate flank had been breached. Union armies could drive easily to the Gulf Coast and capture Mobile or, more importantly, sally to the Atlantic Ocean via Savannah or Charleston and reinforce Grant in the trenches at Petersburg.

Atlanta was not only fairly won, but the war as well.

Appendix A ■ Confederate Valor at the Battle of Ringgold Gap

On November 24, 1863, Joseph Hooker forced Confederate troops from their strong position atop Lookout Mountain, Tennessee, in a glorified skirmish that has been romanticized as the "Battle Above the Clouds" because of the heavy fog that had settled over the mountain. On November 26 Hooker, Thomas, and Sherman stormed Missionary Ridge and routed the remainder of the Confederate Army that was besieging Chattanooga, sending them reeling back into Georgia through Ringgold Gap and on to Dalton.

Irish-born Patrick Cleburne, who had risen from private to general, provided the only measure of Confederate heroism at Missionary Ridge. Sherman's troops advanced to within fifty yards of his line; but Cleburne's hard-pressed warriors forced them back, then counterattacked and threw the Federals off the ridge. While the rest of the Confederate army fled in disorder, Cleburne's 4,000-man division executed an orderly withdrawal from the mountain while protecting the rear of the retreating Confederate army. That night Cleburne received orders to make a stand in the steep gorge of Ringgold Gap.

Braxton Bragg, the commander of the Army of Tennessee, feared that the Federals would organize an immediate pursuit that would destroy his disorganized force. He was particularly concerned about his long and painfully slow train of supply and hospital wagons that stretched for miles along the poor, deeply rutted roads leading to Dalton. Their capture would cripple the army's ability to defend the route to Atlanta, and Cleburne was ordered to check the Federal pursuit until the wagons were safely behind Rocky Face Ridge above Dalton.

Cleburne had only one-half hour to deploy his men in the gap and on both sides of the ridge. It was 8:00 A.M. when Federal skirmishers drove back the Confederate cavalry and Hooker formed his battle lines in front of Cleburne. The Confederate wagon train was still in sight, rocking desperately down the tracks leading south; only Cleburne could stave off total disaster for the demoralized Confederates.

The Federal soldiers advanced confidently; but a well-served Rebel artillery battery delivered a punishing fire that broke one Federal flank, the soldiers diving for cover behind the railroad bed. Hooker's artillery responded; and shells fell in the town, endangering civilians and tearing large chunks of stone from the railroad depot.

A Federal advance up one slope was checked by crackling volleys of Confederate musket fire. Southern soldiers heaved large boulders down the mountain at the enemy and hurled smaller rocks at Federals, taking many of their stunned targets captive. When the Confederates swept down the slope in pursuit, they routed the Federals and captured sixty prisoners.

After the battle had raged for two and one-half hours, the determined Union troops reeled back in confusion with heavy losses. Hooker wisely elected to await reinforcements before renewing the assault. Cleburne's stubborn defense had halted the Federal momentum.

As soon as Cleburne received word that the wagons were safe behind hastily constructed defenses at Dalton, his men withdrew proudly. His casualties had been twenty killed, while Federal losses were estimated at several hundred. For this action Cleburne was thanked by a resolution passed by the Confederate Congress, and he was afterward known as the "Stonewall of the West."

Appendix B ■ "Hold the Fort, for I Am Coming" The Battle of Allatoona

One of the fiercest battles of the Civil War occurred at Allatoona, but not as part of the Atlanta campaign. The Battle of Allatoona occurred five months later, in October 1864. Hood had succeeded to the command of the Army of Tennessee and had dashed his army against Sherman's forces four times, virtually destroying his own command. In September he withdrew from Atlanta, which surrendered and was occupied by the Federals.

Camped at Lovejoy with a disgruntled army that wanted Joseph Johnston returned to command, Hood decided to drive north and destroy the railroad, Sherman's line of supply and communication. Hood intended to invade Tennessee, capture Nashville and regain the state for the Confederacy, and draw Sherman out of Atlanta in pursuit.

Unfortunately for the Confederate cause, after reviewing Hood's near mutinous troops, President Jefferson Davis delivered a speech to the men detailing Hood's plans; and the Confederate press dutifully published the details. Sherman always maintained that his best source of intelligence came from reading Southern newspapers; so, forewarned, he alerted and reinforced his garrisons along the railroad to Chattanooga and dispatched Thomas and his massive army to Tennessee. Two divisions strengthened Chattanooga; another was sent to Rome.

Federal cavalry had occupied Allatoona late in May while Confederate and Union forces were fighting around Dallas. Sherman was so impressed by the natural strength of the position that he ordered the Confederate fortifications expanded and garrisoned the post with 1,000 men. He then established his main supply depot here for the remainder of the Atlanta campaign. By the fall of 1864 the town consisted of eight stores, eight homes, a railroad depot, and several new, large warehouses that contained a million rations of hardtack and 9,000 head of cattle.

There were two main forts at Allatoona, one on either side of the railroad cut. The strongest of the two redoubts, shaped like a star, was on the western side. Both forts were strongly protected by log stockades, abatis, and three rows of outer trenches. The Federals had cleared a field of fire that stretched for hundreds of yards, and artillery emplaced in the redoubts covered all approaches. The deadly new repeating rifles with which many of the Federal soldiers were armed provided a formidable defense. The men had personally bought these guns, which held fifteen shots, for fifty-one dollars each. It turned out to be a wise investment. Confederate soldiers, who would gain a great respect for the guns, said they could be loaded on Sunday and fired the rest of the week!

On September 29 Hood left camp at Lovejoy and moved north to Dallas, and Sherman left Slocum to guard Atlanta and started north after Hood. Hood sent a force to capture a 400-man garrison at Acworth; and a 3,000-man division under Samuel French was dispatched to capture Allatoona, fill the railroad cut with rock, earth, and logs, and destroy a railroad bridge over Allatoona Creek.

Unknown to French, the garrison at Allatoona had been doubled in strength by the arrival of 1,050 men under John M. Corse. Corse had first traveled to Rome but, finding no danger from Rebels there, had returned south to Allatoona just hours before the battle began.

French left Big Shanty and arrived at Allatoona at 1:00 A.M. on October 5. Placing twelve artillery pieces on a hill 1,200 yards south of the pass, he positioned his men to surround the star fort from three sides and waited for dawn to launch the assault.

At 7:00 A.M. French sent a message to the Federal commander informing him that his works were surrounded and demanding the immediate surrender of the Federal garrison to avoid the "needless effusion of blood." French guaranteed that the prisoners would be treated humanely and allowed five minutes for a reply.

Corse rejected the ultimatum, stating that "We are prepared for the 'needless effusion of blood' whenever it is agreeable with you." Confederate artillery immediately opened up a deadly fire on the enemy works.

By 9:00 A.M. all the Confederate troops had been deployed across the rough terrain. Their artillery continued to pound the star fort until the infantry closed on the works; Federal cannon returned the fire briskly.

With a bloodcurdling scream, the Confederates leaped from the forest surrounding the fort and charged forward. Corse later wrote that "a solid mass of gray advanced from the woods and started up the hill, with artillery support from the rear." As Corse ordered his men to fire on the Rebel infantry, he quietly prayed, "Oh, that Sherman might come."

The initial Confederate charge routed the Federals from their first line of outer works, but an intense fire from the second line stopped the Rebels cold. The Confederates regrouped, then charged recklessly, carrying the second line and continuing the mad dash to fall on the third line, which the Union troops defended with desperation. Men were killed in hand-to-hand fighting, using their rifles as clubs, bayoneting their foes, and crashing rocks on their enemies' heads. Some of the defenders were captured; others escaped by scrambling for the cover of the star fort.

The Confederates had suffered heavy casualties, but they dressed their lines and charged the last line of defense. The desperate Federals fired their repeating rifles so quickly that the guns grew too hot to hold, and half the soldiers fired while the other half crouched below the parapets and waited for their rifles to cool. Inside the fort, the ferocity of the Confederate as-

Allatoona Pass, where Corse "held the Fort" in a desperate battle. [HARPER'S WEEKLY]

sault and the pounding from their artillery had taken a heavy toll on the Union soldiers. The dead were propped up against the earthworks to give the false impression that the fort was strongly defended; corpses were hit repeatedly. The artillery crews had been so decimated that the wounded were propped up beside the cannon to pull the lanyards and send charges of grapeshot screaming pointblank into the charging Confederate lines.

The Federal cannon and repeating rifles staggered the bravely advancing gray lines. The Rebels wavered, then reeled back to the third line of trenches. Confederate officers rallied their men, then led them into the storm of hot metal to close on the fort from all directions. They were yards from the final ramparts when they received an incredible order: disengage and withdraw. The dazed, exhausted attackers staggered back into the woods.

French had received a message from Hood advising him that a large force of Federal reinforcements was advancing over the railroad from Kennesaw. French feared that if he did not withdraw then, he would be cut off from Hood and captured. He later reported that the order he gave to withdraw gravely depressed him. After such heroic sacrifice from his men, he had been forced to call off the attack just minutes before the fort would have been overrun or forced to surrender. To the soldiers inside the star fort, it appeared that they had been saved by divine intervention.

The Battle of Allatoona was a relatively minor affair, but no battle in the Civil War was more fiercely fought or brought forth more valor by troops of

The village of Allatoona, a site that Sherman avoided in May and Hood attacked in October 1864. [GEORGE N. BARNARD, LIBRARY OF CONGRESS]

both sides. The carnage was terrible. The Confederates suffered 798 casualties, the Federals 706, or 30 percent of all the men engaged. French lost seventy officers killed or wounded, proving again that in the Civil War officers led their men into battle at the fore.

Hood's maneuver had forced Sherman to leave the comfort of his headquarters in Atlanta temporarily and to take to the field again. The Union commander had just reached his observation post on the crest of Kennesaw Mountain, where months before his men had met disaster, as the battle began. He watched anxiously through his glasses as clouds of smoke marked the scene of a desperate struggle. Starting a column of troops marching north to relieve Corse, Sherman knew they would not arrive in time to alter the course of battle. As they marched, they fired buildings to mark their progress by pillars of fire and smoke for Sherman. They would not arrive at Allatoona until early on the following day.

Sherman recorded: "I followed Hood, reaching Kennesaw Mountain in time to see in the distance the attack on Allatoona, which was handsomely repulsed by Corse." Sherman would later call it "one of the fiercest and more gallant battles of the war."

Hoping to encourage Corse to defend his position and not surrender, Sherman sent this message to Allatoona from Kennesaw Mountain throughout the battle. "Sherman says hold fast; we are coming." Thinking that relief was imminent, Corse held heroically; but he paid a bloody price.

Early in the battle Corse was severly wounded when a minié ball tore away half his face. During the battle he drifted in and out of consciousness, but his subordinates ably carried on the defense. On the following day, he displayed a mixture of bravado and anxiety in a message he signaled to Kennesaw Mountain: "I am short a cheek bone and an ear, but am able to lick all hell yet! My losses are quite heavy. Where is Sherman?"

When Sherman saw Corse after the battle, he remarked: "Corse, they came damn near missing you, didn't they?" Corse was a West Point dropout, but that day he proved himself to be a better man that many who graduated at the top of their class.

On his way to join Hood at New Hope Church, French stopped and bombarded a Federal blockhouse on Allatoona Creek into submission, capturing 250 prisoners. Sherman chased Hood to Rome, Resaca, Dalton, and Tunnel Hill. Hood attacked Sherman's railroad garrisons, capturing several and being driven away from others; but he never stopped to engage Sherman in a pitched battle. Sherman allowed Hood to move into northern Alabama unmolested, happy to have him far from the action. He returned to Atlanta to plan his devastating March to the Sea, which would be unopposed. Hood marched on into Alabama and ultimately Tennessee, failing in his efforts to cut off Sherman's supply route. In Tennessee he would destroy the Army of Tennessee as an effective fighting force by dashing his men in a desperate, but futile, assault at Franklin, then waiting for his army to be shattered at Nashville by Thomas.

Accounts of the battle were given extensive play in Northern newspapers. The Evangelist Phillip Paul Bliss was so inspired that he wrote the moving hymn, "Hold the Fort," which he introduced at a revival meeting in Chicago. It can still be found in some hymnals.

> Ho! my comrades! See the signal, Waving in the sky!
> Reinforcements now appearing, Victory is nigh.
> "Hold the fort, for I am coming," Jesus signals still;
> Wave the answer back to heaven, "By His grace we will."
>
> See the mighty host advancing, Satan leading on;
> Mighty men around us falling, Courage almost gone!
> See the glorious banner waving! Hear the trumpet blow!
> In our Leader's name we triumph, Over every foe.
> Fierce and long the battle rages, But our help is near;
> Onward comes our great Commander, Cheer, my comrades, cheer!

Appendix C ■ Driving Snake Creek Gap

Following the route that McPherson used to sneak around Rocky Face Ridge and threaten Resaca makes a scenic Saturday outing. Begin at the Chickamauga National Battlefield Park, where you may want to spend most of the day exploring the museum and numerous monuments and enjoying a driving tour of the park that marks the largest battle in the western theater of the Civil War.

Exit the battlefield on U.S. 27–GA 1 south. Turn left onto GA 95 and left again on GA 90–151. This intersection was called Chestnut Flat, where McPherson camped for the night of May 7. Continue south to the intersection with GA 136 (Lookout Mountain Scenic Highway) and turn left. Maddox Gap, then called Ship's Gap, winds gently across Taylor's Ridge and enters the beautiful West Armuchee Valley. McPherson seized this strategic gap with no opposition.

At the bottom of the ridge, you might want to take S1030–706 south to Shiloh Church, where Hood recovered from the loss of a leg after the Battle of Chickamauga. This side trip dramatically demonstrates the beauty of Georgia's valley and ridge district. Taylor's Ridge rises to your right; Johns Mountain is to your left.

Return to 136 and continue east to Villanow, which McPherson seized on May 8. The name of the settlement was taken from a Jane Porter novel, *Thaddeus of Warsaw.* If you have the time, just east of Villanow is a sign directing you south on S822–714 six miles to Keown Falls Scenic Area and the Pocket. Keown, on the eastern slope of Johns Mountain, is one of the few waterfalls in this part of Georgia. Picnicking and hiking are the attractions at Keown Falls, and just south of it is a pleasant wooded area with a spring and stream where camping is permitted at the Pocket.

McPherson continued directly from Villanow to seize Snake Creek Gap by surprise on May 8 and threaten Johnston's flank at Dalton. GA 136 shears sharply south in the pass between Mill Creek Mountain to the north and Horn Mountain to the south. The scenic pass is very narrow and several miles long, and the ridges rise spectacularly on both sides of the road. Emerging from the pass you can continue east on 136 to I–75 and the features described at Resaca, or continue south on 136–Connector into Calhoun.

Appendix D ■ Chronology

1863

December 27. Joseph E. Johnston arrives in Dalton to command the Confederate Army of Tennessee.

1864

February 22–27. George Thomas's Federal Army of the Cumberland unsuccessfully probes Dalton's defenses to determine Confederate strength, then withdraws.

March 18. In Nashville, U. S. Grant receives command of all Union armies; he places William T. Sherman in charge of the western armies.

April 9. Grant issues orders that when he attacks Lee in Virginia, Sherman is to move into Georgia and destroy the Army of Tennessee.

May 1–7. Moving south from Chattanooga and Red Clay, Tennessee, the Army of the Cumberland and the Army of the Ohio advance through Ringgold, Catoosa Springs, Varnell, and Tunnel Hill to face Confederate defenses at Rocky Face Ridge near Dalton.

May 8–12. Federals launch diversionary attacks against Buzzard Roost Gap, Dug Gap, and the Crow Creek Valley.

May 9. James McPherson's Federal Army of the Tennessee sneaks through Snake Creek Gap, but pulls back when faced with Confederate resistance at Resaca, wasting a golden opportunity to destroy Johnston.

May 11–13. Sherman advances to Resaca through Snake Creek Gap and Johnston withdraws from Dalton to oppose him.

May 13–15. Sherman's assaults against the Confederate line at Resaca are repulsed, but he successfully places a force behind Johnston.

May 16–18. Confederates retreat through Calhoun and Adairsville, fighting delaying actions against Union pursuit. Federals capture industrial center of Rome.

May 19. Johnston draws the Army of the Ohio into an ambush at Cassville, but John Hood fails to attack. After establishing a second position,

Johnston's generals counsel retreat and the Confederates withdraw across the Etowah River to Allatoona.

May 23–25. Sherman sweeps southwest to Dallas, while Johnston hurries to intercept him.

May 25. Joseph Hooker's Federals launch determined attacks against Hood's corps, but are decimated by concentrated Confederate fire at New Hope Church.

May 27. Sherman, believing he is turning the Confederate flank, is repulsed with loss at Pickett's Mill. Johnston directs Hood to attack Sherman's flank, but he reports unfavorable conditions for the assault.

May 28. Johnston, hoping to catch McPherson withdrawing, attacks a strongly held Union position at Dallas and is thrown back.

June 1–6. After constant skirmishing near Dallas, Sherman shifts to the railroad at Big Shanty and Johnston moves to fortify three high points north of Marietta.

June 14. Confederate General Leonidas Polk is killed on Pine Mountain. Southern forces retreat that night to prevent their encirclement.

June 15–20. Confederates forced to retreat from Lost Mountain. A running battle ensues with encounters at Gilgal Church and Mud Creek.

June 22. Hood leads an unauthorized and unprepared strike against Federals at Kolb's Farm, and loses heavily.

June 27. Weary of the stalemate before Marietta, Sherman attacks Kennesaw Mountain at two points and is soundly defeated, losing 2,000 men to 400 Confederate casualties.

July 2. Finding that Sherman has slipped McPherson and John Schofield between his forces and the Chattahoochee River, Johnston abandons Kennesaw Mountain.

July 3–4. Johnston slows Sherman at a line of fortifications established at Smyrna.

July 5. Flanked out of Smyrna, Johnston withdraws to a strong position on the north bank of the Chattahoochee.

July 9. Federal troops effect two crossings of Johnston's River Line, forcing the Confederates to withdraw south of the river.

July 13. Braxton Bragg arrives in Atlanta to assess the Confederate situation. His report to President Jefferson Davis is critical of Johnston's performance.

July 17. Sherman crosses the Chattahoochee with all three armies; two march directly on Atlanta, while McPherson swings east to Decatur. Jefferson Davis relieves Johnston from command of the Army of Tennessee, replacing him with Hood.

July 20. As Thomas crosses Peachtree Creek, Hood launches a furious attack that is repulsed with a loss of 5,000 men.

July 21. McPherson moves toward Atlanta from Decatur, capturing positions that threaten the city with bombardment.

July 22. Confederate General William Hardee's corps executes a daring night march to reach McPherson's flank, but finds it was extended during the night. In the campaign's fiercest fighting, McPherson is killed and the Union line is temporarily pierced; but Confederate forces are decisively beaten and suffer considerable casualties.

July 22–August 27. Atlanta is besieged and subjected to intense bombardment.

July 28. Sherman sends the Army of the Tennessee west around Atlanta, and Hood dispatches Stephen D. Lee to stop the movement. Lee fails, and Confederate losses are heavy in a battle at Ezra Church.

July 27–August 4. Sherman's grand cavalry strike south of Atlanta is defeated at Brown's Mill, Sunshine Church, and Jug Tavern.

August 6. Sherman's attempt to break a vital railroad by attacking near Utoy Church is thwarted.

August 25–30. Most of Sherman's forces circle south to destroy the two remaining railroads that supply Atlanta. Hood believes Sherman has retreated.

August 30–31. Discovering his rail lines severed, Hood realizes his precarious position and sends Hardee south to dislodge Sherman. Attacking at Jonesboro, Hardee is repulsed.

September 1. Sherman gathers most of his army at Jonesboro and almost destroys Hardee, who escapes south to Lovejoy. That night Hood destroys his military supplies and evacuates Atlanta.

September 2. Federal troops occupy Atlanta.

September 3. Sherman telegraphs Washington, D.C., "So Atlanta is ours, and fairly won."

Appendix E ■ Resources

The Atlanta campaign tour can be completed in as little as two days, or it can be stretched out to a full-length vacation. If your time is limited, the tour can be done in portions. This book has been designed to accommodate either approach. Visits to the sites can be enhanced by contacting any of the following sources for information on what to see and do along the way.

I advise the adventurous traveler to secure county maps from the state, currently available for $1.50 each from the Department of Transportation, 2 Capitol Square, Atlanta, Georgia 30334. The counties covered in the tour are Catoosa, Whitfield, Gordon, Bartow, Paulding, Cobb, Fulton, and Clayton. A good map of Atlanta is also essential. These will enable you to keep up with the tour on maps and will be invaluable if you decide to stray off the tour route.

Basic State Resources

For a free copy of *Georgia on My Mind*, a large magazine-style tour guide to the state. The Georgia Department of Industry, Trade, and Tourism, P.O. Box 1776, Atlanta, GA 30303, (404) 656-3590; (800) 847-4842

For information about state parks:
> Georgia State Parks and Historic Sites, Georgia Department of Natural Resources, 205 Butler Street, S.E., Suite 1352, Atlanta, GA 30334, (404) 656-0779

Resources for a Driving Tour of the Atlanta Campaign

Each is listed in the order it may be needed on the tour

Georgia Visitor Information Center, I-75 Southbound, Ringgold, GA 30736, (706) 937-4211

Chickamauga and Chattanooga National Military Park, P.O. Box 2128, Fort Ogelthorpe, GA 30742, (706) 866-9241

Catoosa County Chamber of Commerce, P.O. Box 52, 306 East Nashville Street, Ringgold, GA 30736, (706) 965-5201

Dalton Convention and Visitors Bureau, (also Northwest Georgia Trade and Convention Center), 2211 Dug Gap Battle Road, (Exit 136 from I-75), P.O. Box 2046, Dalton, GA 30722-2046, (706) 272-7676; (706) 278-5811 (fax)

For information on Dug Gap Battlefield Park and Blunt House, Crown Gardens and Archives, Whitfield-Murry Historical Society, 715 Chattanooga Avenue, Dalton, GA 30720, (706) 278-0217

For a walking tour of the historic downtown district, Dalton Downtown Development Authority, 210 North Pentz Street, P.O. Box 707, Dalton, GA 30722, (706) 278-3332

To order maps for the Armuchee District, which is the western portion of the Chattahoochee National Forest, Forest Supervisor, Chattahoochee National Forest, U.S. Forest Service, 508 Oak Street, N.W., Gainesville, GA 30501, (404) 536-0541

Armuchee Ranger District, 806 East Villanow Street, P.O. Box 465, Lafayette, GA 30728, (706) 638-1085

Gordon County Convention and Visitors Bureau, (also Calhoun Local Welcome Center), 300 South Wall Street, Calhoun, GA 30701, (706) 625-3200

Northwest Georgia Travel Association, P.O. Box 2497, 700 West Lime Street, Calhoun, GA 30701, (706) 629-3406; (706) 625-5062 (fax)

Oakleigh, Gordon County Historical Society, 335 South Wall Street, Calhoun, GA 30701, (706) 629-1515

New Echota Historic Site, 1211 Chatsworth Highway, N.E., Calhoun, GA 30701, (706) 629-8151

Barnsley Gardens, 597 Barnsley Gardens Road, Adairsville, GA 30103, (404) 773-7480

Kingston Confederate Memorial Museum, 13 East Main Street, Kingston, GA 30145

Cartersville-Bartow County Tourism Council, Inc., P.O. Box 200397, 16 West Main Street, Cartersville, GA 30120, (404) 387-1357; (800) 733-2280; (404) 382-2704 (fax)

Etowah Indian Mounds, 813 Indian Mounds Road, S.W., Cartersville, GA 30120, (404) 387-3747

Bartow History Center, 319 East Cherokee Avenue, P.O. Box 1239, Cartersville, GA 30120, (404) 382-3818

Cooper Furnace Day Use Area, Allatoona Dam Visitors Center, Resource Manager's Office, (404) 382-4700

U.S. Corps of Engineers, 30 Pryor Street, S.W., Atlanta, GA 30303, (404) 221-6715

The William Weinman Mineral Museum, Mineral Museum Drive, U.S. 441 & I-75, Exit 126, P.O. Box 1255, Cartersville, GA 30120, (404) 386-0576

Red Top Mountain State Park, 653 Red Top Mountain Road, S.E., Cartersville, GA 30120, (404) 975-0055

Acworth Welcome Center, I-75 and, GA 92, Exit 120, Acworth, GA 30101, (404) 974-7627

Paulding County Chamber of Commerce, 150 East Memorial Drive, Dallas, GA 30132, (404) 445-6016

Pickett's Mill Historic Site, 2640 Mount Tabor Road, Dallas, GA 30132, (404) 443-7850

Marietta Welcome Center and Visitors Bureau, No. 4 Depot Street, Marietta, GA 30060, (404) 429-1115; (800) 835-0445; (404) 933-7220 (fax)

Cobb County Convention and Visitors Bureau, P.O. Box 672827, 1100 Circle 75 Parkway, Marietta, GA 30067-0048, (404) 933-7228; (800) 451-3480; (404) 933-7220 (fax)

Big Shanty Museum, 2829 Cherokee Street, Kennesaw Georgia 30144, (404) 427-4686

Kennesaw Mountain National Battlefield Park, 900 Kennesaw Mountain Drive, Old Highway 41 & Stilesboro Road, Kennesaw Georgia 30144, (404) 427-4686

Marietta National Cemetery, 500 Washington Avenue, N.E., Marietta, GA 30060, (404) 428-5631

Historic Roswell Convention and Visitors Bureau, 617 Atlanta Street, Roswell, GA 3075, (404) 640-3253; (404) 640-3252 (fax)

Roswell Historical Society, Inc., 227 Atlanta Street, Roswell, GA 30075, (404) 992-1665

Tourism Commission, North Fulton Chamber of Commerce, 1025 Old Roswell Road, Roswell, GA 30076, (404) 993-8806

Bulloch Hall, 180 Bulloch Avenue, Roswell, GA 30075, (404) 992-1731

Archibald Smith Plantation Home, 935 Alpharetta Street, Roswell, GA 30075, (404) 640-3253

Chattahoochee National Recreation Area, 1978 Island Ford Parkway, Dunwoody, GA 30350, (404) 399-8070

Atlanta Convention and Visitors Bureau, 223 Peachtree Street, N.E., Suite 2000, Atlanta, GA 30303, (404) 521-6600; (404) 584-6331 (fax)
The Atlanta Convention and Visitors Bureau and its various local centers provide a number of useful maps and brochures to the city's many attractions. Several private companies offer comprehensive sightseeing tours, and the Atlanta Preservation Center sponsors a number of guided walking tours.

Atlanta History Center Downtown, 140 Peachtree Street, N.W., Atlanta, GA 30303, (404) 814-4150

Atlanta Welcome Center, Lenox Square Mall, 3393 Peachtree Road, N.E., Atlanta, GA 30326, (404) 266-1398

Atlanta Welcome Center, Underground Atlanta, Pryor and Alabama Streets, Atlanta, GA 30303, (404) 577-2148

Atlanta History Center and Museum, 130 West Paces Ferry Road, N.W., Atlanta, GA 30303, (404) 814-4000

Historic Oakland Cemetery, 248 Oakland Avenue, S.E., Atlanta, GA 30312, (404) 658-6019

Atlanta Cyclorama, 800 Cherokee Avenue, S.E., Grant Park, Georgia and Cherokee Avenues, Atlanta, GA 30315, (404) 658-7625

Georgia Department of Archives and History, 330 Capitol Avenue, S.E., Atlanta, GA 30334, (404) 656-2350

Georgia Trust for Historic Preservation, 1516 Peachtree Street (Rhodes Hall), Atlanta, GA 30309, (404) 881-9980

State Capitol, Capitol Square, Capitol Hill and Washington Street, Georgia Museum of Science and Industry, Atlanta, GA 30334, (404) 656-2844

Clayton County Convention and Visitors Bureau, P.O. Box 774, Jonesboro, GA 30237

8712 Tara Boulevard, Jonesboro, GA 30236, (404) 478-4800; (404) 478-9226 (fax), Welcome Center (404) 478-6549; (800) 662-7829

Ashley Oaks Mansion, 144 College Street, Jonesboro, GA 30236, (404) 478-8986

Historical Jonesboro, Stately Oaks Plantation Home and Historic Community, P.O. Box 922, 100 Carriage Drive, Jonesboro, GA 30237, (404) 473-0197

Greater Rome Convention and Visitors Center, 402 Civic Center Hill, P.O. Box 5823, Rome, GA 30162-5823, (706) 295-5576; (800) 444-1834; (706) 236-5029 (fax)

Chieftains Museum, 501 Riverside Parkway, P.O. Box 373, Rome, GA 30161, (706) 291-9494

Polk County Chamber of Commerce, 604 Goodyear Street, Rockmart, GA 30153, (404) 684-8774; (404) 684-8760

Atlanta Heritage Row, Underground Atlanta, 55 Upper Alabama Street, Pryor and Alabama Streets, Atlanta , GA 30303, (404) 584-7879

Road to Tara Museum, 659 Peachtree Street, N.E., Suite 600, P.O. Box 2005, Atlanta, GA 30308, (404) 897-1939

Federal Reserve Bank, 104 Marietta Street, N.W., Atlanta, GA 30303, (404) 521-8747

Sweetwater Creek State Park, P.O. Box 816, Mount Vernon Road, Lithia Springs, GA 30057, (404) 732-5871

Douglas County Welcome Center, P.O. Box 395, Douglasville, GA 30133, (404) 942-5022 ext. 1

Coweta County Convention and Visitors Bureau, P.O. Box 1012, Newnan, GA 30264, (800) 826-9382

Male Academy Museum, 30 Temple Avenue, Newnan, GA 30263, (404) 251-0207

DeKalb County Convention and Visitors Bureau, 750 Commerce Drive, Suite 201, Decatur, GA 30030, (404) 378-2424; (800) 999-6055; (404) 378-3387 (fax)

DeKalb Historical Society Museum, Library, and Archives, Old Courthouse on the Square, Decatur, GA 30030, (404) 373-1088; (404) 624-1071; (404) 658-7625

Historic Complex of DeKalb Historical Society, 720 West Trinity Place, Decatur, GA 30030, (404) 373-1088

Georgia's Stone Mountain Park, P.O. Box 778, Highway 78, Stone Mountain, GA 30086, (404) 498-5600; (404) 498-5702

Stone Mountain Village Welcome Center, P.O. Box 667, 891 Main Street, Stone Mountain, GA 30086, (404) 498-2097

Bibliography

Bailey, Ronald H. *Battles for Atlanta*. Alexandria, Virginia: Time-Life Books, 1985.

Barnard, George N. *Photographic Views of Sherman's Campaign*. New York: Dover Publications, 1977.

Brown, Joseph M. *The Mountain Campaigns in Georgia*. Buffalo, New York: Matthews, Northrup, and Company, 1890.

Bull, Rice C. *Soldiering*. San Rafael, California: Presidio Press, 1977.

Carter, Samuel, III. *The Siege of Atlanta*. New York: Ballantine Books, 1973.

Catton, Bruce. *Never Call Retreat*. Garden City: Doubleday and Company, 1965.

Connelly, Thomas L. *Autumn of Glory: The Army of Tennessee*. Baton Rouge: Louisiana State University Press, 1971.

Cox, Jacob D. *Atlanta*. New York: Charles Scribner's Sons, 1882.

Cumming, Kate. *The Journal of a Confederate Nurse*. Savannah: Beehive Press, 1975.

Davis, William C. *The Orphan Brigade*. Baton Rouge: Louisiana State University Press, 1980.

Evans, Clement A., ed. *Confederate Military History*. Vols. VI and XII. Atlanta: Confederate Publishing Company, 1899.

Foote, Shelby. *The Civil War, a Narrative, Red River to Appomattox*. New York: Random House, 1974.

Gay, Mary. *Life in Dixie During the War*. Atlanta: Darby Publishing Company, 1979.

Georgia: A Guide to Its Towns and Countryside. Athens: University of Georgia Press, 1940.

Hoehling, A. A. *Last Train from Atlanta*. New York: Thomas Yoseloff, 1956.

Hood, John B. *Advance and Retreat*. Bloomington: Indiana University Press, 1952.

Horn, Stanley F. *The Army of Tennessee.* Norman: University of Oklahoma Press, 1952.

Johnston, Joseph E. *Narrative of Military Operations.* Bloomington: Indiana University Press, 1959.

Kerksis, Sydney Co, comp. *The Atlanta Papers.* Dayton, Ohio: Morningside Press, 1980.

Kurtz, Wilbur B. *Atlanta and the Old South.* Atlanta: American Lithograph Co., 1969.

McCarley, J. Britt. "Atlanta Is Ours, and Fairly Won." *Atlanta Historical Journal* (Fall 1984).

McInvale, Morton R. *The Battle of Pickett's Mill.* Atlanta: Georgia Department of Natural Resources, 1977.

Nichols, George W. *The Story of the Great March.* New York: Harper and Brothers, 1865.

Nisbet, James C. *Four Years on the Firing Line.* Edited by Irwin W. Bell. Jackson, Tenn.: McCowat-Mercer Press, 1963.

Richardson, Eldon B. *Kolb's Farm: Rehearsal for Atlanta's Doom.* Privately published, 1979.

Rowell, John W. *Yankee Artillerymen.* Knoxville: University of Tennessee Press, 1975.

Scaife, William R. *Campaign for Atlanta.* Atlanta: Privately published, 1985.

Scruggs, Carroll P. *Georgia Historical Markers.* Helen, Ga.: Bay Tree Grove, 1976.

Sherman, William T. *Memoirs of General William T. Sherman.* Westport, Conn.: Greenwood Press, 1957.

Symonds, Craig L. *A Battlefield Atlas of the Civil War.* Baltimore: Nautical and Aviation Publishing Company of America, 1983.

Upson, Theodore F. *With Sherman to the Sea.* Baton Rouge: Louisiana State University Press, 1943.

War of the Rebellion Official Records. Series 1, Vol. 38. Washington, D.C.: Government Printing Office, 1891.

Watkins, Sam R. *Co. Aytch.* New York: Collier Books, 1962.

Yates, Bowling C. *Historical Guide for Kennesaw Mountain National Battlefield Park and Marietta, Georgia.* Marietta: Privately published, 1976.

Index